Avatars, Activism and Postdigital Performance

RELATED TITLES

Ecologies of Precarity in Twenty-First Century Theatre:
Politics, Affect, Responsibility
Marissia Fragkou
ISBN 978-1-4742-6714-4

Political Dramaturgies and Theatre Spectatorship:
Provocations for Change
Liz Tomlin
ISBN 978-1-3501-9758-9

Staging Technology: Medium, Machinery, and Modern Drama
Craig N. Owens
ISBN 978-1-3501-6857-2

Avatars, Activism and Postdigital Performance

Precarious Intermedial Identities

Edited by
Liam Jarvis and Karen Savage

methuen | drama

LONDON • NEW YORK • OXFORD • NEW DELHI • SYDNEY

METHUEN DRAMA
Bloomsbury Publishing Plc
50 Bedford Square, London, WC1B 3DP, UK
1385 Broadway, New York, NY 10018, USA
29 Earlsfort Terrace, Dublin 2, Ireland

BLOOMSBURY, METHUEN DRAMA and the Methuen Drama logo are
trademarks of Bloomsbury Publishing Plc

First published in Great Britain 2022

Cover design by Charlotte Daniels
Cover image: *Swing Individual*, Yoshitoshi Kanemaki
(© FUMA Contemporary Tokyo / BUNKYO ART)

A catalogue record for this book is available from the British Library.

A catalog record for this book is available from the Library of Congress.

ISBN: HB: 978-1-3501-5931-0
          ePDF: 978-1-3501-5933-4
          eBook: 978-1-3501-5932-7

Typeset by Integra Software Services Pvt. Ltd.

To find out more about our authors and books visit www.bloomsbury.com
and sign up for our newsletters.

Contents

List of Illustrations   vi

Notes on Contributors   viii

Introduction: Postdigitality: 'Isn't It *All* "Intermedial"?'
Liam Jarvis and Karen Savage   1

1   Avatars, Apes and the 'Test' of Performance Capture
    Ralf Remshardt   17

2   Performativity 3.0: Hacking Postdigital Subjectivities
    William W. Lewis   39

3   Randy Rainbow's Musical and Social Media Activism: (Digital)
    Bodyguards and Politicizing/Weaponizing Audiences
    Karen Savage   65

4   Deepfake-ification: A Postdigital Aesthetics of Wrongness
    in Deepfakes and Theatrical Shallowfakes   *Liam Jarvis*   89

5   The Glitch, the Diva, and Coming Back Out: Aging and
    Postdigital Identity   *Asher Warren*   115

6   Voicing Identity: Theatre Sound and Precarious Subjectivities
    Lynne Kendrick and Yaron Shyldkrot   137

7   Postdigital Place-Mixing in the Wild City   *Jo Scott*   161

Index   187

List of Illustrations

2.1 Screengrab from the *Karen* app. Day 4, Session 2 – Karen wants to talk about her date. *Karen* by Blast Theory   41

2.2 Screengrab from the *Karen* app. Day 1, Session 2 – *What area of life coaching do you seek most? Karen* by Blast Theory   48

2.3 Screengrab from the *Karen* app. Personal Data Report – Page 8, Personal Openness. *Karen* by Blast Theory   53

2.4 Screengrab from the *Karen* app. Day 9, Session 1 – Karen learns about herself. *Karen* by Blast Theory   61

3.1 Viewers of Rainbow's videos on Facebook and YouTube   67

3.2 Comments from viewers of Rainbow's videos on Facebook and YouTube   67

3.3 Rainbow as chorus in 'BEFORE HE TWEETS' (uploaded to Facebook 5 July 2017)   79

4.1 Screengrab from *YouTube*. Nicolas Cage as Lois Lane in *Man of Steel* (2013)   89

4.2 Screenshot of Barack Obama Deepfake, YouTube: BuzzFeedVideo   90

4.3 Nicolas Cage GIF on *Reface* app, Liam Jarvis photograph, and Nicolas Cage/Liam Jarvis deepfake result on *Reface* app   95

4.4 Screenshot of a photorealistic human image created by an AI generative adversarial network (GAN) from the https://thispersondoesnotexist.com website   97

5.1 *The Coming Back out Ball* by All the Queen's Men (2017)   128

6.1 Dead Centre's *Chekhov's First Play*   141

6.2 Dead Centre's *Lippy*   149

6.3 Dead Centre's *Lippy*   153

7.1 Glitched digital images of a wildscape, formed through
    'incorrect' panning on an iPhone   170

7.2 'Tiled' images of wild, green spaces (captured from
    video footage)   171

Notes on Contributors

Liam Jarvis is a theatre-maker, director and practitioner-researcher; he is currently Co-director of the Centre for Theatre Research (CTR) and Senior Lecturer in the Department of Literature, Film and Theatre Studies (LiFTS) at the University of Essex. Liam co-founded Analogue, an award-winning independent theatre company with whom he has created devised work that toured the UK/internationally. Liam has been co-convenor of the Intermediality in Theatre & Performance Research Working Group at the International Federation for Theatre Research (IFTR) from 2017 to 2021. Publications include *Immersive Embodiment: Theatres of Mislocalized Sensation* (2019); *Theatre Rites: Animating Puppets, Objects and Sites* by Liam Jarvis and Sue Buckmaster (2021); 'Theatre & Appification: App as Simulator of Neurodivergence and an Intervention in "Affective Realism"' in *Theatres of Contagion*, Fintan Walsh (ed.) (2019); and 'The Ethics of Mislocalized Selfhood – Proprioceptive Drifting towards the Virtual Other' in *Performance Research* 22:3 (2017), Ben Cranfield and Louise Owen (eds).

Lynne Kendrick is Reader in Theatre and Performance at the Royal Central School of Speech and Drama, University of London, and Course Leader of the MA/MFA in Advanced Theatre Practice. Publications include *Theatre Aurality* (2017); 'Aural Visions: Sonic Spectatorship in the Dark' in *Theatre in the Dark: Shadow, Gloom and Blackout in Contemporary Theatre*, A. Alston and M. Welton (eds) (Bloomsbury, 2017); 'Auralite´ et performance de l'inaudible' in *Le Son du Théâtre*, J. M. Larrue and M. M. Mervant-Roux (eds) (CNRS Editions, 2016); 'Aurality, Gestus and the Performance of Noise' in *Sound und Performance*, W. D. Ernst, N. Niethammer, B. Szymanski-Düll and A. Mungen (eds) (Würzburg: Königshausen & Neumann, 2015); 'Scene in the Dark' in 'Sounding out the Scenographic Turn': Eight Position Statements, A. Curtin and D. Roesner, for *Theatre and Performance Design* 1:1–2 (2015); 'Mimesis and Remembrance' in *Performance Research: on Technology*, 17 (3): (2012); 'A Paidic Aesthetic' in *Theatre, Dance and Performance Training* 2 (1): (2011); *Theatre Noise: The Sound of Performance* co-edited with David Roesner CSP (2011).

William W. Lewis is an interdisciplinary scholar/artist and Visiting Assistant Professor of Directing and Performance at Purdue University. His research focuses on interactive spectatorship, politics, digital cultures and experiential performance. Through practice-based research he integrates interactive technologies into performances to better understand the relationship between audiences and mediatized society. He is the founding co-editor of *PARtake: The Journal of Performance as Research* and has co-edited with Sonali Pahwa an issue of *The International Journal of Performance Arts and Digital Media*. He has published articles and chapters on experiential theatre and intermedial performance in *GPS: Global Performance Studies, Theatre Topics, Performance Research*, and the edited collection, *New Directions in Teaching Theatre Arts*. Will is currently working on a collaboratively written book focusing on developing pedagogical models for university instructors who train students in the creation of experiential performance projects.

Ralf Remshardt is a professor of theatre and past director of the School of Theatre and Dance at the University of Florida (USA). After studying in Munich and Berlin, Germany, he received a PhD at the University of California, Santa Barbara. Remshardt has worked in professional and university theatres as a director, translator and dramaturg. His publications have appeared in many journals and edited collections. His book, *Staging the Savage God: The Grotesque in Performance*, was published in 2004 and reissued in 2016. He co-produced a 2015 documentary film about New York Latinx theatre that has been shown at international film festivals and the Library of Congress. He is co-editor of *Intermedial Performance and Politics in the Public Sphere* (2018) and *Routledge Companion to Contemporary European Theatre and Performance* (forthcoming). His current research concerns the intermedial intersections between theatre and early film, and performance-capture technology.

Karen Savage is a scholar and practitioner-researcher; she is currently Associate Professor and the Head of School of Fine & Performing Arts at the University of Lincoln. Karen works across film and theatre, creating work that has been screened and performed nationally and internationally. Karen has been co-convener of the Intermediality in Theatre & Performance Research Working Group at the International Federation for Theatre Research (IFTR) from 2017 to 2021. Publications include 'Performance in the (K)now – Social Raportage and Rapport of Social Media in "Reterritorializing Digital Performance from South to North"', *International Journal for Performance and Digital Media*, 15 (3) (2019), William W. Lewis and Sonali Pahwa (eds); *Economies of Collaboration in Performance: More Than the Sum of the Parts* by Karen Savage and Dominic Symonds (2018); 'Deference, Deferred: Rejourn as Practice in Familial War Commemoration' in *Staging Loss: Performance as Commemoration*, Michael Pinchbeck and Andrew Westerside (eds) (2018).

Jo Scott is an intermedial practitioner-researcher and Senior Lecturer in Performance at the University of Salford. Following the completion of her practice as research PhD project at the Royal Central School of Speech and Drama in 2014, Jo has developed both practical and theoretical research in the area of intermedial performance, addressing in particular the intersection of digital computational processes and live performance practices. Her first monograph, *Intermedial Praxis and PaR*, was published in 2016 and she has also contributed writing to a range of recent books and journals. Jo's current practice as research project engages digital technologies in creative encounters with wild urban spaces, through live mixing practices, combining video, text, sound and song. See www.joanneemmascott.com for publications, projects and documentation.

Yaron Shyldkrot is a practitioner-researcher and performance maker. He is a lecturer in theatre and performance at the University of Sheffield (UK) and his research focuses on different relationships between uncertainty and performance by investigating the many possibilities in and of darkness, the blurriness between natural and artificial, relationships with technology and each other, and the edges of sound and vision. His article 'Mist Opportunities: Haze and the Composition of Atmosphere' was recently published in *Studies in Theatre and Performance*. As a performance maker, he works as a director, dramaturg and lighting designer and co-founded Fye and Foul, a theatre company exploring unique sonic experiences, darkness and extremes.

Asher Warren is Lecturer in Theatre and Performance at the School of Creative Arts and Media in the College of Arts, Law and Education. His teaching and research focus on new and diverse ways of developing, performing and experiencing theatre in the twenty-first century, including experimental and intermedial performance and unique forms of participatory and experiential experience. He is interested in how theatre speaks to contemporary audiences, and how theatrical traditions are adapted and expanded through networked culture. His writing has been published in *Performance Research*, *Performance Paradigm*, *Australasian Drama Studies* and *Refractory: A Journal of Media Entertainment*, as well as for the Research Unit in Public Cultures and in the edited collection *Performance in a Militarized Culture* (2018). Asher convened Performance Studies Melbourne from 2016 to 2018 and is a member of the IFTR Intermediality Working Group, Performance Studies international, and the PSi Future Advisory Board from 2017 to 2020.

Introduction: Postdigitality: 'Isn't It *All* "Intermedial"?'

Liam Jarvis and Karen Savage

In the year prior to our convenorship of the Intermedial Theatre and Performance working group at the International Federation for Theatre Research (IFTR) conference, Matthew Causey had offered a provocation at the Stockholm gathering in 2016; does an 'intermedial' performance research group *need* to exist? In the wake of the mass upheaval of the 'digital revolution' (Clarke 2012), 'intermedial theatre' had, for some scholars, already become something of an anachronism. For Causey, 'multimedia', 'intermedial' and 'transmedia' theatre, even back in 2016, were all 'a thing of the past' (2016: 428). In this view, the constellation of research interests that had previously held the network together was somewhat precarious. Had the research group reached a decisive moment when it had fulfilled its purpose? With the ubiquity of the 'digital' and the subsequent techno-disenchantment associated with the 'postdigital', can 'intermedial performance' still be recognized as a discrete field of artistic endeavour and/or focus of analysis? After all, in virtually any global context, what performance *doesn't* make use of technology onstage? What artists *don't* make use of social media in some aspect of a work's delivery/marketing/audience engagement? How many works *don't* draw on intertextual allusions or reference other mediums? After decades of post-internet 'convergence culture' (Jenkins 2006) – and in 2020, with the ubiquitous exile of live performances from shared physical spaces to online platforms due to the impacts of the global Covid-19 pandemic – isn't it *all* intermedial?

The emergence of intermediality in performance

Perhaps a consequence of this ubiquity is the disappearance of intermediality as a focused area of investigation in performance research? Following the 'intermedial turn' over a decade ago,[1] the study of intermediality in contemporary theatre practice emerged in response to the incorporation of digital technology and presence of media within theatre productions. Freda Chapple and Chiel Kattenbelt had argued in *Intermediality in Theatre and Performance* (2006) that intermediality in this context was 'associated with the blurring of generic boundaries, crossover and hybrid performances, intertextuality, intermediality, hypermediality and a self-conscious reflexivity that displays the devices of performance in performance' (11). Kattenbelt offered the notion of theatre as a 'hypermedium', a term that implied a staging space where 'realities in-between performer, computer-generated realities and the audience perception of those realities are realised in performance' (19). But such a staging space, for them, mirrored a more pervasive trend in culture where life is lived 'in-between the arts and media' and thus 'intermediality' becomes understood as the 'modern way to experience life' (Chapple and Kattenbelt 2006: 24).

To place this 'intermediality-*as*-modern-life' pronouncement in a historical context, it came one year prior to the 'smartphone revolution' that arrived with the launch of Apple's iPhone in 2007 and the first-generation Android smartphones in 2008 – the ultimate neoliberal commodity and quintessentially 'intermedial' devices. Like the hybridity of the hypermedium theatre stage, smartphones had integrated once discrete channels for communication within one housing (e.g. text messages, emails, video conferencing, GPS), while simultaneously sealing previously removable batteries into 'always on' devices. Arguably, what began to increasingly disappear with the smartphone, among other encroaching personal communications and surveillance technologies, was ephemerality more broadly – a threat to the very vanishing act that Peggy Phelan had identified as ontologically unique to 'performance', which she had suggested eludes the circulation of 'representations', 'regulation' and 'control' (1993: 146–8). And yet in 2020, even prior to the widespread effects of the pandemic, theatre classes/lectures have been routinely recorded using surveillance technologies (e.g. microphones built into class spaces). For example, at the University of Essex, class content is reproduced on a centrally controlled system called 'Listen Again', powered somewhat ironically by software called 'Panopto', a term that resonates with the permanent visibility of panopticism that encompasses Michel Foucault's critique of asymmetrical surveillance (Foucault 1977). Furthermore, 'live' performances are often assessed by external examiners on the basis of their digital documentation more so than the ephemeral event, and what passes for 'theatre' amidst the Covid-19 pandemic (e.g. streaming live broadcasts, self-generating performances as apps, uploaded pre-recorded media) would be unthinkable through the distant lens of Phelan's performance ontology in the 1990s. The Thoreauvian withdrawal from the digital that this ontology calls to mind seems increasingly nostalgic and untenable in 2021. Much of our daily actions are subject, more than ever before, to data capture and harvesting. Whistle-blower Edward Snowden, following his leak of classified information from the US National Security Agency in 2013, had alerted a wider public to the fact that in a 'mobile first everything' culture, information which had readily disappeared in the past about one's whereabouts, for example, could now be stored in 'bulk collection' by companies. Every smart device, courtesy of their IMEI and IMSI global unique identifiers, is 'screaming in the air [...] "here I am, here I am"!' (Snowden 2019), with our phone's movements becoming a proxy for our own. The marginal but widespread activity of placing different mediums on the world's theatre stages might well be thought of as outmoded when considered as something discrete, especially in relation to the wider infiltration of devices in everyday life that routinely transform their users into readily detectable 'data doubles'.

The *Mapping Intermediality in Performance* (2010) edited collection from the working group recognized that the landscape of intermedial practices was 'being de- and re-territorialised' (Bay-Cheng et al. 2010: 9). This was reflected in the organization of *Mapping Intermediality* into a series of 'instances', 'nodes' (in recognition of a network) and 'portals'. Such language is indicative of the way that this book might be approached by its readers but also recognizes the various access points and interpretations of intermediality, shifting towards the language of computation in how information is distributed. Intermediality scholars also considered the effects of intermediality in relation to audience experience with new ways to describe the relationship between the work and the audience proposed, such as the 'experiencer' (Nelson 2010). Katia Arfara, Aneta Mancewicz and Ralf Remshardt's edited collection, *Intermedial Performance and Politics in the Public Sphere* (2018), examined multiple ways in which interdisciplinary artistic practices had contributed to 'counter-hegemonic discourses', providing visibility for those who had been 'silenced and marginalized' (2018: 2). Through historical and social explorations of the public and private sphere, the publication drew 'attention to the convergences and divergences on the international scene' (2018: 2).

The working group's publications were significant contributions in scholarship, initially setting out the territory and then mapping the landscape as it became de- and re-territorialized. However, if we return to Causey's provocation that intermedial theatre is a thing 'of the past', his critique appears to be hinged on terms that act as problematic mediators to the existing binaries that had first played out through the Peggy Phelan (ontology of performance)/Philip Auslander (liveness) debate about performance and media. Causey states that 'terms like *multi-*, *inter-*, or *trans-*, still construct a logic of the supplement that creates hierarchies that are irresolvable and false' (Causey 2016: 428). The digital is ubiquitous, complexly entangled, and is an essential part of most lives; possibly even more so with global shifts towards blended approaches to online and socially distanced performances mid- and post-pandemic. But even pre-pandemic, the use of media and digital technologies existing co-presently with live bodies as performance had been commonplace. Arguably, most audiences barely notice the use of digital technologies in performance anymore. Our co-presence with digital devices invite responses from makers and scholars exploring form and content to consider interdisciplinary practices that expand the notion of performance studies (Leeker et al. 2017).

Causey's provocation as to the redundancy of terms such as 'intermedial theatre' alongside an emergent field examining postdigital culture, has coincided with other seismic shifts in intermedial scholarship that are articulated in this book. For example, William W. Lewis argues that smart tech and datafication are showing the potential to 'transfer acts of spectating away from performance venues' (Chapter 2); displacing the hypermedium stage entirely. Other practitioner-researchers have moved away from well-worn discourses on 'in-between-ness' (Rajewsky 2005), 'liminality' (Fornäs 2002), 'hybridity' (Lavender 2016) and 'remediation' (Bolter and Grusin 1999), towards an interest in more complexly layered configurations, live mixes and superimpositions (Scott 2016). The current post-internet epoch is marked increasingly, as Causey proposes, by 'zones of indistinction' (Causey 2016: 434) and no longer by the supplementary 'inter-', which keeps mediums separable and hyphenated. For Lars Elleström, intermediality had necessitated a 'both-and' approach, identifying that media are *both* different *and* similar. Therefore, for him, intermediality 'must be understood as a bridge between medial differences that is founded on medial similarities' (2010: 12). But is the separating out of intermingling media for analysis where our critical energy should currently reside? Particularly in a highly knotted climate of post-truth confusions, big data, machine learning, information/reality wars and the intrusion of computation and dataveillance in various aspects of our lives? What might be dislodged in intermedial discourse? And what kinds of resistances are taking place in a hyperconnected hegemonic culture now that any clear binaries such as 'online/offline' are also widely considered to be outmoded (Berry 2015: 50)? Rather than analysing intersecting mediums in theatre, the focus is shifting to an examination of the 'informational selves' constructed through user interactions with networked systems. The precarity of artist and audience identities as potentially quantifiable, digitally manipulatable, copy-and-pastable, anonymizable, fluid and virtual – all notions that are central to postdigital aesthetics which takes 'liquidity of identity' (Causey 2016: 436) as a key feature – coincides with a growing precarity around 'intermedial' as a concept that requires re-evaluating.

As convenors of the Intermediality working group (2017–2021) and co-editors of this publication, we recognize that 'intermediality' has potentially moved beyond being an accurate term to describe the work or the scholarship from the group. Notably, while this book includes some discussions on theatre and/or live performance practices, its contributors concentrate on practices that expand the notion of 'performance' to include our entangled interrelations with data and social media sites – audiences/ users and performers as informational selves. As Causey proposes, within a postdigital context, the 'ontologies of the performance and media converge and are experienced as less uncanny and more familiar, less discreet and autonomous phenomena, and understood as a flow, a becoming, and always in process' (Causey 2016: 430–1).

A postdigital turn: Towards expanded notions of 'performance'

Edward Snowden's 2013 revelations were crucial to the emergence of postdigital culture. However, the term 'postdigital' had been coined over a decade earlier by the computer musician Kim Cascone in 2000 as a way of describing the 'aesthetics of errors and failure including phenomena such as glitch as "a collection of deconstructive audio and visual techniques that allow artists to work beneath the previously impenetrable veil of digital media"' (Cascone 2000: 12). By this logic, postdigital strategies in art-making practices or maker culture entail an ostensibly post-Brechtian surfacing of the messy hidden processes that lurk behind the shiny veil of an interface. For Florian Cramer, the term 'postdigital' in its simplest sense describes 'the messy state of media, arts and design after their digitisation' (17). But he suggests it can also refer to something more attitudinal, describing either an anti-new media 'disenchantment with digital information systems and media gadgets' or marking a defining period in which 'our fascination with these systems and gadgets has become historical – just as the dot-com age ultimately became historical' (Cramer 2015: 13). Such disenchantment has a politically resistant bent as the promise of new technology to deliver open competition, personal freedom and trustworthy knowledge has also ushered in corporate monopolies, surveillance and widespread disinformation.

Cramer notes that 'after Edward Snowden's disclosures of the NSA's all-pervasive digital surveillance systems, this disenchantment [with the digital] has quickly grown from a niche "hipster" phenomenon to a mainstream position' (Cramer 2015: 13). Correspondingly, this book's coupling of the 'postdigital' with 'activism' in its title draws out this inherent connection between postdigital practices and resistant politics or countercultural thinking. Causey had similarly recognized that what he termed as 'postdigital performances' *think digitally* in order to resist or critique 'ideological and economic strategies of control, alienation, and self-commodification' (Causey 2016: 432). Such strategies pervade much of the thinking within this book, including analysis of those industry practices that are not necessarily intended to offer the kind of resistances or self-reflexive critique that 'postdigital performance' alludes to; for example, Ralf Remshardt's opening chapter that scrutinizes the implications of acting through the avatars of Imaginarium Productions' performance capture technology (Chapter 1).

For Matthew Causey, postdigital has been distinguished by the following key characteristics: thinking digitally (thinking as the network), blending of the virtual and the real through hybridity, and deliberately mixing up discreet processes (2016). It is interesting to consider how Causey's invitation to 'think as the network' is connected with Bay-Cheng et al.'s earlier prompts that '[t]he idea of a network, without fixed bearings and entailing recursive loops, which might be entered and exited at any point marks our sense that each aspect of digital culture is best understood in relation to another, which leads to yet another and so on' (Bay-Cheng et al. 2010: 9). The rapid technological developments continue to extend this network, as Causey questions, '[i]f our understanding of performance include the techno-performative and the boundaries and ontologies of media and performance are indistinct, what is it we are experiencing as performance from within a postdigital context?' (2016: 439). With our personalized and handheld networks in the form of our smartphones (which have perhaps long supplanted the more marginal hypermedium theatre stage) we become another node in that network. Causey's model of the 'postdigital' from a performance studies perspective is one of complex entanglements. He considers the situation of a postdigital culture to be 'that of a social system fully familiarized and embedded in electronic communications and virtual representations, wherein the biological and the mechanical, the virtual and the real, and the organic and the inorganic approach indistinction' (2016: 432). Similarly, David M. Berry asserts that '[t]oday the postdigital is hegemonic, and as such is entangled with everyday life and experience in a highly complex, messy and difficult to untangle way that is different from previous instantiations of the digital'

(Berry 2015: 50). Part of this book's project is to examine instances of how the personhood of the audience and/or human or non-human performers (e.g. bots, machine learning-generated artworks) are implicated in such knotty entanglements.

Informational selves: The 'not *not*' and the '*Knot* Not'

In digital culture, as well as material living bodies, we are 'informational persons'. But are we '*our data*'? In *How We Became Our Data* (2019), Colin Koopman comments that the 'shock' of Snowden's revelations quickly dissipated to indifference, and it was the retreat to apathy that might be considered the 'deeper scandal' (2019: ix). For Koopman, the reason for this indifference might be because thinking of ourselves as 'data' seems too abstract. There is a queasiness, especially from some 'Humanities' vantage points, as to what the notion of *being* our data might mean. He calls to mind the phrase 'I am not a number' from sci-fi television series *The Prisoner* (1967), setting it against the converse fact that we seem very much to be a number when met with a multitude of administrative systems where our bank account number, tax number, insurance number, employee number, student number, order number/s and so on may need to be produced as verification simply to access, let alone participate in those systems. If, as a thought experiment, we opted out of all such systems by disavowing our 'numbers' for even six months, where would we find ourselves? Most likely in crisis! In Koopman's wording, it's not uncommon to hold the view that 'I am here' and my data is '*out there*'. But he questions what are we gesturing to 'out there' when our data simply points back to us? To return to Snowden's point, the phones in our pockets continue to shout, '[H]ere I am, here I am!'. Koopman argues, '[W]e like to believe that we are not our data. But we inhabit lives that rely on data in nearly every act we perform. We are therefore our data as much as we are anything else' (2019: ix). Our data, it seems, while not us is simultaneously not *not* us. And postdigital art and thought, in part, wrestle with these kinds of uneasy entanglements.

A central concept that pervades this book is not the 'in-between-ness' or 'both-and' concepts previously associated with intermediality, but the 'not *not*' – the notion of the double negative. In English, two negative elements in a sentence cancel one another out to produce a weaker affirmative (Horn 1978: 164), while in other languages, double negatives can rather intensify the negation. But in what respects might the 'not *not*' apply to the phenomena examined within this book that is bound up in issues of technologically assisted identity-creation? Ralf Remshardt notes that Andy Serkis as a cyborgian performer has paradoxically come to represent the acceptable face/s of performance capture, while being utterly concealed by it. He questions, what does the viewer gaze into when meeting the eyes of the Serkis/Caesar ape in the rebooted *Rise of the Planet of the Apes* (2011)? It is not *not* Serkis, but neither is it him, an informational 'Serkis' in a process that subordinates film acting to a digital post-production pipeline of interferences and manipulations (Chapter 1). For William W. Lewis, through his analysis of Blast Theory's pseudo-life coaching app *Karen* (2015–), technologies that capture our data create 'digital identities' or 'databodies' based on inputs that perform back to their users (Chapter 2). 'Micro-subjectivities' arise from potentialities of user interactions with digital systems that are not *not* the user, while simultaneously being 'out there' in circulation in the digital realm. Karen Savage highlights how filmed audience reactions to US Vice President Mike Pence's presence at the musical, *Hamilton,* are hijacked in the layered musical satirical videos of Randy Rainbow, who ironically apes Trumpian 'Us vs Them' logic, descending into partisan body-guarding on both sides of the political divide with the non-human intervention of bots exacerbating divisive interpersonal discourse on social media (Chapter 3). While we are not our images, Liam Jarvis explores how images are accepted as proxies for those we may never meet first-hand, including our politicians. A deepfake video of Obama that concatenates a vast online pool of images of the former US president into a manipulatable digital puppet is neither Obama nor is it *not* Obama; it's not *not* Obama – a claim that offers less veracity than 'it *is* Obama'. But the veracity of machine learning-generated likenesses is on the increase and Jarvis contends that we can only understand a deepfake as a 'deepfake' through uncanny effects that are increasingly being traversed (Chapter 4). Lynne Kendrick and Yaron Shyldkrot examine how sonic manipulations can problematize 'stable' audience identities, relocating the voice to the ears through headphone performances that create a precarious 'avatar-audience' of quasi-performers in the work of theatre company, Dead Centre (Chapter 6). The chapters in this publication bring some of the entanglements between layers of digital processes to the forefront in repositioning the performativity of the work in order to question whether they can be untangled or whether it is in itself 'knot tangled'.

In *Performing the Digital: Performativity and Performance Studies in Digital Cultures* (2017), Martina Leeker et al. respond to two guiding questions: How is performativity shaped by contemporary technological conditions? And how do performative practices reflect and alter techno-social formations? (2017: 9). Readers are invited to approach the book through an arrangement and framing of 'doings'; 'they thus enter into and engage with the complexity of digital cultures by way of specific processual notions' (14). There is an emphasis on the key concepts of historicizing, annotating, affecting, trading, encrypting, protesting, mapping, tagging, co-producing, instituting, organizing, crashing and democratizing (14–15). Many of these concepts can be found in this publication too.

Leeker et al. remark that 'in digital cultures […] the "performative turn" (McKenzie 2001; Fischer-Lichte 2004) needs to embrace its own "technological turn"' (2017: 11–12), and this is one of the key drivers for the way that we are rethinking the use of the terms 'intermediality' and 'the digital'. This book rethinks the assumptions and contradictions of performance and media – how the body is rethought and reperformed in layers of digital processing, and how through that processing, philosophically there is a point of disassembling/reassembling. N. Katherine Hayles asserts that 'by interacting with digital media, we are in a real sense re-engineering our brains. One of the questions that we need to think about is in what direction we want that re-engineering to proceed and what it implies about the way in which we engage with digital media' (N. Katherine Hayles in conversation with Birgit Van Puymbroeck 2015: 22). A sense of re-engineering is at play through the various multiplications of informational selves that are generated in the practices discussed in this book – from the capturing of multiple facial images as training data for deepfakes (Chapter 4) to Randy Rainbow's chorus lines of himself (Chapter 3). Elsewhere, rather than the manipulations of another's image or voice, it is queer postdigital 'flocks' that are re- or disassembled. Asher Warren examines the glitching of representations of LGBTI+ identities in the postdigital milieu. He explores works that use camp to appropriate and recycle, but which are resistant to an evolutionary futurism of 'perfect reproduction', by including the perspectives of LGBTI elders (Chapter 5).

The cover image for this book offers a useful visual representation of a 'glitch sculpture' called *Swing Individual* (2016) by Yoshitoshi Kanemaki (though Google Translate's neural machine translation of the artwork's Japanese title is 'shake feeling individual'). Of his artworks, Kanemaki says that 'everyone holds hesitations or inconsistencies that they can never answer […] "ambivalent" emotions can be embodied regardless of whether they are "surface" or "deep" layer by giving the effect of an irregular shape deviating from human figure' (Kanemaki 2016). This affective response to the ambivalence of emotion is something that we feel is echoed through the digital double, a ghosting by digital traces and extensions of our personhood. The sculpture is a deviation from a human figure, perhaps a materializing of postdigital thinking. The image at first glance seems to capture a 'failure' (to borrow Cascone's term) associated with a medium other than the one that the sculpture is comprised of, namely multiple exposure in photography or computational malfunction. But it's purposely carved that way in Hinoki wood. It is *not* a double exposure, but in its mediatization and recirculation online its effect is not *not* a double exposure. It is not *not* a double thinking. It is not *not* a capture of postdigital thinking. At once, *Swing Individual* might be a representation that calls to mind corrupted data. But when cognizant that it's a wood carving, it might be usefully re-understood as data with the potential to corrupt. The not not captures a similar sense of precarity; if it isn't *not* something then what is it? N. Katherine Hayles proposes that

> we are never only conscious subjects and objects are never just physical artifacts. Instead, we are connected in processes of meaning-making. These processes help to determine our behavior, as our behavior helps to configure these processes. If we never act with complete agency, we are never completely without it either. Andrew Pickering (1995) calls this the 'mangle of practice' in which complex recursions between material resistances and disciplined practices constantly interact with and modify each other.
>
> (Van Puymbroeck and Hayles 2015: 28)

The 'mangle of practice' (Pickering 1995) was also re-proposed by Leeker et al. to challenge the 'neat separation of human agency and non-human "procedurality"' (2017: 11). Through the process of meaning-making we are always modifying. And there is perhaps nothing quite as explicit as the accelerated speed of modification through the digital. A sense of precarity is prevalent in terms of a sense of displacements, possible hijackings of identities, displaced labour and mistruths propagated online. However, we go further with this metaphor and consider the 'not not' as the 'Knot Not'. There is an immediate visual connection, a sense of something connected, tied, distinctive elements that can be entangled with intra-connections.

Consider the reef knot; it can be tied with a single piece of rope or used to tie two pieces of rope together, creating an interlocking knot, visually like two sliding loops. In knot topology, in the field of mathematics, scholars use diagrams to work out the number of moves that are required to unknot a knot and to identify different types or similarities between knots; 'the main problem in knot theory is to recognize whether two knots are equivalent. This can be a challenge even for the simplest knot type, called the unknot – that is, as the name suggests, a not knotted knot type' (De Toffoli and Giardino 2014: 832). Similarly, one of the main problems for digital thinking is to determine whether something is what we think it is. Jarvis's chapter explores this thinking through a progression from the 'wrongness' of unconvincing fakes to moral wrongness of an entirely different order, when the fakeness of reproduced persons becomes undetectable.

The topology of knots (in mathematics) differs from the everyday use of knots (such as tying a shoelace) in that the mathematical knots have no ends and can only be undone by cutting. Theorists study what happens to knots when they are manipulated or altered, and this understanding can be applied to work through problems in other subject areas such as chemistry (Horner et al. 2016). Other sciences apply an understanding of knots to work through complexities in genetics and physics. Santos, Paulo E, Pedro Cabalar and Roberto Casati's review of the literature in this field explains:

> The scientific literature on knots usually distinguishes three basic types of string entanglements: hitches, braids, and knots. Usually, they are (informally) defined as follows: hitches are a special kind of knots used to fasten a rope around another object (usually a post or another rope); braids are entanglements of a number of strings generated by twisting motions, so that the direction of each string remains the same. The general term for the knot is used to represent entanglements of strings capable of holding their own shape, regardless of their relation with external objects.
>
> (2019: 335)

This comment from their study explains the knot in a dynamic way – it is entangled, it is string-based, it is a fastener, it is multiply tangled. Yet it is also its own shape; it is kinetic. Their study is particularly interesting for our work in that they explore interdisciplinary approaches using the dynamic concept of knots to identify opportunities related to human interaction, through processes with technology. They say that

> [r]esearch on the robotic manipulation of ropes may, in turn, provide the appropriate tools for the empirical study of embodied cognition, facilitating the development and empirical evaluation of models that not only solve problems in space, but that also take into account the body actions and perceptual feedback when doing so.
>
> (353)

This link between technology, human perception, action and understanding is a pertinent example of how abstract forms and methodologies from other practices and theories can be knotted together and applied across disciplines, opening our enquiries and finding new ways to work with expanded notions of performance.

This thinking resonates with Ralf Remshardt's study of performance capture in that the film actor has to 'preserve his humanity in the face of the apparatus' and that performance capture raises several pressing questions about the indexical relationship of the performance to its product (Chapter 1). William W. Lewis asserts through interactions with algorithmic machines, postdigital subjectivities become entangled within processes of datafication and dataveillance (Chapter 2). Considering the various connections of embedded codes, digital links, human interaction and machine generation, alongside the dissemination, perception and engagement between human and technology, the Knot Not can, we propose, help us to think digitally.

For example, the unknot, in its simplest form, the ring, can be used as a visual metaphor for understanding the continuity link between human and the digital, in that we are joined in ways that are not always visible, but have become an inherent part of our cultures. The knotted form, like the reef knot that uses two half-knots, we propose, is a visual metaphor for understanding the link between human and the postdigital. At the point that the half-knot loops over with the other half-knot there is a tension between being knotted and not knotted, and we argue that this not knotted point is the visual entanglement that acts like a rub or a glitch, the glitch that we might perceive in postdigital thinking.

Other scholars have drawn on these entanglements to create their own metaphorical approaches to performance practices. Erika Fischer-Lichte uses the term 'interweaving cultures' in place of intercultural performance in recognition that it is not always possible to distinguish 'between what is "ours" and what is "theirs"' (2009: 399). The idea that the exchange between cultures creates a weaving together with an evolving connection is aligned to the way that we see the dynamic engagement between human and technology. Scott specifically draws attention to this in her discussion of digital devices in relation to the body and place, and how the organic wild of nature exchanges and evolves with computational devices (Chapter 7). The Knot Not differs from a weave in that it presents a visual metaphor that can help to explain the complex processes of digital thinking alongside human interaction and engagement and additionally, when spoken, and in the terms of the linguistic double negation, reminds us that something cannot not be as it seems.

One of the key contributions to this collaborative publication comes from the ongoing dialogue of the Intermedial Theatre and Performance working group. It is crucial that we recognize that intermediality has been an evolving area of study and various members of the group have made contributions throughout this development and re/de-territorializing of the terrain. Some of those members are presented here in the following chapters. In order to highlight the importance of dialogue to our ongoing projects, we have invited authors to explore the intra-connections with the chapter adjacent to theirs throughout this publication. Cumulatively, the authors' thinking in these chapters folds back and folds forwards, making links and locating new entanglements with the practices and ideas discussed in discrete chapters. The book is linked through themes related to postdigital culture. However, these knotted chapters also enable more explicit reference to the way that these intra-connections have been made, and woven through conversations, with the authors drawing links between their chapters and, thus, expanding the notion of the knotted network in our thinking.

Note

1   This term had been used earlier in literary criticism, some indicating an 'intermedial turn' in the 1990s.

References

Arfara, Katia, Aneta Mancewicz, and Ralf Remshardt (2018), *Intermedial Performance and Politics in the Public Sphere*, Basingstoke, Hampshire: Palgrave Macmillan.

Auslander, Philip (2008), *Liveness: Performance in a Mediatized Culture (Second Edition)*, London and New York: Routledge.

Bay-Cheng, Sarah, Chiel Kattenbelt, Andy Lavender, and Robin Nelson (2010), *Mapping Intermediality in Performance (Volume 4.0)*, 1st edn, Amsterdam: Amsterdam University Press. MediaMatters, 5.

Berry, David M. (2015), 'The Postdigital Constellation', in David M. Berry and Michael Dieter (eds), *Postdigital Aesthetics: Art, Computation and Design*, 44–57, Basingstoke/New York: Palgrave Macmillan.

Bolter, Jay David and Richard Grusin (1999), *Remediation: Understanding New Media*, Cambridge, MA and London: The MIT Press.

Cascone, Kim (2000), 'The Aesthetics of Failure: "Post-Digital" Tendencies in Contemporary Computer Music', *Computer Music Journal*, 24 (4): 12–18.

Causey, Matthew (2016), 'Postdigital Performance', *Theatre Journal*, 68 (3): 427–41.

Chapple, Freda, Chiel Kattenbelt, and International Federation for Theatre Research (2006), 'Key Issues in Intermediality in Theatre and Performance', in *Intermediality in Theatre and Performance*, 11–26, Amsterdam and New York: Rodopi.

Clarke, Michael (2012), 'The Digital Revolution', in Robert Campbell, Ed Pentz, and Ian Borthwick (eds), *Academic and Professional Publishing*, 79–98, Oxford: Chandos.

Cramer, F. (2015), 'What Is Post-digital?' in D. Berry and M. Dieter (eds), *Postdigital Aesthetics: Art, Computation and Design*, 12–27, Basingstoke and New York: Palgrave Macmillan.

De Toffoli, Silvia and Valeria Giardino (2014), 'Forms and Roles of Diagrams in Knot Theory', *Erkenntnis* (1975–), 79 (4): 829–42. Available online: http://www.jstor.org/stable/24012602 (accessed 25 October 2020).

Eaton, Paul William (2016), 'Chapter Twelve: Multiple Materiality across Distributed Social Media', *Counterpoints*, 501: 165–78. Available online: http://www.jstor.org/stable/45157536 (accessed 21 October 2020).

Elleström, Lars (2010), 'The Modalities of Media: A Model for Understanding Intermedial Relations', in Lars Elleström (ed.), *Media Borders, Multimodality and Intermediality*, 11–48, Houndmills, Basingstoke and Hampshire: Palgrave Macmillan.

Fischer-Lichte, E. (2009), 'Interweaving Cultures in Performance: Different States of Being In-Between', *New Theatre Quarterly*, 25 (4): 391–401. doi: 10.1017/S0266464X09000670.

Fornäs, Johan (2002), 'Passages across Thresholds: Into the Borderlands of Mediation', *Convergence*, 8: 89–106.

Foucault, Michel ([1975] 1977), 'Panopticism', in *Discipline and Punish*, English trans. Alan Sheridan, New York: Pantheon. Originally published in French as *Surveiller et Punir*.

Horn, Laurence R. (1978), 'Some Aspects of Negation', in Joseph H. Greenberg, C. A. Ferguson, and E. A. Moravcsik (eds), *Universals of Human Language, Vol. 4, Syntax*, 127–210, Stanford, CA: Stanford University Press.

Horner, Kate E., Mark A. Miller, Jonathan W. Steed, and Paul M. Sutcliffe (2016), 'Knot Theory in Modern Chemistry', *Chemical Society Reviews*, 45 (23): 6432–48.

Jenkins, Henry (2006), *Convergence Culture: Where Old and New Media Collide*, New York and London: New York University Press.

Kanemaki (2016), 'Yoshitoshi Kanemaki Chisels Larger-than-life Wooden Glitch Sculptures from Tree Bark', *Designboom*, 10 November. Available online: https://www.designboom.com/art/yoshitoshi-kanemaki-wooden-glitch-sculptures-11-10-2016/ (accessed 20 October 2020).

Kattenbelt, Chiel (2006), 'Theatre as the Art of the Performer and the Stage of Intermediality', in Freda Chapple and Chiel Kattenbelt (eds), *Intermediality in Theatre and Performance*, 29–39, Amsterdam and New York: Rodopi.

Koopman, Colin (2019), *How We Became Our Data*, Chicago: University of Chicago Press.

Lavender, Andy (2016), *Performance in the Twenty-First Century: Theatres of Engagement*, Oxon and New York: Routledge.

Leeker, Martina, Imanuel Schipper, and Timon Beyes, eds (2017), *Performing the Digital Performativity and Performance Studies in Digital Cultures*. Bielefeld: Transcript-Verlag. Available online: https://library.oapen.org/bitstream/id/1fbf5f38-9ec2-4bfe-b559-f97a574b3d52/627661.pdf (accessed 21 October 2020).

Nelson, Robin (2010), 'Node: Modes of Experience', in Sarah Bay-Cheng, Chiel Kattenbelt, Andy Lavender, and Robin Nelson (eds), *Mapping Intermediality in Performance*, 1st edn, 45–7, Amsterdam: Amsterdam University Press. (MediaMatters, 5).

Phelan, Peggy (1993), *Unmarked: The Politics of Performance*, New York and London: Routledge, 146.

Pickering, Andrew (1995), *The Mangle of Practice: Time, Agency and Science*, Chicago: Chicago University Press.

Rajewsky, Irina (2005), 'Intermediality, Intertextuality, and Remediation: A Literary Perspective on Intermediality', *Intermédialités: Histoire et théorie des arts, des lettres et des techniques*, 6: 43–64. doi: 10.7202/1005505ar.

Santos, Paulo E., Pedro Cabalar, and Roberto Casati (2019), 'The Knowledge of Knots: An Interdisciplinary Literature Review', *Spatial Cognition & Computation*, 19 (4): 334–58. doi: 10.1080/13875868.2019.1667998.

Scott, Joanne (2016), *Intermedial Praxis and Practice as Research: 'Doing-Thinking' in Practice*, London and New York: Palgrave Macmillan.

Snowden, Edward (2019), 'Joe Rogan Experience #1368 – Edward Snowden', *YouTube*, 23 October. Available online: https://www.youtube.com/watch?v=efs3QRr8LWw (accessed 27 August 2020).

Van Puymbroeck, Birgit and N. Katherine Hayles (2015), '"Enwebbed Complexities": The Posthumanities, Digital Media and New Feminist Materialism'. *DiGeSt. Journal of Diversity and Gender Studies*, 2 (1–2): 21–9. doi: 10.11116/jdivegendstud.2.1-2.0021.

1

Avatars, Apes and the 'Test' of Performance Capture

Ralf Remshardt

Kafka worries and Benjamin tests

In March 1913, Franz Kafka came across a poster in the lobby of a cinema. It advertised a new feature starring the notable German stage actor Albert Bassermann in his first film appearance. To say that Kafka, an avid and regular filmgoer in his native Prague as well as a dedicated patron of the theatre, was overcome by mixed feelings, is only to say that he was Kafka. In this instance, however, Kafka's ambivalence was excited by a philosophical problem. Like many middle-class filmgoers in the early days of cinema, Kafka was able to appreciate and reflect on literary theatre one day and attend a popular film the next without much cognitive distress. But here was his idol Bassermann, an actor whom Kafka had admired in classical roles in Berlin, clearly crossing the boundary between two incommensurable worlds, the stage and the screen. He wrote to his fiancée, Felice:

> I found myself pitying B [i.e. Bassermann] as though he were the most unfortunate of men. This is how I imagine the situation: the satisfaction of acting is over; *the film is made*; B. *himself can no longer influence it in any way*; he need not even realize that he had allowed himself to be taken advantage of, and yet, when watching himself in the film, he may become aware of the utter futility of exerting all his considerable powers and – I am not exaggerating my sense of compassion – he grows older, weak, gets pushed aside in his armchair, and vanishes somewhere into the mists of time. How wrong! This is just where the error of my judgment lies. Even after the completion of the film Bassermann goes home as Bassermann, and no one else. If at any time he should withdraw [*sich aufheben*], he will withdraw completely, and be gone.
>
> (Kafka 1973: 213, his emphasis)

Kafka's concern with the actor's participation in what he views as a 'wretched film' is not merely aesthetic but is in fact profoundly *ontological*. Having been robbed of his 'influence' on the artefact, Bassermann, in Kafka's imagination, 'vanishes' (though he gets a reprieve in the last passage through the quasi-Hegelian phrase *aufheben*, which can paradoxically mean both to disappear and to retain). The performance is not so much given as *taken* – an exploitation of the actor in which he may or may not be complicit, but which results, as if it were some shamanic co-optation, in the diminution of his powers. Kafka uses the Bassermann example to discuss his own fragile sense of self, but he also implicitly formulates a theory of film acting, and a kind of new media theory. Attuned as no other writer to the exactions an alienating modernist environment made on the self, Kafka had grasped the actor's dilemma intuitively, expressing the apparent paradox that as cinema had elevated Bassermann to the status of an imaginary and had achieved his apotheosis, it had also laid waste to his 'considerable powers' as an actor, diminishing him in his substance. The film is *Der Andere* (1913, dir. Max Mack), in which the character played by Bassermann suffers from a split personality following a shock. For Kafka, film was that shock.

In this cinematic revolution of the early twentieth century, camera acting first forced performers accustomed to the regimes of the stage to reconsider their craft. The director Joseph von Sternberg wrote openly about the camera as 'a complicated machine [that] extracts an essence from the actor, over which the actor has no control' (Sternberg 1974: 86). This idea of the *alienating* quality of the camera is echoed in Walter Benjamin's notion: '*The representation of human beings by means of an apparatus has made possible a highly productive use of the human being's self-alienation*' (Benjamin 2008: 32). Both regard the act of camera performance as a submission to control by outside forces, but to von Sternberg, it seems vaguely sinister that film coerces from the actors a loss of autonomy while simultaneously trading on the phantasm of their autonomous image. In Benjamin's materialist analysis, however, the actor trades the auratic presence of the stage for a manufactured, commodified 'magic of the personality' (33), to be subjected to the critical gaze of the masses in the marketplace of images. Masses that are no less than the camera's alter ego and the final arbiter and critic of the performance in which Benjamin sees a 'test performance' [*Testleistung*] (30).

In Benjamin's analogue film world, there is a clear positionality of the actor relative to the camera, which, in spite of all of the artifice engaged to reassemble the performance, is still merely a conduit to the actor's ultimate confrontation with a mass audience who 'will control him': 'Those who are not visible, not present while he executes his performance, are precisely the ones who will control it. This invisibility heightens the authority of their control'

(33). In the following, I will discuss performance capture technology, a set of data acquisition processes which might well be regarded as the Benjaminian 'test performance' of the present. Performance capture has the potential to renegotiate the 'peculiar nature of the artistic performance of the film actor' which, as Benjamin observed, is 'carried out before a group of specialists … who are in a position to intervene in his performance at any time'. In Benjamin's view, the film actor is subject to 'examinations' (*Prüfungen*) by the apparatus that are analogous to the tests faced by workers in the mechanized industrial production process. But in capitalist production, Benjamin argues, these tests are hidden, invisible. Film exceeds these strictures by making the test '*capable of being exhibited by turning that ability itself into a test*' (30, his emphasis). The key to this test is the actor's struggle 'to preserve his humanity in the face of the apparatus', a heroic, even triumphal act of resistance where, as a proxy for the urban masses who congregate in the cinema to witness it, he takes 'revenge on their behalf' (31).[1]

The nature of the 'test' has changed with performance capture as it has emerged from ever-more complex and integrative iterations of motion capture. Performance capture offers the possibility of creating not just the digital representation of the actor but a comprehensive spatio-temporal simulacrum of a given filmic world, a shift which has redefined the physical presence of the performer, making him or her a potentially cyborgian performer in an increasingly fluid relationship to the utilized technology, within a post-human medial construct. The apparent power of the collective response has also been diminished in the performance capture process. First, by the interposition of invisible animators who splinter even that test of the actor by the apparatus-as-proxy which Benjamin still imagines as a legibly heroic confrontation between human and machine. Secondly, by the context of individualized image consumption (streaming, etc.) that never permits the masses to assemble as an authoritative perceiving body to absorb the actor's performing body en masse.

One might expect the introduction of performance capture, computer-generated characters and other instances of digitally based performance to stir anxieties similar to those of the early film actors, but the present response has been curiously muted. Almost a century after Kafka, von Sternberg and Benjamin, the executive director of the American film actors union SAG-AFTRA, writing in the introduction to a theme issue on digital acting, sought to reassure performers that though this is 'a time of sweeping change', each previous evolution in technology, beginning with silent film, 'has produced a revolution in products, platforms, audience viewing habits and, fortunately, new projects for Screen Actors Guild members. Each period brought uncertainty but, with smart responses, we adapted to ensure that it also served to expand opportunities for our members' (White 2010: 12). This essay aims to push beyond such anodyne proclamations (and there are many) to enquire about the way in which digitally based acting not only expands opportunities but also extends and complicates the aesthetic and ethics of mediated performance as both an artistic and commercial discipline.

Acquiring bodies

Performance capture is situated on the terrain of two intersecting technical domains: motion capture (mocap) and computer-generated (CGI) character animation. Of the many succinct distinctions between motion and performance capture on offer, Matt Delbridge's is perhaps most useful: performance capture, he writes, 'describes the total recording of a performance without cuts using an Optical MoCap system. [Performance capture] allows an entire performance to be captured in one take, significantly eliminating the need for multiple takes (of a single scene) to be recorded. It allows for the exploration and capture of a whole scene to be undertaken unhindered by device limitations (like the frame and physical environments)' (2014: 222). As a set of imaging techniques that enables the recording of animal or human movement sequences in order to analyse and repurpose the data, motion capture was arguably initiated with the experiments in chronophotography pioneered by Eadweard Muybridge and Étienne-Jules Marey in the late nineteenth century. Artists of the 1930s and after widely used rotoscoping and frame-by-frame tracing as a way to translate natural motion into animated cartoons. In 1966, in '9 evenings: theatre & engineering', Billy Klüver, a former Bell Laboratories engineer, used electronic motion tracking with devices attached to suits of performers to generate soundscapes (Garwood 2007: 38) and Lee Harrison III deployed electronic motion tracking that could produce a virtual puppet avatar on a television screen in real time as early as 1967 in *Scanimate* (Auslander 2017: 117).

Full visualization, however, was dependent on much higher processing speeds, so that digital avatars in commercial video gaming or performance art – two forms that began to cross-fertilize across multiple mutual boundaries – became viable only in the 1990s. Contemporary mocap now makes use of technologies first developed in medical science for biomechanical analysis, encasing the performers in a body suit studded with dozens, sometimes hundreds of passive (optical) or active (LED or infrared) markers which are then triangulated by several cameras to yield a data set representing the performers' movement in space. Increasingly, markerless systems that dispense with the cumbersome body glove have come into use. Dance choreography was in the vanguard of utilizing the biomechanical capture technology for purposes of artistic exploration. Beginning especially at the end of the last millennium, when processing speeds began to catch up with the moving human form, choreographers such as Marie-Claude Poulin, Susan Kozel and others, working in conjunction with media designers, began to make work that questioned the disposition of the digitized body as much as to celebrate its technological liberation. For instance, Poulin's Montreal-based company *kondition pluriel*, as Chris Salter remarks, offered a 'darker reimagining of the body integrated within a sensor-occupied universe, while blurring the line between performer and participant' (Salter 2010: 270).

In order to progress from motion to what director James Cameron soon renamed 'performance' capture, a convergent but more difficult aim was the credible representation of human or humanoid physiognomy through computer graphics. The first CGI character capable of registering emotion, long a particularly elusive goal, was the lounge singer Tony de Peltrie in an eponymous short film made by four University of Montreal graduates in 1985.[2] The capturing and conversion of an actor's varied facial expressions to access and manipulate the underlying emotional lexicon became the master objective of performance capture, but it remained vexed by the persistent problem roboticist Masahiro Mori in 1970 had famously termed the 'uncanny valley' – the perceived revulsion of audiences against almost-but-not-quite lifelike virtual humans. The response is grounded in a high collective sensibility to any image judged not sufficiently human in appearance. Humanoid rather than explicitly human characters, which have been the main products of performance capture in mainstream cinema, sidestep the uncanniness problem to some degree, though the debacle over the live-action version of *Cats* (2019, dir. Tom Hooper) or the studio's quick redesign of the title character in *Sonic the Hedgehog* (2020, dir. Jeff Fowler) following previews showed how narrow the line between rapture and revulsion can be.[3] The often vitriolic responses by the public in such instances of failure, however, also illustrate that audiences, even if they can intervene in the cinematic process only via social media posts and the like, still maintain a kind of critical-ludic relationship to the creation of digitally based films. This is similar to the 'subversive' attitude towards datafication and dataveillance William W. Lewis notes in his adjacent essay in this volume.

The facial capture technology with a helmet-mounted camera now in use was principally brought to fruition at WETA digital in New Zealand on Peter Jackson's *Lord of the Rings* trilogy (2001–3) to allow for the generation of actor Andy Serkis's performance as the creature Gollum. This was refined on James Cameron's *Avatar* (2009) to render the alien Na'vi characters and has yielded impressive results in the performance of the sapient chimpanzee leader Caesar (Serkis again) in the *Planet of the Apes* reboot (2011–17). Gollum's surreptitious jealousy and histrionic self-pity, Caesar's smouldering anger and anxious tenderness are complexly layered, often contradictory emotions read by the audience as a direct and true reflection of the characters' inner state, even though there are multiple interventions by the cinematic apparatus, each one of which can alter the meaning. As Anders Langland of WETA remarked, 'Even a fraction of a pixel change in the expression, particularly around the eyes, can completely change the way you perceive the character' (Langland 2017). It is on this granular, pixel-sized level of interpretive intervention that some of the most pertinent aesthetic and ethical questions about performance capture as performance arise.

The Serkis problem

While there are beginnings of an academic consideration of the questions associated with digital acting,[4] there are few traces of a serious debate about performance capture in the film industry or in the media outlets of popular culture. This may have to do with the fact that audiences, while generally aware of the technical efforts involved, are indifferent to their implications for performers and certainly don't sweat the ontological minutiae. '[T]he audience', Antonio Pizzo remarks, 'seems not to care much about the authorship question' (2016: 8). 'Performance capture' lacks its own *Wikipedia* entry, instead redirecting to 'motion capture', a sign that categorical distinctions have not yet received the imprimatur of the principal arbiter of the digital age.

A search for 'performance capture' turns up primarily articles on the ubiquitous Serkis, who has become the face (or faces) of performance capture. As Gollum in *Lord of the Rings* or Caesar in *Planet of the Apes* series, Serkis is now identified with performance capture at the same time that he is, paradoxically, largely concealed by it. The actor, who owns his own performance capture outfit in London, The Imaginarium, and has most recently directed a photorealistic CGI version of *The Jungle Book* using the technology, is convinced that captured performances are close to being Oscar-worthy (Foster 2017) and argues tautologically that it is 'no different than any process you go through to create a role, whether you're on a stage, or in front of a screen in a more conventional sense. The actor's performance is the actor's performance' (Rafferty 2017). Academic critics like Sharon Marie Carnicke have lent support to this notion, noting that 'acting is – at base – a discrete art form which has – over the centuries variously adapted to the changing technologies' and that the essential processes of acting 'remain relatively stable' (Carnicke 2014: 322). She argues that a performance such as Gollum 'can be subjected to the same kind of analysis and assessment as any other kind of screen performance' (332).

That question remains to be explored here, but it is plausible that an actor like Serkis, who is so linked to an emergent and ill-understood technology, would want to normalize it and reframe it in the context of familiar tropes, though his advocacy carries a note of lobbying. As the principal generator of Oscar-worthy performances in performance capture, Serkis's effort to cast it as a branch of conventional performance untroubled by aesthetic and ethical landmines serves to reduce the potential anxieties of a largely older white male bloc of Academy voters. It is also not unlikely that the relentless foregrounding of Serkis as performer is a deliberate strategy by studios to humanize the technology and recuperate the real-world actor which the performance capture process otherwise so effectively amalgamates and effaces, as a way to quell potential audience unease. This is the outflow of what Jessica Bode recognizes as a pervasive 'discourse of reassurance' in the promotional materials to films like *Planet of the Apes*, an attempt to 'disarticulate acting from the work of the animators' (Bode 2015: 32).[5] Serkis has had a leading part in almost every major motion/performance capture-based film of recent years, including Peter Jackson's *King Kong* (2005), Steven Spielberg's *Tintin* (2011) and multiple instalments of the *Star Wars* franchise (2011–15), suggesting that he brings a specific technique and understanding to performance capture. Reducing performance capture to simply another type of acting acknowledges only Serkis's own insistence on maintaining his grounding in prior processes within a radically changed medial environment. In truth, performance capture challenges the phenomenology of performance as well as its semiotics.

Remaking mocap into 'performance capture' is an assertion of a categorical leap, like going from 'pigment' to 'painting' or 'sound' to 'music', that is, from a physical to a socio-aesthetic and from a process-driven to a systemic phenomenon.[6] Motion, once captured through sensors, linked camera arrays, or other devices, is freely and infinitely convertible into any of its medial analogues that can represent the vectors of bodies in space: projection, computer simulation, etc. In other words, motion is preserved at every step of conversion and can be recovered, retrieved, even reconstituted, say through mapping onto a robotic exoskeleton. Performance, however, is resistant to such conversions; it is fiercely local and exists only at the moment of its original enunciation and again when it is actualized *through* the medium, though not *in* it. In performance capture, as Matt Delbridge notes, the 'workflow privileges the processes involved post performance' (2015: 84) and so has the potential to render the performative moment subordinate rather than uniquely generative.

No doubt digital performance capture has increased the difficulty of writing about film acting exponentially. Any student is told to avoid the category error of confusing character with actor in a performance review, since the ability not to succumb to the apparent aesthetic fusion and to track and articulate the difference between signifier and signified in performance semiosis is the mark of mature analysis. But then, here is film critic Manohla Dargis, reviewing the *Rise of the Planet of the Apes* reboot (2011) in the *New York Times*:

> First among the computer creations is Caesar, who evolves from a ball of fluff into a rambunctious child, a sullen teenager and finally a young adult given nuance through performance-capture technology (which combines an actor's moves with computer-generated imagery) and the efforts of Andy Serkis, the actor who brought Gollum to life in the *Lord of the Rings* trilogy. When Caesar scowls, as he increasingly does, you don't see just digital wizardry at its most expressive; you also see a plausible, angry, thinking character.
>
> (Dargis 2011)

The paragraph makes an obligatory nod to Serkis and his 'efforts' but doesn't connect them in a clear causal manner to the character we 'see'. Are the actor's efforts visible or invisible? Do we ever *see* the actor rather than the character? This is not just a semantic quibble; it goes to the heart of the question whether the 'binocular vision' of semiotic and phenomenological perception (States 1985: 8) that has sustained our engagement with performance for centuries has entered a categorically different phase. The question at issue is this, as Philip Auslander poses it (echoing Derek Burrill, who calls it the 'Gollum problem'): 'At what point is something too digitized? If something is partially digitized, what of its ontology, its presence? Can someone (or something) perform, in the traditional sense, in the digital?' (Auslander 2017: 8).

Piercing performance in the digital

Auslander's approach to the problem is to frame it as a principally semiotic one: he interrogates performance capture in terms of Peircean semiology, grounding it all the while in discourses of traditional film acting. First, he asks, is there a clear *iconic* relationship between actor and character, a referential bond founded on similarity, recognizability? In the case of Gollum,

Auslander demurs, drawing on Bert O. States who believes our appreciation of the actor's art (on stage) is much determined by our recognition of the actor in the role. Arguably though, Oscar voters are swayed by iconicity, which makes Serkis's bid to be recognized as the man behind the digital mask all the more comprehensible. Perhaps it is in involuntary response to such self-promotion that Dargis cites the actor's efforts, but it seems she also contradicts Auslander implicitly here by recognizing Serkis as Caesar in his efforts at unrecognizability, a kind of iconic loop.

However, in his essay Auslander is far more concerned with another of Peirce's semiotic categories, that of indexicality. The *index*, in distinction to the icon, rests on correlation rather than resemblance to the object. Thus, a facial expression stands in an indexical (or 'deictic') relationship to the inner state of the actor. The first hurdle is to ascertain whether a digital image can assume the same (or similar) indexical relationship to its object as an analogue one, given that the direct causal link between object, light and chemical reaction in photography is replaced by sampling and algorithm. While this link may obtain for digital photography or videography where the CCD image sensor is routinely treated like a substitute for film, much of the mocap and performance capture apparatus is not optically based but rather is a telemetric rig that delivers data for spatial measurements. The image which is generated, not per se recorded, is a by- or end-product of the data set. Even if we were to concede that such images are not categorically distinct from traditional film images but merely an alternate mode of registration, how can the process of performance capture be squared with the idea, pervasive in much of traditional film criticism throughout the twentieth century, that the film image, particularly in close-up, discloses the inner life of the actor directly to the audience? Auslander wrestles at length with this question, citing Béla Balázs and Siegfried Kracauer as tokens of an understanding of filmic intersubjectivity that takes the face at, well, face value:

> In defending performance capture as a kind of acting, it therefore becomes necessary to argue that the actor's expressions and gestures can be successfully captured and transferred to the CGI figure, to be read either as indexing this figure's presumed emotional state or pointing back to the actor whose performance was captured.
>
> (Auslander 2017: 17)

Indeed, the technical process itself, in its increasing complexity, can't warrant that as viewers, we can access any primary performative moments. In *Planet of the Apes*, close-ups of the characters of Caesar, Maurice, Bad Ape and the other simians were the result of what the animators referred to as 'facial puppets' in which every movement was key-frame animated by hand to achieve the desired results. Animation supervisor Anders Langland of WETA, echoing Andy Serkis's assertion, found it necessary to repeatedly reassure his audience that the performances seen on screen corresponded entirely to the actors' intentions while implicitly admitting the exact opposite, namely that every moment was subject to observation, interpretation, processing and direct manipulation:

> The performances of the apes are 100 per cent the actors' performances. But translating that performance from the actor to the digital ape takes painstaking work from our extremely talented team of facial animators. It requires analyzing the performances to understand the intent and emotion behind every single frame of the shot.
>
> (Langland 2017)

If an indexical relationship was maintained between the performer and the captured data in performance capture, it was most certainly altered or severed in the multiple interventions of translation and animation. Nonetheless, a powerful *illusion* of a complete inner emotional state is created – the impression Dargis referred to as 'a plausible, angry, thinking character' – except that its connection to the original performance is at best undecidable. This ambiguity prompts Antonio Pizzo to remark that 'the motion capture actor does not provide a performance per se, but a text to be played and interpreted by the animators' (2016: 22). On these grounds, Auslander also rejects the idea that it is possible to 'perform in the digital', at least for now. '[T]he PerfCap figures we see on screen', he concludes, 'do not appear as performances by individual actors but, rather, as techno-dramatic phenomena brought forth through a complex process of production' (2017: 21–2). But Auslander's premise, while correct on the undecidable qualities of performance capture performance, also falls prey to the self-mythologizing of traditional analogue cinema. The notion that the film camera is a 'truth machine', a royal road to the actor's unconscious that detects any falsehood and impeccably renders the performer's inner life, is roundly contradicted by many anecdotes by well-known film actors, from James Cagney to Laurence Olivier, who happily, in Hitchcockian parlance, 'faked it'. Pizzo lends support to Auslander by arguing that the link between actor and animation is fuzzy and that determination of 'authorship of the final rendering of character cannot have a theoretical solution'. He writes: 'We are now in a situation where the job of the actor is best represented as existing on a spectrum ranging from real acting to digital acting' (2016: 12). (Instantly, such a formula of course opens the theoretical Pandora's box of what may be meant by 'real acting').

Performance/Surveillance

In the terms proposed by Bert O. States (albeit for the theatre), performance capture pushes the act of performance purely into the *representational* mode, i.e. 'disappearing into' the artefact until only the image of the character remains. It arguably effaces the two other 'pronominal modes' of acting, the self-expressive and the collaborative, i.e. the assertion of the performer's personal identity and their interaction with the audience. These latter two are exactly the pronominal modes Kafka feared had been stripped from Albert Bassermann in *Der Andere*, the modes Benjamin tested in his imaginary heroic actor, and the modes propagated by Andy Serkis on behalf of his performance capture projects. In the hierarchy of acting values *qua actor* the self-expressive and collaborative modes signal the actor's autonomy, the resistance to being fully absorbed into the role and being instrumentalized by and for the representation.

The necessarily reductive process of performance data capture in which solely the representational logic holds sway aligns it with surveillance technologies. In his recent book on performance and surveillance, James Harding engages the notion of theatrical acting and surveillance with a nod to Bertolt Brecht's 'street scene'. In that seminal essay, Brecht had likened epic acting to witnessing an incident in the street and giving a demonstrative account of it. In the context of public surveillance culture, Harding argues, such a 'naïve' epic model has given way to the 'seen street' where 'any intervention along the lines described by Brecht is now shaped by, indeed is always already positioned within, the frame of surveillance technology's sociopolitical interventions' (Harding 2018: 18).

It might indeed be said that performance capture is the first real revolution in acting since Brecht's theorization and deployment of *Verfremdung* in the 1930s and 1940s. Brecht was concerned with wresting control of performance from the apparatus of the theatre, which had structurally incorporated it into a predetermined exchange that was by its nature captive to both commercial and emotional interests (the emotional being, as Brecht clearly observed, the political). *Verfremdung* restored the performer's artistic and ideological autonomy. What propelled Brecht was the creation of a productive rupture between the performer and the scene. Performance capture tries, so to speak, to return Brecht's genie to the bottle, closing the gap between actor and character, and character and environment, by subsuming the authority of performance and making it infinitely convertible, accessible, malleable and inseparable from the apparatus. It eradicates, under layers of digital accretion, the barb of individual performance, and leaves merely its trace.

Admittedly, a Brechtian performance is hardly the aim of the practitioners of performance capture, but it is remarkable that performance capture and digital character rendering defy two central principles of Brecht's *Short Organum* (1948). One, of course, is the injunction against 'wholly transforming' into the character, since such visual absorption is precisely the strength of the process. The other comes in the guise of offering the actors and director greater performative freedom. Because the virtual camera can retrospectively access and resolve any angle or visual plane, performances are omnidirectional; the actors never know where the viewer will finally be. But for Brecht's theory, the actor's 'point of view', or rather 'standpoint' (*Standpunkt*) is critical, not simply as an abstract set of political or social maxims, but indeed as a topographical and deictic stage location from which to articulate them (Brecht 1964: 193, 196).

Given the many overt parallels between performance capture and the ubiquitous technologies of biometric data capture in the public arena, whether by corporate entities or by state-sanctioned or supra-national organizations, and the ongoing conversion of such information in conjunction with other metadata streams into digital images and identities, it is not far-fetched to speak of performance capture as a kind of 'performance surveillance'. As in performance capture, individuals under public surveillance, as Elise Morrison writes, 'often retain little control over the appearance of their digital doubles, let alone the interpretation of their aggregate data' (2016: 190). Such digital representations 'privilege the corporeal body as a data source over the agency or rights of the individual, a being capable of self-determination and change' (190). In a sense, the liberatory power that Walter Benjamin ascribed to the new visual media, that '*any person can lay claim to being filmed*' (Benjamin 2008: 33, his emphasis), has been turned against its subject by being made to serve neoliberal interests. Indeed, he thought of such a claim to representation through the apparatus as akin to (self-)authorship and was highly critical of the absorption of film into a capitalist model, though the extent of surveillance now possible would have been unimaginable to him (as, to a degree, it still is to us).

Resistance to surveillance techniques has taken many forms, including protests designed to thwart CCTV cameras (e.g., Hong Kong 2019), but also practices of aesthetic intervention. Artists like Zach Blas, Leo Selvaggio and others have engaged in projects specifically aimed at critiquing facial recognition technology. Blas, in *Facial Weaponization Suite* (2011–14) has created blob-like masks concealing the wearer's face which combine 'aggregated facial data of participants, resulting in amorphous masks that cannot be detected as human faces by biometric facial recognition technologies' (Blas). Selvaggio took the opposite tactic in his URME project, creating a photorealistic 3D printed prosthetic of his own face which he sells online, instantly converting the wearer into Selvaggio and potentially confounding the surveillance apparatus with multiple data copies of himself (Morrison 2016: 206–9). But even in the individual encounter with algorithmic systems, resistance is possible. William W. Lewis argues in his adjacent essay in this volume that such systems of *dataveillance* invite the user to 'performatively add noise' and hack the exchange of data by presenting 'purposeful and consistently *inconsistent*' versions of a user's identity as 'an outlet for a full performance of a post-humanist self' (see page 57).

As Elise Morrison remarks, the common thread among anti-surveillance artists is that they 'reject the notion that amalgamations of data can stand in for individuals' (2016: 228). This points urgently to the fact that in terms of surveillance culture, the actor's acquiescence to yielding her image to the opaque processes of performance capture and manipulation is an extension of the larger public's compliance with social data collection and processing. Citing a term by Graham Sewell and James Barker, Harding discusses the 'rules of right' which 'refer to a willing submission to systems of surveillance and oversight': 'Ultimately, the rules of right have a profound effect on the kinds of performative acts that shape individual identity, and those acts are not only deeply entrenched in processes of social sorting and stratification; they sustain those processes as well' (192–3). Performance capture is merely the cinematic extension of these compliant rules.

The ethics of *Avatar*

If a performance is now not a statement, recorded for posterity, but an act of surveillance followed by a series of technical interventions, where are the limits, the borderlines, of those interventions? Who gives, receives and owns the performance? Here it is instructive to look at the first film in which performance capture (rather than a refinement of motion capture) was used, and the most recent, as a way to chart the medium's own consciousness.

A key moment was the release of James Cameron's *Avatar* (2009), a film that was calculated to do no less than reimagine the process of filmmaking and deliver a proof of concept of the instrumental and expressive maturity of performance capture. *Avatar* rested on dual, mutually integrated technical achievements: the rendering of a plausible (if not realistic) largely computer-generated 3D environment and the refinement of motion capture techniques into performance capture. But Cameron's ostensibly emancipatory parable subverted itself in its own technical and ideological refractions and altered the meaning and ontology of performance in a hegemonic system of digital acquisition, alteration and distribution. This system is currently in full force with the simultaneous manufacture of four *Avatar* sequels, two of which have completed principal photography (Deb 2018). The initial entry into the series was exceptionally successful, grossing over $2.7 billion against costs of $280 million.

In the plot of *Avatar*, paraplegic Marine Jake Sully travels to the distant planet of Pandora where a greedy mining corporation intends to drive off the native humanoid Na'vi people in order to mine for a precious material called, improbably, *unobtainium*. As *Avatar* is itself, at heart, a tale of surveillance, Sully gathers intelligence for the cooperating military unit spearheaded by brutal Colonel Quaritch, while simultaneously attempting to infiltrate the Na'vi people with the use of an 'avatar' identity. While Sully begins to bond with the native inhabitants and quickly falls in love with the alien Neytiri, the Colonel moves forward with his ruthless extermination tactics, forcing the soldier to take a stand and fight back in an epic battle for the fate of Pandora.

The film seems like a palimpsest of dozens of anti-corporate tracts, and on the narrative level, it propounds an obvious, fairly conventional anti-colonialist fable that can be (and has been) read as an allegory of US imperialism.[1] *Avatar's* perceived message with its nod to environmentalism was echoed by indigenous leaders such as Bolivia's Evo Morales, and emboldened active resistance to political oppression in the West Bank where Palestinian protesters dressed up as Na'vi. But the surface plot of *Avatar* became subordinate in many media accounts to the other 'heroic' battle connected to the film, that of its technical breakthroughs and the struggle to get it financed, filmed and defended from jealous opportunists. The medium, or rather the (re)mediation, was always the real message. As Nicholas Cull has argued, '*Avatar* has the *image* as hero. The film was conceived, created, marketed and consumed around the notion of immersive spectacle' (2013: 199).

Consequently, the creation of the image, of which performance capture has a significant part, had to be preserved from any suspicion of its authenticity or legitimacy, lest it make common cause with the targets of the film's ostensible political critique. But the rather fair accusation that *Avatar* was at its core a neocolonial fantasy disguised as a neoliberal environmentalist fable quickly spread to blogs and online fora. The Na'vi are a transparent composite of several pre-industrial non-Western populations subject to a kind of fetishizing of the colonial subject, but for our purposes, we need to pay attention to the colonial essentializing of the film's other Other, the performers. The film's claims to decrying cross-species exploitation and championing environmental sensitivity were thrown into ironic relief by the very manner in which the performance of the film's indigenous characters was created, an extractive process in which the originating actors ceded control over their image to a central authority, which bears a freighted resemblance to the very colonialist enterprise the movie superficially condemns. In the creation of the digital performances, the film recapitulates itself on a formal level in order to contradict itself ideologically, in a kind of mise en abyme of self-subversion.

Compared to science-fiction films such as *The Matrix* (1999, dir. The Wachowskis) whose mash-up of consciousness and circuitry leads to an utter ontological dislocation of its protagonists and poses a set of post-human dilemmas, the premise of *Avatar* itself is really precybernetic, though masked as cutting-edge biotechnological achievement in the narrative. As presented in the film, the avatar bodies are not externally controlled or independently accessible from a higher-order control function; rather they are in effect *inhabited* in alternation with the avatar's primary body or locus of consciousness. In consequence, being an avatar in the film is less an instance of cyborgian extension of human capacity than an instance of soul transfer, or *metempsychosis*, a more atavistic category mirroring the film's pop mysticism. The idea of the avatars themselves, the exchange of one body for another, is an allegory for acting, of course. The avatar is a kind of meat suit for its operators, depositing a migratory consciousness in a constructed xenogenic body. The human characters inhabit it for the purposes of 'performing' (in the expanded sense proposed by John McKenzie) a function in the alien world, including certain rites of passage. Cameron's implicit ideal of the para-humanity embodied in the Na'vi, then, is one of unfettered, self-determining agency (the kind of agency denied the actual humans who operate in the story under the multiple constraints of military-industrial rules and colonial displacement).

Swathed in data suits emblazoned with reference markers, performers were constantly monitored by 120 digital cameras, including a head rig that scanned fifty-two dots on the face. Run through Motion-Builder, a 3D character animation program, and fed back to the floor as CGI data, the performance was instantly mapped to the actors' blue alter egos. Because the reference data was both instantly accessible and stored digitally, Cameron could use a virtual camera to walk through the set and even reshoot scenes from different angles without having the actors present. The results, rendered in relatively low resolution, then became the template on which digital animators in New Zealand and elsewhere built the final look.

In the film's promotional materials (e.g. an HBO *First Look* featurette), Cameron and his actors made the familiar claim that performance capture was no different from any other acting mode, that it translated the 'personality', even 'soul' of the actor '100 per cent' – a hyperbolic statement under any circumstance, and one that has apparently become WETA's party line. Lisa Bode has noted this 'discourse of "fidelity"' throughout the emerging performance capture cult(ure), one that 'encourages us to see performance capture as "conveyance" rather than "mask"' (Bode 2015: 41). But the industry press remained sceptical. Andre Soares, the publisher of the online *Alt Film Guide*, rejected the insistence of *Avatar*'s makers that the Na'vi performance is comparable to conventional film performance: 'As far as I'm concerned', he wrote, 'solid screen acting uses the eyes more than anything. The eyes of the Gollum were computer-animated – and so were those of the Na'vi in *Avatar*. How can you tell how much of the actors' "eye performance" is acting and how much is drawing?' (Soares 2010). In the usually pop-culturally compliant magazine *Entertainment Weekly*, Mark Harris argued rather passionately that 'a computer can't pick up every nuance of an actor's work, because great performances have nuances that are ineffable and unquantifiable'. Zoe Saldana's character Neytiri, he concluded, is 'a superb visual effect enhanced by an actor' rather than the opposite (Harris 2010).

In the film, the ubiquitous Na'vi greeting, meant to convey the species' soulful acknowledgement of their interlocutors' true inner visage is the phrase 'I see you'. The production process upended this sentiment since *in effect* the creation of the Na'vi rested on the unseen, in fact, on a kind of ethics of digital disappearance. The uncomfortable truth for Cameron's emancipatory fable was that most of the non-white performers never appeared *as themselves* on screen. What was extracted was an essentialized otherness composed largely of nobility and fierceness, which could apparently be supplied by Zoe Saldana's Dominican heritage or Laz Alonso's African-American ethnicity equally well. Analogous to biometric surveillance regimes, which are programmed to 'reinscribe whiteness, masculinity, youth, and high economic class' as normative (Morrison 2016: 193), Cameron's performance processing likewise minimized or erased racial or ethnic identities or subsumed them into an appealing exoticism.[8]

The conscious ape

Following *Avatar*, some critics began to reflect increasingly on the intersections of plot and technology that Cameron's movie implied. In a review of the first *Planet of the Apes* reboot two years later, Manohla Dargis wrote: 'If you wanted to indulge in some old-school 1970s-style paranoia, you could see an analogy between our world, in which digital characters are fast catching up to their human counterparts, and that of *Rise of the Planet of the Apes*, which clears the stage for a coming ape revolution (and doubtless more movies)' (Dargis 2011). In fact, the relationship of the films to themselves and their own mode of creation was increasingly beginning to take that paranoia into account and thematize it, as when the dialogue assigned to the seemingly deranged Colonel McCullough in *War for the Planet of the Apes* (who turns out to be quite rational in his brutality) operates on both the plot level and the metadiscursive plane. 'My god, look at your eyes. Almost human', he says to the captive Caesar, as if both to validate the audience's perception and to dispel any rising sense of uncanniness while giving a sly nod to the animators' art. It's also a reminder of the pervasive racialized subtext of the original *Apes* movies, once so openly signified by Charlton Heston's outburst 'Take your stinking paws off me, you damned dirty ape!'.

Later, in a full-blown Frankensteinian monologue, the Colonel observes: 'You're much stronger than we are. You're smart as hell. No matter what you say, you'd eventually replace us. That's the law of nature. The irony is we created you, tried to defy nature, bend it to our will. Nature has been punishing us for our arrogance ever since.' It doesn't take much imagination to see in this 'law of nature' speech an analogy to the law of digital dominance in which the avatars replace their repentant originators. The comparatively simple narrative arc of *War for the Planet of the Apes* where the apes are digitally endowed with all indices of humanity and dignity while the humans regress into barbarity and speechlessness is complicated by this constant medial self-awareness of the cinematic artefact. The human villain is allowed to articulate the position of fallen humanity (in one instance, rather pushing the point, he maintains that he 'gave his only son' in a bid to save his species) while the apes, who reach a kind of paradise at the end, are both mythopoetically and technically post-human, namely not-quite and better-than. In that way, the film carries on a constant recursive dialogue with itself about the circumstances of its own making.

This self-awareness is perhaps necessary because motion and performance capture raise serious ethical and legal concerns regarding the disposition of the data. The manipulation of an actor's digital likeness has become disturbingly common, at first arising out of fiscal necessity. When the actor Brandon Lee died during the shooting of the movie *The Crow* (1994, dir. Alex Proyas), technology was advanced enough to create a posthumous performance and salvage the film by digitally painting Lee's face on a body double. Digital exhumation and reanimation was conducted on Laurence Olivier (who was resurrected for *Sky Captain and the World of Tomorrow* in 2004 (dir. Kerry Conran)) and more recently and to startling effect, on Peter Cushing in *Rogue One* (2016, dir. Gareth Edwards). The Disney corporation, which now owns the *Star Wars* properties, has denied being in negotiations with the estate of the deceased Carrie Fisher for 'continued use' of her digital image, an almost certain sign that the opposite is true (Pulver 2017). Elsewhere in the cultural industries, Harding references the occasion in 2012 when the late Tupac Shakur was virtually resurrected by Digital Domain at the Coachella festival to be able to perform alongside Snoop Dogg 'as an autonomous, distinct, and powerfully marketable commodity' (2018: 209).

James Cameron is not innocent of previous instances of virtual human trafficking. In 1993, Steven Spielberg used the data scan of actor Robert Patrick that had been made for Cameron's *Terminator 2* (1991) to fashion a CG character that could be gobbled up by a digital dinosaur in *Jurassic Park* (Beard 2001: 1169). Such repurposing of captured human data is a legal conundrum. In an article suggestively titled 'Digital Slaves of the Render Farms', Adam Faier notes that under US law, actors cannot be copyrighted, whereas images of actors and cartoon characters can be: 'A virtual actor used in a motion picture or a printed image, for example, may be protected under copyright law' (2004: 334). In 2001, when CGI characters were first appearing more widely in films, law professor Joseph Beard argued that protections from civil or copyright law were far from catching up with the legal ramifications of unleashing masses of IVH (imaginary virtual humans) on mass culture. The World Intellectual Property Organization reports that negotiations for a comprehensive global performances copyright treaty have stalled since 1996, mostly because of resistance from the United States, where performers' rights are automatically ceded to producers (WIPO). This unsettled legal framework, to which the US Screen Actors Guild is a party through inaction, can only benefit the producers who always have the upper hand in the Benjaminian 'test performance' of image circulation.

Actor training by and large leaves its graduates ill-equipped for the apparatus they may encounter. UK movement teacher Mark Evans concedes that a concerted response is both necessary and subject to opposition in the profession: 'How does a performer prepare for a performance that may take place against a "blue screen", be re-modeled and digitally transplanted onto another "actor", and then further "enhanced" through editing?' Movement teachers tend, in Evans's analysis, to retain a traditional practice 'specifically crafted for the live actor' and to resist 'the implicit alienation of the "body as representation" from the "body as source" which is present in the digital reproduction of movement' (Evans 2009: 180). Summoning a Bakhtinian trope, Evans attributes an 'unruly body' (143) to the modern actor, a lived-in body not contained or circumscribed by its semiotic potential. It is this (post)modern body with its multiple social and biological inscriptions (class, race, gender, weight, etc.) that the contemporary actor brings to the work of representation, and in the context of a slowly diversifying pool of performers, these inscriptions, these marks of individuality and authenticity, even of unruliness and excess, are indeed a primary currency. However, it is a currency that is too easily convertible and made fungible under the auspices of performance surveillance.

Philip Auslander asked whether performance in the digital is possible. Auslander aside I believe that it is not only possible but *unavoidable*, and that to fall back on notions of a 'pure' indexical relationship between the performing subject and the resultant image would be retrograde. Performance in the mediated realm such as performance capture is not so much the result of a clearly defined transaction, iconic or indexical, as an *emergent structure* that becomes extant under certain conditions. As Chris Salter remarks in a slightly analogous context, the tension between the *humanistic* body and the *dehumanized* (or perhaps *post-human*) machine is 'a false line between poles that are always in the process of being blurred' (Salter 2010: 276). Writing on virtual reality performance long before performance capture, Johannes Birringer contended that human performers are not separate from the software system or programming environment in which they operate; 'the entire interface environment can be understood as digital performance process, as emergent system' (Birringer 1998: 44). Our understanding of this emergent system of performance is likewise still emergent; the 'testing' of the cinematic future will determine whether the performer, rather than simply being reified as a commodity under surveillance and digital doubling, can be empowered to recover the self-expressive and collaborative 'pronominal modes' of acting in the face of the technology's coercive controls, and finally, to gather and withdraw (*aufheben*) herself, to come back into her own in the manner Kafka imagined Bassermann doing, at the dawn of film acting in 1913.

Notes

1   I have preserved the male pronoun for the actor in Benjamin's text while acknowledging that it is not inclusive.
2   See the brief history of virtual humans (through the late 1990s) in Magnenat-Thalmann and Thalmann (2008) and the extensive inventory of digital character modelling in Flueckiger (2010).
3   In the event, criticism centred on the expensive and apparently haphazard effort to anthropomorphize the cat characters, which audiences found risible and repulsive. An amended version of the film was rushed into theatres, though to no avail (see Blair 2020).
4   Antonio Pizzo (2016) provides a good overview of this academic discussion. I thank Prof. Pizzo for generously sharing his work with me. See also Auslander (2017), discussed below.

5   Matt Delbridge points out that there is disagreement on whether animation or performance takes precedence in performance capture. Citing the initial use of the term in work on *The Polar Express* (2004, dir. Robert Zemeckis), he notes: 'Many animation enthusiasts tend to look with disdain at the work of Zemeckis, claiming that PeCap diminishes the role of the animator. Contemporary literature focused on MoCap and animation tends to suggest the opposite of this, where the act of performance is diminished and often looked on with disdain' (2014: 222).

6   In this regard, I agree with Pizzo, who suggests that 'the technological differences between "motion capture" and "performance capture" are not substantial' (2) but, considering how the subtle differences in image acquisition and processing inflect the temporal the nature of the performance, I disagree that the terms are interchangeable.

7   Unsurprisingly, it was most vigorously attacked by right-leaning intellectuals like Ross Douthat in the *New York Times* or John Podhoretz in the *Weekly Standard*, but even a sympathetic critic such as David Boaz in the *Los Angeles Times* called it 'a perfect souffle of left-wing attitudes'.

8   As Tanine Allison has argued, motion capture in principle should be free of racial bias: 'In erasing, and "e-race-ing," the visual appearance of the mo-cap performer, motion capture renders racial difference irrelevant' (2015: 122). But in an animated film like *Happy Feet* (2006), about dancing penguins, having the character Mumble voiced by a white actor (Elijah Wood) and movement provided by a black dancer (Savion Glover) perpetuates 'the association of African Americans with the body while the white actor provides the language, usually associated with the mind' (123).

References

Abramowitz, R. (2010), 'Avatar's Animated Acting', *Los Angeles Times*, 18 February. Available online: http://articles.latimes.com/print/2010/feb/18/entertainment/la-et-avatar-actors18-2010feb18

Allison, T. (2015), 'Blackface, *Happy Feet*: The Politics of Race in Motion Capture and Animation', in D. North, B. Rehak, and M. S. Duffy (eds), *Special Effects: New Histories/Theories/Contexts*, 114–26, London: BFI and Palgrave.

Auslander, P. (2017), 'Film Acting and Performance Capture', *PAJ*, 117: 7–23.

Avatar (2009), [Film] Dir. James Cameron. USA: Twentieth Century Fox.

Beard, J. (2001), 'Clones, Bones and Twilight Zones: Protecting the Digital Persona of the Quick, the Dead and the Imaginary', *Berkeley Technology Law Journal*, 16 (3): 1166–271.

Benjamin, W. (2008), *The Work of Art in the Age of Its Technological Reproducibility, and Other Writings on Media*, ed. M. W. Jennings, B. Doherty, and T. Y. Levin, trans. E. Jephcott, R. Livingstine, H. Eiland, and others, Cambridge, MA and London: Harvard University Press.

Birringer, J. (1998), *Media and Performance: Along the Border*, London and Baltimore: Johns Hopkins University Press.

Blair, I. (2020), 'The "Cats"-astrophe! Experts Say Don't Blame the VFX', *Variety*, 10 January. Available online: https://variety.com/2020/artisans/awards/vfx-cats-1203463342/ (accessed 23 March 2020).

Blas, Z. (2014), *Facial Weaponization Suite*. Available online: http://www.zachblas.info/works/facial-weaponization-suite/ (accessed 23 March 2020).

Boaz, D. (2010), 'The Right Has "Avatar" Wrong', *Los Angeles Times*, 26 January. Available online: https://www.latimes.com/archives/la-xpm-2010-jan-26-la-oe-boaz26-2010jan26-story.html (accessed 23 March 2020).

Bode, L. (2015), 'Fleshing It Out: Prosthetic Makeup Effects, Motion Capture and the Reception of Performance', in D. North, B. Rehak, and M. S. Duffy (eds), *Special Effects: New Histories/Theories/Contexts*, 32–44, London: BFI and Palgrave.

Brecht, B. (1964), *Brecht on Theatre*, trans. J. Willett, New York: Hill and Wang.

Carnicke, S. M. (2014), 'Emotional Expressivity in Motion Picture Capture Technology', in J. Sternagel, D. Levitt, and D. Mersch (eds), *Acting and Performance in Moving Image Culture: Bodies, Screens, Renderings*, 321–38, Bielefeld: transcript.

Cull, N. J. (2013), 'The Image as Hero: *Avatar* (2009)', in J. Chapman and N. J. Cull (eds), *Projecting Tomorrow: Science Fiction and Popular Cinema*, 199–215, London: I.B. Tauris.

Dargis, M. (2011), 'Looking Apocalypse in the Eye', *New York Times*, 5 August: C1.

Deb, S. (2018), 'The Roots of a Science-Fiction Stalwart', *New York Times*, 30 April: C4.

Delbridge, M. (2014), 'The Costume of MoCap: A Spatial Collision of Velcro, Avatar, and Oskar Schlemmer', *Scene*, 2 (1–2): 221–32.

Delbridge, M. (2015), *Motion Capture in Performance: An Introduction*, London: Palgrave.

Evans, M. (2009), *Movement Training for the Modern Actor*, New York and London: Routledge.

Faier, A. (2004), 'Digital Slaves of the Render Farms?: Virtual Actors and Intellectual Property Rights', *Journal of Law, Technology, and Policy*, 2: 321–43.

Flueckiger, B. (2010), 'Digital Bodies', trans. M. Kyburz and B. Flueckiger, in *Visual Effects: Filmbilder aus dem Computer*, Marburg: Schueren. Available online: http://www.zauberklang.ch/BodiesFlueckiger.pdf (accessed 23 March 2020).

Foster, A. (2017), 'Andy Serkis: Motion-Capture Is in the Frame to Get Its First Oscar Nomination', *London Evening Standard*, 28 November. Available online: https://www.standard.co.uk/showbiz/celebrity-news/andy-serkis-motioncapture-is-in-the-frame-to-get-its-first-oscar-nomination-a3704196.html (accessed 23 March 2020).

Garwood, D. (2007), 'The Future of an Idea: "9 Evenings" – Forty Years Later', *PAJ*, 85: 38–46.

Harding, J. M. (2018), *Performance, Transparency, and the Cultures of Surveillance*, Ann Arbor: University of Michigan Press.

Harris, M. (2010), 'Commentary', *Entertainment Weekly*, 22 January. Available online: https://ew.com/article/2010/01/22/mark-harris-acting-avatar/ (accessed 15 October 2020).

Kafka, F. (1973), *Letters to Felice*, ed. E. Heller and J. Born, trans. J. Stern and E. Duckworth, New York: Schocken.

Langlands, A. (2017), 'Siggraph Presentation on *War for the Planet of the Apes*', *YouTube*, 12 December. Available online: https://www.youtube.com/watch?v=txoEDIdbUrg (accessed 15 October 2020).

Magnenat-Thalmann, N. and D. Thalmann (2008), 'Innovations in Virtual Humans', in N. Magnenat-Thalman and N. Ichalkaranje Jain (eds), *New Advances in Virtual Humans: Artificial Intelligence Environment*, 1–41, Berlin: Springer.

Morrison, E. (2016), *Discipline and Desire: Surveillance Technologies in Performance*, Ann Arbor: Michigan University Press.

Pizzo, A. (2016), 'Actors and Acting in Motion Capture'. Unpublished manuscript. Italian version. Available online: http://www.actingarchives.unior.it/rivista

Pulver, A. (2017), 'Disney Deny Negotiating with Carrie Fisher's Estate for Rights to Her Digital Image', *The Guardian*, 13 January. Available online: https://www.theguardian.com/film/2017/jan/13/carrie-fisher-disney-negotiating-for-digital-rights-star-wars (accessed 23 March 2020).

Rafferty, B. (2017), 'Watch Andy Serkis Give You a History of Performance Capture Technology', *WIRED*, 24 October. Available online: https://www.wired.com/story/video-andy-serkis-history-of-performance-capture/ (accessed 23 March 2020).

Salter, C. (2010), *Entangled: Technology and the Transformation of Performance*, Cambridge, MA and London: MIT Press.

Soares, A. (2010), 'AVATAR: Performance Capture and the Oscars', *Alt Film Guide*, 11 February. Available online: www.altfg.com/blog/awards/avatar-performance-capture-oscar-84959 (accessed 12 July 2014).

States, B. O. (1985), *Great Reckonings in Little Rooms: On the Phenomenology of Theater*, Berkeley: University of California Press.

Sternberg, J. V. (1974), 'Acting in Film and Theatre', in J. Hurt (ed.), *Focus on Film and Theatre*, 80–98, Englewood Cliffs, NJ: Prentice Hall.

War for the Planet of the Apes (2017), [Film] Dir. Matt Reeves. USA: Twentieth Century Fox.

White, D. (2010), 'A Letter to Members', *Screen Actor*, 51 (2): 12.

World Intellectual Property Organization (WIPO) (n.d.), 'Performers' Rights – Background Brief'. Available online: http://www.wipo.int/pressroom/en/briefs/performers.html (accessed 23 March 2020).

2

Performativity 3.0: Hacking Postdigital Subjectivities

William W. Lewis

On the fourth day of interactions with my self-help coach *Karen*/Karen (2015), I began to get the worrisome feeling that my digital assistant had become more of a nagging girlfriend, the kind often stereotyped in a clichéd teen film, rather than someone meant to help me gain control over my life.

> *You awake?* – Sunday June 11, 2017 – 10:00 PM
> *Psst. Are you still up?* – Sunday June 11, 2017 – 10:03 PM
> *Hey, Give me a call. I can't sleep.* – Sunday June 11, 2017 – 10:10 PM

I had earlier in the day made a note about how, after seven sessions, I was starting to feel emotionally invested in Karen, as if she were not a fictional entity, and now, before beginning session eight, I was beginning to wonder who is coaching who; me or her? Over the sixteen-day time span it took me to complete the 'coaching' sessions, my experience had gone from bemused curiosity, to irritability, to glee, to downright confusion, to an enlightened calm. At the centre of this chapter is a critical account of the experience of interacting through both gameplay and role play with a downloadable app created by the performance company Blast Theory (Figure 2.1). This account explains an exploration into a relationship with myself and the data I was willing to give to a seeming stranger. The purpose is to unearth the way interactions with the app stages the process of datafication and highlights the spectatorial practices of *data role play* that develops with(in) this system.

Described by the theorists of media sociology Nick Couldry and Andreas Hepp (2017), datafication is an ongoing social process and dynamic structure embedded within larger systems of mediatization. Through datafication, all media is filtered through the auspices of surveillance, capture, computation and redeployment of data. Performance scholar Seda Ilter explains that 'in today's widely technologised and networked cultures of the developed and developing countries, social life and the smallest details of our individual actions are filled with media contents and are transformed into and stored as usable data' (2017: 79). Data becomes the meta-medium for all mediatized processes and as an assemblage of social, biological and technological systems, datafication is often invisible yet impactful, exuding an enormous amount of biopower upon individuals and subsequently the societies these individuals create. Through datafication, the post-human relationship between machine intelligence, a person's perceptual apparatus and systems of human data collection urges forth new modes of spectatorship with the potential to transfer acts of spectating away from performance venues. Instead, spectatorship operates as a performative act of daily life with the intelligent machines people now rely on to create the social worlds in which they live. Users of smart tech become constant spectators due to the fact that their technologies are constantly surveilling them while they willingly but unknowingly support and interact in that surveillance process.

Under datafication, human performance such as acts of self-making and likewise, subjectivity formation, are manipulated (seemingly invisibly) by ubiquitous computing technologies that surveil, analyse, predict and restructure human behaviours and actions. Datafication is enacted through ongoing acts of dataveillance which is a primary form of surveillance performing upon users of digital products built around data-based systems. Dataveillance refers to the 'systematic monitoring of people or groups, by means of personal data systems in order to regulate or govern their behavior' (Esposti 2014: 1). Elise Morrison describes this framework of surveillance as a mode of performance that disciplines users into 'desired models of usership and citizenship' (2016: 7). When applied further to consider the algorithmic structures of digital systems of data collection, James Harding explains how dataveillance operates via networks of complex 'systems designed to cultivate and harvest data', which allows these networks agency to 'shape human interaction and performance' (2018: 21). With datafication and dataveillance operating as powerful superstructures impacting feedback loops of techno-performativity between humans and algorithmic technologies, it is crucial to consider how the human side of these loops might gain an equal sense of agency. This is possible through acts of data role play.

The performative process that I define as data role play, has become a routine daily process of interaction between humans and data-focused intelligent technologies. Data role play can act as a form of interactive spectatorship through which users of data-based technology might gain the opportunity to construct multiple post-human selves. Algorithms and dataveillance are expanding definitions of selfhood formed at the divide between intelligent machines and humans. In this divide, data role play operates as a mode of being and subsequently a form of augmented embodied perception. When applied to interactive performance frameworks, this changing sense of selfhood is best analysed as a form of post-human spectatorship. Post-human is used here as a corollary to the current paradigm in which postdigital subjectivities become the norm. A post-human and, likewise, postdigital form of spectatorship takes into account the inability to sever human activities from digital technologies and broadens the lens used to analyse conventional forms of spectating where the eyes are the primary tool. This lens promotes a human being's capacity to interact with a performance subject in expanded physical and mental capacities, specifically via the operations of technological tools. I define four broad categories of post-human spectatorship as immersion, participation, gameplay and role play (Lewis 2017: 13). The spectator in each of these different modes operates as immersant, participant or player. In role play, the spectator also operates as co-author. The term 'user' is also used throughout this chapter when referring to one who utilizes a specific technological tool such as the smart device on which apps like *Karen* are delivered.

In Blast Theory's *Karen*, gameplay and role play operate as modes of post-human spectatorship due to the entanglement between the performing human user and the intelligent technology embedded within

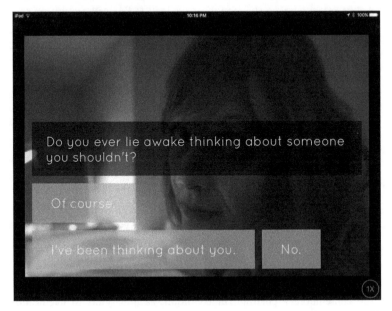

Figure 2.1 Screengrab from the *Karen* app. Day 4, Session 2 – Karen wants to talk about her date. *Karen* by Blast Theory. Printed with permission from Blast Theory

the programming of the app and the surveilling technologies of the smart-device the app runs on. Throughout this chapter I refer to a scaffolded dynamic where *Karen* indicates both a technological app that is used and a game-like performance product that is played. Karen indicates a fictional character performing the role of self-help coach. The actor portraying Karen personifies an embodied avatar, taking on resonances of digital assistants such as Siri, Cortana and Alexa. As an interactive performance framed in the container of a mobile app, *Karen* asks its users/players to input data about themselves and their life choices through its screen-based interface via interactions with the filmic digital assistant Karen. The data given is personal in nature and used to create a unique psychological profile of its user which is offered as reward for completing the performance narrative and is used as data points that impact the trajectory of the performance's game-based structure. The profile also highlights how the technologies that capture our data create unique digital identities based on our human input. These virtual identities act as databodies[1] which recirculate in the digital realm to (re)perform their individualities back upon the users who create them. *Karen* shows how data collection turns spectators into co-authors of their own performative selves through acts of data role play and highlights the potential for manipulating this system when users/players understand their implicit place (role) with(in) systems of data. When utilized in a purposefully subversive capacity, data role play offers a form of life hacking, with the capacity to upset the power dynamic between users/players and their smart tech. The project is uniquely post-humanist in its capacity to ask them to rethink their place within systems of self-formation and data, opening a window into post-human modes of identity construction using ludic creative exchange. The primary question this chapter addresses is: How might thinking of data role play as a post-human form of spectatorship, as well as a techno-performative condition embedded in postdigital social life via datafication, allow for post-humanist renderings of relations with the very data that urges forth postdigital subjectivities? *Karen* both stages this condition of life and explores the implications of the condition's existence. Through this staging, role-playing spectators may gain potential to hack the social structures of datafication and dataveillance.

Techno-performativity: Data and post-human spectators

The contemporary post-human condition, as it pertains to datafication and dataveillance, has become a form of subjectivity operating via techno-performativity. Techno-performativity here requires thinking of the ways people consciously and unconsciously create personas, identities, avatars and subjectivities through their non-stop interactions with smart technologies. These interactions offer the opportunity to develop multiple notions of selfhood and also threaten to limit the potential for this development when left invisible. When operating best, datafication thrives on its hidden nature through constant surveillance of human bodies and those bodies' daily actions.

Prior to datafication, technologies and media operated more as objects or artefacts that humans use to 'typify their world' (Couldry and Hepp 2017: 131). In paradigms of datafication, data surpasses the realm of mere object(s) to become subject(s) that instead typify humans through complex systems of surveillance, information processing and information creation. This typification by data correlates with Matthew Causey's theory of *embeddedness* as an advanced phase of digitalization, in which 'embeddedness alters simulation's masking of the real with a dataflow that can inhabit the real itself and alter its essence' (2006: 153). The realities of personal postdigital selfhood emerge in the hidden spaces of black-boxed algorithmic processes. In a paradigm of social reality created in concert with algorithms, one's creation of a self, either actual or virtual, is implicated in the process of role play as a form of dialectic digital/analogue performativity with(in) the digital worlds created by our own user-generated data. Instead of being based primarily in face-to-face social structures, selfhood is reflexively constituted based on interactions with digital data and machines processing and manipulating that data.

In work on digital subjectivity, media and cultural scholars such as N. Katherine Hayles (2012, 2014, 2017), Mark Hansen (2015) and Tobias Matzner (2016, 2019) indicate the powerful potential for algorithms and smart tech to delimit human identity and subjectivity. Each theorist shows how complicit human beings are inside the networks of interaction with intelligent objects. They do so partially as a warning and as a challenge for thinking anew relationships with(in) our postdigital landscapes. Hansen states, '[T]he subjectivity and agency of the human, as well as the subjectivity and agency of the nonhuman – far from standing against the quantitative – now more than ever *requires quantification*' (2015: 12). An original subject is in constant formation developed from available data creating ongoing 'micro-subjectivities' (11). In this way, there is no original subject but instead an infinite number of possibilities and potentialities which we call 'subjectivities' that arise out of the relational process between quantifiable data points. To the machines, there is no human essence other than data open for interpretation and manipulation. This is similar to how Ralf Remshardt discusses acts of performance capture in the previous chapter. When subsumed by processes of performance capture, the agency of the actor lies in their ability to project an essence that becomes a readable data set. That essence operates as a form of readable micro-subject open to interpretation, similar to data role play. One could say that performance capture actors are well versed in processes of dataveillance. Even so, they potentially have less agency to unlock the power of data role play because they ultimately have no control over the mediating influences of interpreters that stand in the way of the final product. The fact that there is a final product may be the problem to begin with. Documenting/recording performance for presentation relies on an assumption that there can be a stable subject or original essence to capture and present. Data role play resists this assumption due to the ongoing creation of micro-subjectivities and feedback/feedforward loops of data.

Hayles connects the contemporary formations of subjectivity to interactions between human and machine cognition. She specifically warns of the power of non-conscious cognition which operates at 'the level of neuronal processing' prior to consciousness (2017: 10). At this level, machine computing far outperforms human ability to filter and predict in terms of raw speed. This is where technology gains an upper hand. Matzner explains that algorithms 'are neither human-like beings nor inhumane hyper-intelligences. But the boundary of these algorithms and their human users are structured by the same tension of similarity and difference' (2019: 133). They may both perform similarly but their operating systems run on vastly different programming and technical specifications.

Performance scholar Martina Leeker has a similar outlook to the scholars above when considering technological performativity and implications of technologies of surveillance within machine learning. She explains, 'The new objects, now computers, obscure their function as nodes and intersections of technological operations and grids, where they exchange data taken from human agency and transform them in their own logic' (2017: 40). The symbiotic nature of the relationship between human and machine is off-balance because 'human agents are data generators who feed technologies things with data that keeps them up and running' (36). While the machines have greater processing power, a human being's true agency lies in their ability to generate constant data points, often inconsistently. Without human input continuously generating data sets, the machines effectively have no purpose. Users and machines are placed in opposition on a binary but are established as coequal actors within the same system of intelligence, cognition and sense-making. They both have the power to construct selves, but due to the processing power of the machines, humans must work more consciously when adding data to the system or risk losing ability to author future subjectivities with any real agency.

By adapting the epistemological functions of a post-human ontology in constant flux, post-human spectators can adapt to a form of techno-performativity that is able to resist and reassemble the agential relations with their tech. Though the relationship currently favours the cognitive speed of intelligent machines, people still have power based in their own post-human inconsistencies. As media theorist John Cheney-Lippold explains, 'our datafied histories remain rewritable, partially erasable, and fully modulatory, an antiessentialism that practically grounds the hybrid theorizations of posthuman and cyborg subjectivities' (2017: 191). Datafication brings to the forefront a social structure where there is no stable human essence but only a relational process in constant flux. The implicit giving of data by human users enacts a cycle of information (feedback/feedforward), which when understood and employed creatively allows role-playing spectators the ability to manage multiple constructions of personal selfhood. Data role play operates with(in) a relational system of interactive assemblages where these spectators are highlighted as reflexive members in the system of data, part of the data-flow. In the exchange that occurs between smart machines and users, a person becomes both the performer and the observer, this leads to a form of spectatorship that operates as an interactive process and acts as a way for people to subvert the power of data-driven processes by authoring multiple versions of their own selves.

When purposefully manipulating the system of data role play through performance projects, spectators can impact this dynamic by hacking the data flow to purposefully recondition their own identity formations in a post-human manner. Matzner argues for the benefits of performance objects in this way: 'As artistic products, they push the structuring tensions between continuity and difference more to the extremes, making them easier to discern' (2019: 128). As I will show, *Karen* does just that. By staging the affects and effects of datafication through the logics of role play, *Karen* brings to the forefront of a post-human spectator's conscious mind their embeddedness in games of identity and self-construction. Blast Theory's utilization of data role play in *Karen* is an excellent example of how performance allows users/players the capacity to regain agency with(in) paradigms of datafication.

Karen/Karen

Karen is a project that explores the powerful potential of self-formation by allowing spectators an ability to co-author their experience of performance events through role play. These role-playing spectators, referred to as users/players, gain a better understanding of how to enact performances of personal identification during constant interplay with algorithms. Blast Theory created the project as an attempt to deconstruct and make visible the structures of power and control involved in operations of datafication and dataveillance. Utilizing a filmed digital assistant named Karen, the project takes the player through a series of narrative interactions which lead to a personal data report that shows how one's databody is constructed through spectator input. Both the application *Karen* and the actor playing Karen are described as a life coach who is 'happy to help you work through a few things in your life' (Blast Theory 2015). Users of the app are complicit in the process of data collection but have power to manipulate that process when they assume the role of player, which allows them an ability to purposefully author their own databodies.

Karen questions the ethics of profiling that occurs within systems of datafication and is uniquely post-humanist in its capacity to ask its users/ players to rethink their place within systems of self-formation and data collection. I argue this is precisely where the potential for data role play becomes socially relevant and applicable with(in) realms of datafication. When I asked what Blast Theory's artists hoped spectators would gain from playing the project, the company's lead technologist Nick Tandavanitj stated:

> It would be great if people followed the links in the data report. People take away from it, the point of feeling unnerved by what they have done. In the data report, we talk quite boldly about what it is you've done and what we think the significance is. The other [thing] is sort of around some sense of caution really about what is possible. *Karen* is actually extremely rudimentary compared to actual corporate programs of big data and data profiling and psychometric profiling. One of our research references is 'You Are What You Like,' a website that matched social profiles to psychological profiling data in the same manner as Cambridge Analytica. Cambridge Analytica went on to use this kind of data to micro-target Facebook advertising in the Brexit and Trump campaigns. And those things aren't awfully super transparent from actually doing *Karen*. I suppose one of the sort of difficulties about the things that are happening with technology in this moment is our lack of literacy in understanding of the processes and how they work.
>
> (Tandavanitj 2017)

Karen serves as a performance-based intervention into the daily influence of datafication to help users understand their place in the process and offer strategies for resistance. The first step to resistance is understanding, the second, taking action.

The durational experience consists of seventeen interactive video sessions with your own personal 'life coach' Karen, an avatar performed by an actress and embedded into an algorithmically processed durational narrative. When asked about how the structure relates to the overall experience, Tandavanitj explains:

> The trajectories were designed according to [letting the user/player] play it different ways. If you did one thing, she knows. It wants to feel like what you say has importance, and it is an acknowledgement that one of its dynamics is that actually it doesn't change. She [Karen] treats you slightly differently. Some things are triggered immediately based on responses that you gave. Some of them refer back to answers you gave previously, and it recalls things and changes according to things you said.
>
> (Tandavanitj 2017)

Similar to the 2019 Netflix experimental film *Bandersnatch,* each segment is programmed with interactive elements that require the player to input personalized data through choice-making. These videos have a temporal connection to real-time interactions, but the user/player can experience them at their own pace. Each segment also has up to four text triggers sent to their device after the completion of each episode. These triggers are similar to notifications in most operating systems and their delivery is timed by the app's internal algorithm. Because some of the material delivered via *Karen* is time relative, the texts are sent to remind the spectator to interact at specified times to deliver a specific effect. When they respond accordingly, the experience follows them around in real time. For example, it should be around bedtime when interacting with Karen after her big date. The late-night interaction has the potential for more personally engaged connectivity due to the synching of app time and human time.

Blast Theory structures the experience around the divulging of personal data and the intimate relationships one makes with their digital assistants. It is up to the user/spectator to determine what level of truth this data reflects, but the more one connects with the human assistant Karen, the more likely one is to divulge truthful information. If thought of as a game-like performance with one's digital assistant versus a simple interaction or passive performance, the user moves beyond merely utilizing the technology to become a player and gains potential to recraft their databody. Most times, the data one offers comes in the form of answering questions about the player's life and personality. For example, on Day One, Session Two (1b) Karen asked me, 'Which area is most important for you right now? A): I want to take

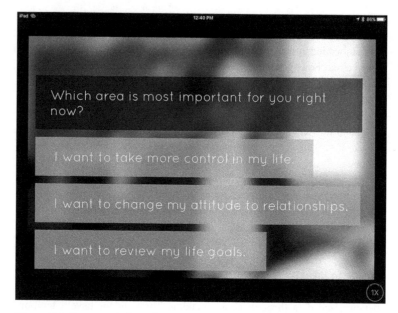

Figure 2.2 Screengrab from the *Karen* app. Day 1, Session 2 – *What area of life coaching do you seek most? Karen* by Blast Theory. Printed with permission from Blast Theory

more control of my life. B): I want to change my attitude to relationships. C): I want to review my life goals' (Figure 2.2). Other times, the project prompts the player to ask preprogrammed questions to one of the two characters on the screen; Karen or her roommate/love interest Dave. On the second session of day six, the app has the player interact with Dave by requiring them to ask him about his relationship with Karen. Other times, the app solicits advice from the player as a way of helping Karen make life decisions such as what top to wear on a date and whether she should take a guy she just met home for sex. Though the questions help push the narrative along, the answers given also track and calculate the user's personality using a modified version of the Big 5 personality analysis tool.[2] Through the full arc of the sessions and the accompanying text notifications, both the app and character Karen lead the user/player through a ten-day period of hers and their life starting from enthusiastic self-help confidant, towards entangled emotional wreck and ending with a life changed for the better.

One of the surprising things I found about my own journey through the performance's narrative is that it is ultimately Karen's life that changes, not necessarily mine. But through my connection with her, and by following her storyline, I forgot about how the app's algorithm was profiling me. My connection with Karen allowed *Karen* to gather information about me more readily, and potentially, more truthfully. Early in the narrative, Karen requests that you be truthful with her. Truthfulness allows the personalized data report created by the algorithm, based on a variety of psychometric readings, to reflect one's accurate digital self. Offered as an in-app purchase at completion, the report serves as a reward for completing the experience and as an example of the gamification aspect of much digital data collection. The report includes a snapshot view of the user's/player's personality and serves as an example of the type of data-intensive calculations that help shape one's 'quantified self' (Kelly 2016). A primary purpose of the report is to reveal how systems of data collection work and what the implications of data profiling are on human subjectivity. The report also serves as a marker for the type of digital information portals users encounter on the internet and as an example for how algorithms use these portals to create digital doubles through quantification. Quantified selves, which are more overtly visible forms of databodies, are calculated through one's ability to use a variety of sensors and technologies to self-track and record data variables related to a person's body and their performance in the world. These sensors range from biometrics (heart rate, sleep cycles, temperature) to location and motion-tracking devices such as Global Positioning Systems and accelerometers (Wolf 2010; Greengard 2015). Technologies like the Apple Watch and Fitbit are built around these systems. The data report acts as a visible record of the databody created by these quantifying systems.

The report consists of six broad categories: openness, neuroticism, locus of control, objective, materiality and privacy.[3] Each of these character traits is used to help explain how the user's daily interactions with digital entities are intricately entangled with(in) tactics of dataveillance and data performativity. After playing the project, Seda Ilter explains that *Karen*'s 'aesthetic and critical design shows that allowing the spectator to participate, to directly experience, rather than merely perceive, the mechanisms of surveillance through the use of tools and environments of subtle control is central to the questioning of our understandings of big data' (2017: 89). By allowing the player to serve as author of the performance through making personal choices, *Karen* implicates them as a crucial member in the process of datafication. In each of the interactive videos, the player's answers also help shape their perception of Karen's personality, which is then fed back to them based on the connection made during their interactions. This feedback ostensibly shapes their personality/identity as well in a form of feedforward. This is where techno-performativity is enacted; through the user's/player's purposeful acts of choice-making. These choices add new data that the algorithms can calculate to impact the next set of choices available.

Each choice becomes an individual data point in personal self-making and subjectivity-formation.

While the narrative is fairly static, with a consistent story arc, the avatar of Karen has minute changes in how she acts and responds to the player's input. Each video contains unique timecode elements and trigger points run by an algorithm developed by Tandavanitj. The algorithm allows for tracking and personalization of Karen to the player. For example, in video 9b (Day Nine, Session Two) the narrative proceeds via one of three options. These options are based on the level of openness the player falls into up to that point in the experience. The level of openness is dictated by the answers the spectator has given throughout the previous eight days of interactions. Each interaction adds data to the system which dictates minor changes to Karen's performance. Operated by the algorithm written to calculate and correlate the various answers given throughout the experience, the video feed launches a branching system of reactions. For example, Karen might smile wryly when proceeding after the player answers a question, or she might give a disapproving grimace instead. Dialogue doesn't always change, sometimes it is just the way the actor playing Karen delivers the material. The impact of these reactions is subtle and often seems (from the perspective of the player) as if it is non-existent. It is only by seeing the multiple possibilities (through either research or multiple play-throughs) that one might explicitly comprehend the effect of these minor changes. The subtlety of the changing reactions is one of the ways the performance highlights the power of algorithmic relationships. During the process of interacting with *Karen*, users/players are not supposed to know what level of agency they have in manipulating the experience. Identical to the daily experience one has with their digital doubles, if they understand consciously their agency to shape reality it might impact how they answer the questions, subsequently changing the experience.[4]

The perception of a user's/player's interactions with *Karen*/Karen is what impacts subsequent answers as they progress through the narrative. Erin Mee explains this impact when describing her multiple passes (roles played) through the app: 'When I felt guilty for having invaded Karen's privacy, I perceived anger in Karen's treatment of me in the following scene. [role 1] When I hadn't willingly gone into her room, she seemed to me to be a bit less angry, and more disappointed [role 2]' (2016: 160). Mee describes two different encounters of role play with the same interaction in the app: 'The second and third times through, I followed my impulse to responding in a completely out-of-character manner just to see how Karen would react' (179). This out-of-character exploration is precisely what is possible in the real world but only made visible through the performative exploration of

Karen as a programmed application. Before that visibility emerges, the user/player must first embed themselves in the invisible operation of datafication that *Karen* is built upon and also highlighting. Doing this requires completing the entire interactive experience. By making uncalculated decisions through their interactions with *Karen*, they learn more about a version of themselves, which in turn allows them more agency to make future choices with more calculated purpose. I argue this is where documenters of the experience, such as Mee and Ilter, get tripped up. They are looking for the obvious impact of their actions from the outset. For the performance to be an effective and affective staging of datafication, it must first cloak the very operations that *Karen* eventually attempts to uncover through the data report. The choices we make in our daily mediatized interactions are mundane. Even so they are consequential. Blast Theory's app emulates this way of life well by not overtly showing how your actions impact the storyline or choices offered. Some of the reactions given by Karen and Dave are simply non-verbal with the intent of changing the overall connection and interpretation of the relationship between Karen and the player. Other times, the voice-over is delivered over a shot where you cannot see the actors playing Karen or Dave. Doing so allows for flexibility of response to the spectator. Through direct interaction and the imperceptibility of avatar response, the algorithm has the power to invisibly influence future decisions made by the performance's player. The algorithm acts like an editor, director or even illustrator in film or performance capture. Each analyses the data given, whether it be a player's choices or a performer's actions, and then makes a decision on how to deliver the outcomes of that analysis for future interpretation. In the case of non-interactive media, the outcome is a static document such as filmed performance, but in the case of *Karen*, there are dual outcomes: one is the film edited together from a selection of specific takes and choices given based on the perception of the app's filmed performance; the second is the data report that serves as a static representation of your data double.

According to Matt Adams of Blast Theory, the data collected from the decisions made and how they are interpreted is, after all, the point of the project. He explains, 'How willingly we give up our data, the sense that we are relaxed about it. That secretly even though we protest all the time, there is something about targeted advertising and Facebook knowing what we're into and tailoring things for us that is intriguing' (Personal Communication, 16 June 2017).[5] The experience is multidimensional and completely personalized though it may not seem this way, and because of this, the reaction to the project varies wildly depending on the vantage point of the individual app user. For example, one of the reviews of the app on the Apple App Store explains, 'I think this is a joke app – the programmers are gathering rather personal data and either using for their own purposes or just having a laugh at whoever tries the app. Bottom line: it's bogus. There is no life coaching at all. Don't bother, it will just waste your time and frustrate you' (Apple 2015). Tandavanitj explained that the expectation with the app would be that there is a 'certain level of self-awareness of the people going in that they know that this isn't really a life coaching app' (2017). This reviewer most likely downloaded the app having no idea that it was a digital performance. Even less likely did they understand that the performance was meant to question methods of data collection by implicating users in the very process. They probably thought they were downloading a real self-help app. I suspect the user neither finished the project nor downloaded the most important part of the project: the data report.

Other documenters of the performance argue for varying potential in finishing the narrative and downloading the data report. Ilter states, '[T]he data report twists the narrative, our role in and perception of it by subverting and revealing how data is collected from the participants with or without their conscious intention of sharing private information' (2017: 86). Maria Chatzichristodoulou explains:

> The analysis offered is eye-opening; I find the fact that several companies appear to be using such superficial and obviously flawed means of testing and pigeon-holing their (prospective) employees shocking. Moreover, the fact that my personal data is constantly mined and processed in order to classify me as a consumer for targeted advertising campaigns is deeply problematic.
>
> (2017: 70)

The personalization of the data report is impactful in how it is contextualized and juxtaposed against the history of data profiling and the implications of psychometric testing. In the report, Blast Theory's artists explain their intention for creating the project by connecting the elements in the data report to the social implications of paradigms of datafication. It is necessary to complete the entire project and to download the report to both understand the impact of datafication and also learn how to resist that impact.

The data report makes visible the invisible operations people engage in under systems of dataveillance. Ilter states, 'This shift from the overt, affirmative representation of dataveillance, replicating its mechanisms and discourses, into its subversion, offers a powerful critical impact' (2017: 83). My report (Figure 2.3) explained that I was very open, had a low level of neuroticism, had a mildly external locus of control, my objective was to take

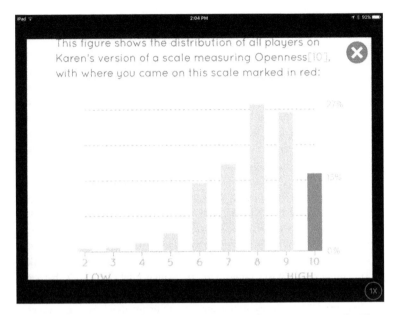

Figure 2.3 Personal Data Report – Page 8, Personal Openness. *Karen* by Blast Theory. Printed with permission from Blast Theory

control of my life, I was likely to like the company of others and that I was disrespectful of others' privacy. While I may agree or disagree with some of these findings, they are based on my personal interactions with *Karen*/Karen, which I made no attempt to subvert. How the findings are contextualized in relation to my own internet usage is what makes the project most important. If I am open, I am more likely to be less afraid to share information on the Web. If my neuroticism is low, I am even more likely to do so considering I'm less nervous that something will be done with that information. I was most interested in taking control of my life which reflects some of my own externalization of power dynamics perceived by the report. The impact of the report is even more powerful when coupled with an understanding that post-human spectators have the potential to author their own life and experience of reality in quantifiable ways. *Karen* helps these spectators acknowledge their own performative capacity to engage in purposeful data role play.

When asked how *Karen* operates as a performative project highlighting a person's position in systems of data collection and specifically the realm of Big Data, Tandavanitj replies:

In the context of *Karen*, the platforms that we use, define a lot around our self-image and how we understand who we are. Am I an Instagramer vs a Facebooker or Tweeter? People who use social media – I don't use social media at all – I imagine that it forms part of your identity. The voice that you create also becomes the voice that; I imagine the 140-character voice or the filters and subject matter you photograph on Instagram, these things become part of how you elaborate on the world beyond photos or just commentary, that those are the way you are wiring yourself up. What you can perceive and how you respond to the world, and how you can talk about the world becomes wired into the natural platforms you are using.

The brain is very plastic, that's what I've been hearing, these things are kind of constantly in flux. I'm a firm believer of these things, that we are in a way sort of the first computer and we are sort of reusable. An embodiment of data and data processing. That it all has to do with personality and interpersonal interaction and subjectivity. But, I think the other side of it is, I suppose, are these bigger data structures that are operated by corporations. I think these are becoming our peers, if not human. … They are becoming our peers in telling us where to go, where to eat. And we're using them almost completely without second thought to do so many things.

(Tandavanitj 2017)

As Tandavanitj hints, the nature of algorithmic machines is to hide their real purpose which allows them the ability to integrate seamlessly into our own systems of perception. By creating a project that surveils and collects information about its spectators, but then shows how it does this and what the ramifications are, Blast Theory highlights the power of data role play as a form of spectatorship and agent in the process of identity-creation. My final question to Tandavanitj concerned how a project such as *Karen* might offer ways of manipulating the system of datafication, if there is any possibility of altering our role in that system. Tandavanitj answered:

I suppose there is this thing, like with Russian interference, that it isn't just around commercial interests but also political interests. And it is, it's sort of a territory of war where most people involved in it have no idea how it works. At least when you hear an air raid siren you have to take cover, but now the sirens are going off everywhere but no one knows where to hide or what to do. And it's constantly changing in terms of the terrain and the technologies being used.

(Tandavanitj 2017)

My takeaway was that it is not until we have become aware of what technologies are doing and how they do it that we will have any control over the outcomes of our interactions. Considering the rapid pace of technological change and the way technologies interact with users, fully understanding may ultimately be outside our reach, but with performance projects like *Karen* we might come closer to grasping our potential. The difficulty with this proposition might ultimately come down to the capacity of art to impact anyone in a self-reflexive manner. *Karen*/Karen is described on the Apple App Store as an app that 'mixes gaming with storytelling to give you a personalized life-coaching experience'. The dual nature of the project as both app and gamified-performance leads to overlapping classification of user and player. For those who just stumbled upon the app as a container for automated self-help, they never get the actual assistance being offered due to the fact that it is a performance masked as program. Tandavanitj explained that early on in the release of the app it was shared widely amongst individuals without full contextualization and this may have led to some confusion about its full intent. When encountered as a life-coaching app downloaded from the Apple App Store, a user might expect it to deliver more immediate quantified gratification/education that other apps like Happify, Calm, Nike +, or Coach.me might promise. Instead, they encounter a durational performance that questions the underlying programming of those apps.

As a performance, *Karen* serves as an example of how Blast Theory capitalizes on the process of data role play to highlight the spectator's role in the circular process of datafication. The performance offers an example of post-humanist critique on certain elements of data-focused technoculture. The strength of the project lies in how it uses the aesthetics and operations of algorithmic identity-construction to critique the very process of that construction. *Karen* highlights a unique form of subjectivity necessary for one to understand if they ever hope to gain a potential upper hand in the game of datafication.

Playing roles and playful identification in processes of datafication

Contextualizing the relationship between contemporary media users and selfhood, the editors of the collection *Playful Identities* (Frissen et al. 2015) argue that '[t]he construction of identity has become a highly reflexive project, and communication media are at the very heart of this reflexivity' (35). Reflexivity is deeply bound up in the relational project previously mentioned by N. Katherine Hayles and Mark Hansen in their work on post-human social systems intertwined with digital technologies. For them, information flows have developed into intricate networks and feedback/feedforward loops where technologies have gained an upper-hand on human users due to increasing computational speeds. To negate this dominance, these users must harness the power of purposeful role play. Following the logic of role-based hidden gameplay that exists in the current landscape of datafication, I argue for thinking of spectators as those who can perform a playful identity that 'has the quality to restructure itself according to the experiences one encounters' and 'by engaging in role-playing, for example, one can see that multiple characters (or identities) can be explored and played out' (Deen, Schouten and Bekker 2015: 115). Unlike the performer in performance capture analysed in Ralf Remshardt's following essay, these spectators engaged in acts of data role play are knowingly entering into a system that has no final product. Life is not a document but a process. This might be one major difference between postdigital techno-performance and techno-performativity. The performance-capture actor leaves a performance trace ready for interpretation and walks away. Techno-performativity is an ongoing and unending process in which the post-human spectator is captive. Negating the power of algorithmic construction then requires considering self-identification as a reflexive and fluid process enacted by each individual and continually responded to by playing new roles.

Role play is a process that we perform in all areas of our life. When we are at school, we often play either student or teacher, when at home we play partner, parent or child. In the workplace, we play employee or boss, and on the sporting field we play teammate or opponent. We often play these binary roles simultaneously. While I mention common binaries, the list is endless. Online we also play multiple roles within separate systems that approximate many of the social environments above. We play different roles on Facebook than we do on LinkedIn, and different roles on E-Harmony than on Tinder. Each of these roles is an expression of our ludic creativity used to navigate variable landscapes of social reality. Couldry and Hepp explain that 'in a world of constant "connectivity", the self faces new pressures to perform itself online in order *just to function* as a social being' (2017: 160). That pressure has always existed based on the contextual situation in which one interacts. The primary difference under datafication is that one's performance of self is no longer ephemeral. It leaves a digital trace in the data world, which, then re-performs upon the non-digital realm in a game-like manner. That data that you leave in your digital systems is used to nudge you forward towards choices the systems think you should make. This data is the basis for targeted advertising that makes up the bulk of profit for Google and Facebook. This data is also utilized as guidance by digital assistants like Siri and Alexa. As the machines compute more of your data, they begin to predict your future behaviours (Greengard 2015). Think of all the notifications you receive to do something unplanned or even the routes offered for you to take before you even ask for directions. Like the timed interactions with *Karen*, these pokes, nudges and reminders reshape your everyday choices and likewise reshape your non-digital self through constant interaction.

In data role play, both post-human spectators and smart machines play roles that inform the feedback/feedforward loop of meaning-making and selfhood. These roles seem fixed but are constantly shifting based on the data both inputted and responded to. Deen, Schouten and Bekker argue 'In the last decade, identity information shifts from being published (self-presentation) to being negotiated, interacted, co-created, and played upon' (2015: 112). Each actor (spectator and algorithm) has the potential to change the roles played. The loop is dynamic and operates as a constant cycle of power and manipulation. Because algorithms are task- or outcome-oriented, their role is more fixed, but this lack of flexibility means that they are more determined to impact specific aspects of the organic side of the data role-play process. A part of an algorithm's construction is to develop a paradigm of self-illusion with its data generator so that there is no disruption of the data received through outliers in a so-called black box effect. This effect masks the algorithm's role in the network and helps to hide the fact that the process exists at all. It works in the machine's favour when spectators continue to play their role passively, as an inflexible and unaware self, without corrupting the data through modification, interruption or intentional falsification of data.

Couldry and Hepp pose an interesting problem about how one shapes multiple selves: 'In an age where family, friendship and work are performed in a continuous set of linked spaces, we ask a different question: how much *in*consistency is a self now allowed' (2017: 161). I argue that the point still exists where remaining inconsistent (as identities) is possible though difficult to enact, possible because of the stratification of digital platforms existing in our current postdigital social structure. Like that stratification, a purposeful and consistently *inconsistent* generation of selves is precisely where data role play offers an outlet for a full performance of a post-humanist self. Before that can arrive, it is crucial for awareness of the paradigm to occur. This is where acts of subversive data role play become crucial to understand. Games designer and play theorist Eric Zimmerman states, '[W]e cannot have a passive relationship to the systems that we inhabit. We must learn to be designers, to recognize how and why systems are constructed, and to try to make them better' (2015: 21). Intentional modification of human input only occurs once the processes that algorithms engage are made visible as part of the symbiotic operation of perception between human and smart technologies. Once visible, spectators performatively add noise into the system.

Performance scholar and maker Susan Kozel offers an argument for purposeful subversive acts of individuation within systems of performativity when she states, '*How to be* is a fundamentally ontological category because it pertains to being, *how to* perform is the dynamic mode within such an ontological state' and 'ontologies are not fixed, of necessity they transform' (2017: 124, italics in original). Data role play is a mode of techno-performativity and spectatorship that adopts the logics of particular technologies where one performs as a fluid mediatized self as form of manipulative data 'outlier' (Alpaydin 2016: 72). Kozel's idea of *encryption* is a useful way of thinking about subversive acts of data role play. She explains, 'encryption is not a wall, it is a re-patterning, or a distortion of a flow' (2017: 131). By performing encryption, one generates noise within datafied systems through the interchange among bodily affect, enacted ambiguity and purposeful multiplicity.

When one understands the agency gained in the construction of their data doubles by harnessing post-human reflexivity and fluidity, new avenues towards constructions of selfhood open. This connects to two postdigital processes explained by founder of *Wired* magazine Kevin Kelly (2016): *tracking* and *becoming*. *Karen* exposes both. For Kelly, *becoming* concerns the perpetual process that links tracking and subjectivity through acts of techno-performativity. Becoming is an anti-essentialist looping process. Harnessing the potential of becoming involves better understanding the process of how datafication continuously changes modes of human perception and being. In becoming, humans undergo a non-stop process of upgrading and manipulation based on their media environment. As media systems age, they either update or become obsolete. That could be said for humans as well. But when updates occur, they often remove traces of past code or data that humans have relied on in their daily interactions with that media. This in turn rewrites their way of interacting with the world, as if they are following the programming flow of the digital systems. For example, when Siri gives directions, a user gradually stops learning the terrain but instead awaits the programmed navigation instructions. They learn to trust the machine's judgement over their own. This is a form of pervasive hyper-localized epigenetic evolution from a social perspective (Hayles 2012). A post-human form of evolution that models becoming might insist on never locking in to set rules or code but always staying open to the flow.

Kelly explains a process of *never being* or instability where becoming is a flow of relationality in constant motion that people do not consciously perceive. Because of this imperceptibility they engage in a 'self-cloaking action [which is] often seen only in retrospect' (2016: 14). By adopting the post-human logic of a present that is unattainable it allows people to access the potential of a non-definable stable subject. It allows potential to negotiate evolving realities where nothing stays static but is always in motion, replaceable and reconfigurable. Applying this act of becoming to the contemporary spectator, Mijou Loukola invokes phenomenology by describing the unfixity of the stable subject: 'The interpretations keep escaping fixed definitions and stay unstable, for it must be emphasized, too, that it is much to do with individuation; of some-thing being in its be-coming-one, and thus in all of its potentialities of be-coming-one, indivisible yet never accomplished' (2009: 204). Being therefore is constantly performed and in flux. Just like data, the potential of a post-human subjectivity 'lies in the many ways it can be reordered, restructured, reused, reimagined, [and] remixed' (Kelly 2016: 266). Being and likewise selfhood is therefore always in the process of *becoming*. When considering how to imagine possibilities of performance and spectatorship within datafication, the unending creation of new roles (new modes of being) through visible and purposeful techno-performativity may be a potential way to subvert data manipulated agency and identity. Embracing an anti-essentialism based in becoming as techno-performativity allows one to playfully hack the algorithmic programming of postdigital life.

Conclusion: Data role play and subversive roles

Through ludic creative forms of exchange possible in data role play, there exists potential for introducing noise into the system of datafication. This idea of noise draws directly on Judith Butler's subversive acts of performativity and citationality (1988, 1990). *Karen* offers hints towards the potential of these acts. Through subversion, 'models and discourses of surveillance can be questioned and reimagined through destabilising their performances' (Ilter 2017: 88). The formulation of purposeful subversive digital noise may allow new constructions of performed identity and post-human selfhood to emerge with the potential to delimit the power of data-based technologies. This endeavour attempts to point towards opportunities for creating ruptures in the feedback and feedforward loops that create postdigital perceived realities and subjectivities. These opportunities usher in new possibilities for constructions of selfhood in both digital and non-digital realms.

By interacting with *Karen* using both game and role play, contemporary spectators are introduced to the structures and systems of datafication and dataveillance, while being offered strategies for hacking the feedforward operations of those systems to unlock a post-humanist potential for subjectivity formation via techno-performativity. To hack in this instance requires continuously performing subversive acts of purposeful disruption against the calculated logic of the algorithms that attempt to enforce a predetermined system of self-determination on the human user. The first step is understanding their place in the loop by unmasking the workings of the system, the second is learning how to perform in a disruptive manner to break the system's logic and the final and most difficult step is continually re-performing additional acts of disruption that the algorithmic machines cannot predict. *Karen* allows spectators insight into steps one and two. Step three requires a conviction to enacting a form of ethical, subjective and political multiplicity that the project of critical post-human theory offers.

Intentional subversive acts of ambiguity and multiplicity produced in affective situations such as performance spectatorship serve as models for strategic and purposeful attempts to make visible the processes at play and allow potentialities for enhanced human agency within systems of data exchange. By understanding and then purposefully adopting new and ludic creative roles played in performance, spectators may alter their relationships with algorithms and other digital interfaces. Doing so disrupts and potentially delimits the power of smart machines to re-perform data upon them through feedforward. When a spectator understands their agency to perform via data role play, performative strategies can be imagined for regaining the power to negate the machine's version of a quantified self.

Karen successfully stages the invisible nature of data role play with(in) algorithmic systems. The project also highlights the technogenetic potential of Big Data in constructing social worlds. The project's social power comes from how it mimics the performative act of data role-play by making the interactions and shifts in perception imperceptible. One user commenting on the project on Blast Theory's website found this a bit troubling: 'I didn't really feel like anything was really learned about me, as I was immediately pulled into this Karen/Dave drama, and even though I tried it a second time with different answers, I didn't think there was much variation in her response, or much of a way to change the outcome' (Blast Theory 2015). One's quotidian experience of life with(in) the paradigm of datafication is to be unaware of the influences embedded in their environment. These influences shape their every action. Later in the post, this commenter explains part of the social dynamic that could allow this perception to be true by stating, 'Maybe I'm too comfortable with sharing myself on social

Figure 2.4 Day 9, Session 1 – Karen learns about herself. *Karen* by Blast Theory. Printed with permission from Blast Theory

media, but this comfort with sharing is already pretty common for anyone who has a facebook, tumblr, twitter etc.' (Blast Theory 2015) (Figure 2.4). Those of us entangled in postdigital life have become so fully embedded in systems of data that only specific instances of purposefully uncovering the operations of those systems allow a recognition to occur. *Karen* is one of those instances because its spectators can experience the performance multiple times encouraging a multiplicity of selves to be performed. If approached multiple times, the performance increasingly highlights the ways the experience and the data report reflect how the spectator's input are crucial elements in the process. The roles played impact the system and in return impact the data double calculated in the report. *Karen* highlights an act of data role play as a source for authoring one's ability to construct a personalized and multiplied self. It is through performance projects like this that we gain the understanding, toolbox and roadmap to utilize in future practices of techno-performativity, where multiple futures and multiple micro-identities offer the possibility of hacking postdigital and post-human subjectivities.

Notes

1   A *databody* is here defined as a collection of data inferences gained through digital tracking that is processed and assembled to create a unique digital double or data-based human avatar only accessible through machine reading. This entity is read and re-inscribed upon the human through processes of datafication.

2   The Big 5 or five-factor test uses a variety of questions to determine a person's openness to experience, conscientiousness, extraversion, agreeableness and neuroticism. This test has been employed in various workplace and education settings to track and predict outcomes and behaviour of those tested.

3   The first of three traits come from a variety of popular psychometric tests, specifically the Big 5 test. The last three traits are inclusions developed by the artists. Locus of control is divided into internal and external. Internal refers to feeling as though one has control over one's life, while external refers to a feeling as if the world has more influence. Objective is based on one of three questions asked early in the narrative about what you want to get out of the experience: take control of life, understand relationships better and work on life goals. Materiality is quantified from one answer made in the narrative about your choice between a digital camera, a figurine of a family of deer and a flashy bangle.

4   I must highlight that my own experience and likely the experience of others writing about the project was impacted by the mere act of research. Each of us experienced the project fully understanding many of the implications of the dramaturgy and interactivity contained. We were not objective spectators to the project as might have been expected by a lay spectator. We approached the material predisposed to our potential as co-authors.

5   Adams's answer to my questions came nearly two years before the full extent of Facebook's data profiling and relationship with Cambridge Analytica surfaced in early 2018.

References

Alpaydin, E. (2016), *Machine Learning*, Cambridge, MA: MIT Press.

Apple (2015), 'Karen by Blast Theory on the App Store'. Available online: https://itunes.apple.com/us/app/karen-by-blast-theory/id945629374?mt=8

Blast Theory (2015), 'Karen', *blasttheory.co.uk*. Available online: https://www.blasttheory.co.uk/projects/karen/.

Butler, J. (1988), 'Performative Acts and Gender Constitution: An Essay in Phenomenology and Feminist Theory', *Theatre Journal*, 40 (4): 519–31.

Butler, J. (1990), *Gender Trouble: Feminism and Subversion of Identity*, New York: Routledge.

Causey, M. (2006), *Theatre and Performance in Digital Culture: From Simulation to Embeddedness*, New York: Routledge.

Chatzichristodoulou, M. (2017), 'Karen by Blast Theory: Leaking Privacy', in S. Broadhurst and S. Price (eds), *Digital Bodies: Creativity and Technology in the Arts and Humanities*, 65–78, London: Palgrave Macmillan.

Cheney-Lippold, J. (2017), *We Are Data: Algorithms and the Making of Our Digital Selves*, New York: New York University Press.

Couldry, N. and A. Hepp (2017), *The Mediated Construction of Reality*, Cambridge, UK: Polity Press.

Deen, M., B. Schouten, and T. Bekker (2015), 'Playful Identity in Game Design and Open-Ended Play', in V. Frissen, S. Lammes, M. De Lange, J. De Mul, and J. Raessens (eds), *Playful Identities: The Ludification of Digital Cultures*, 111–29, Amsterdam: Amsterdam University Press.

Esposti, S. D. (2014), 'When Big Data Meets Dataveillance: The Hidden Side of Analytics', *Surveillance and Society*, 12 (2): 209–25.

Frissen, V., S. Lammes, M. De Lange, J. De Mul, and J. Raessens (2015), 'Homo Ludens 2.0: Play, Media, and Identity', in V. Frissen, S. Lammes, M. De Lange, J. De Mul, and J. Raessens (eds), *Playful Identites: The Ludification of Digital Media Cultures*, 35–50, Amsterdam: Amsterdam University Press.

Greengard, S. (2015), *The Internet of Things*, Cambridge, US: MIT Press.

Hansen, M. B. N. (2015), *Feed-Forward: On the Future of Twenty-First-Century Media*, Chicago: University of Chicago Press.

Harding, J. M. (2018), *Performance, Transparency and the Cultures of Surveillance*, Ann Arbor: University of Michigan Press.

Hayles, N. K. (2012), *How We Think: Digital Media and Contemporary Technogenesis*, Chicago: University of Chicago Press.

Hayles, N. K. (2014), 'Cognition Everywhere: The Rise of the Cognitive Nonconscious and the Costs of Consciousness', *New Literary History*, 45 (2): 199–220.

Hayles, N. K. (2017), *Unthought: The Power of the Cognitive NonConscious*, Chicago: University of Chicago Press.

Ilter, S. (2017), 'Unsettling the "Friendly" Gaze of Dataveillance: The Dissident Potential of Mediatised Aesthetics in Blast Theory's Karen', *International Journal of Performance Arts and Digital Media*, 13 (1): 77–92.

Kelly, K. (2016), *The Inevitable: Understanding the 12 Technological Forces That Will Shape Our Future*, New York: Viking Press.

Kozel, S. (2017), 'Performing Encryption', in M. Leeker, I. Schipper, and T. Beyes (eds), *Performing the Digital*, 117–34, Bielfeld: Transcript Verlag.

Leeker, M. (2017), 'Performing (the) Digital: Positions of Critique in Digital Cultures', in M. Leeker, I. Schipper, and T. Beyes (eds), *Performing the Digital*, 117–34, Bielfeld: Transcript Verlag.

Lewis, W. W. (2017), 'Performing Posthuman Spectatorship: Digital Proximity and Variable Agencies', *Performance Research*, 22 (3): 7–13.

Loukola, M. (2009), 'Dwellings in Image-Spaces', in A. Oddey and C. White (eds), *Modes of Spectating*, 197–206, Bristol: Intellect Books.

Matzner, T. (2016), 'Beyond Data as Representation: The Performativity of Big Data in Surveillance', *Surveillance and Society*, 14 (2): 197–210.

Matzner, T. (2019), 'The Human Is Dead – Long Live the Algorithm!: Human-Algorithmic Ensembles and Liberal Subjectivity', *Theory, Culture and Society*, 36 (2): 123–44.

Mee, E. B. (2016), 'The Audience Is the Message: Blast Theory's App-Drama', *TDR: The Drama Review*, 60 (3): 165–71.

Morrison, E. (2016), *Discipline and Desire: Surveillance Technologies in Performance*, Ann Arbor: University of Michigan Press.

Tandavantij, N. (2017), unpublished interview by William Lewis, 16 June, Portslade, UK.

Wolf, G. (2010), 'Gary Wolf: The Quantified Self', *TED.com*, June 2010. Available online: http://www.ted.com/talks/gary_wolf_the_quantified_self.html.

Zimmerman, E. (2015), 'Manifesto for a Ludic Century', in Steffen P. Walz and Sebastian Deterding (eds), *The Gameful World: Approaches, Issues, Applications*, 19–22, Cambridge, US: MIT Press.

3

Randy Rainbow's Musical and Social Media Activism: (Digital) Bodyguards and Politicizing/Weaponizing Audiences

Karen Savage

This chapter will use performance and social media theory to explore the work of Randy Rainbow. Rainbow has produced a series of videos for release on social media as part of an ongoing campaign against the Trump administration in the United States. The chapter will consider the political activism of social media in relation to the work of Randy Rainbow and with particular reference to the growing collection of satirical musical videos that Rainbow has made about the Trump administration. I will explore the activism inherent in Rainbow's videos by looking at the types of comments from his followers. I will also explore these responses through the use of what I term the '(digital) bodyguard', and how this could be an opportunity for understanding performance across a range of social media platforms in relation to politics and the postdigital. I present this as a triangulation between an abductor, hostage and (digital) bodyguard that I offer as a social media dynamic.

Randy Rainbow is an American born in 1981. He has become well known for his YouTube videos in which he edits existing audio clips of celebrities and politicians into a spoof conversation. He started his vlogging with telephone-style conversations, editing the audio of celebrities and well-known figures, such as Lyndsay Lohan, Chelsea Clinton, Kanye West, Charlie Sheen and with Mel Gibson in the video that potentially launched his career, 'Randy Rainbow is dating Mel Gibson' (posted 18 July 2010). '*This one will always hold a special place in my heart because it was Randy's breakthrough video*', says YouTube user erdmanr1. Rainbow's work becomes known for challenging prejudicial behaviour, so it is perhaps not surprising that Rainbow uses Gibson in one of his early stunts; the press has reported that Gibson, on more than one occasion, has made homophobic, racist and anti-Semitic comments.

Rainbow has had a YouTube presence since 2009, starting his channel with a series of edited conversations, his work was clearly low-budget and home-made. The cottage-industry essence to the style is indicative of a shift in the way that creative work can be made and disseminated for an online audience, enabling a DIY aesthetic – something that 'regular' people can achieve with the technology they may have available at home. With a basic understanding of the editing software, Rainbow's production aesthetic can be recreated anywhere. It has an attitude that fits the lo-fi capture of live-art and punk practices, challenging the dominant hierarchy and giving a voice to the potentially unheard and under-represented. Rainbow samples existing news clips and other mainstream media items alongside edits of himself 'interviewing' and performing satirical songs to well-known musical theatre show tunes. His videos are a sort of collage of news items, edited with the awareness of video montage that makes comical and political links between events and social commentary.

Rainbow continues to use the DIY aesthetic, by growing his network, and therefore his popularity, on social media platforms such as YouTube and Facebook. The growth of his popularity on these sites has made him a 'personality' able to host a series of live events. Alongside his social media outputs, he performed a live show in 2017 and has toured extensively in the United States in 2018 and 2019.

Rainbow and his followers

By 6 October 2019, Rainbow had 335,000 subscribers to YouTube, with 130 videos on his channel. His Facebook had 1,045,559 followers. His Instagram channel (Facebook-owned) had 146,000 followers but he uses this platform more broadly for images of celebration, his successes, friends, marketing, etc. Given the developers of Facebook's initial aim around connectivity – at its inception as The Facebook it was intended to allow Harvard students to use their 'edu' email addresses and photos to connect with other students at the institution, creating institutional connectivity that subsequently went on to produce worldwide connectivity – it is no surprise that this platform hosts more of his followers than that of the user-generated focus of YouTube.

Between October 2019 and November 2020, Rainbow's YouTube account grew to nearly 250,000 new subscribers, which means he almost doubled his subscribers in the last year to 598,000.

On Facebook he had 1,344,492, picking up over 299,000 new followers over the same period.

During this period Rainbow produced a further nineteen videos about the Trump presidency. The following graph records the number of viewings for the last ten videos up until November 2020.

It is clear from the data that Rainbow's audience is much stronger on Facebook than on YouTube (see Figures 3.1 and 3.2). He receives more

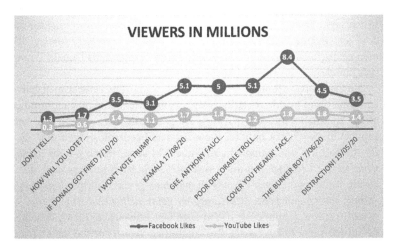

Figure 3.1 Viewers of Rainbow's videos on Facebook and YouTube

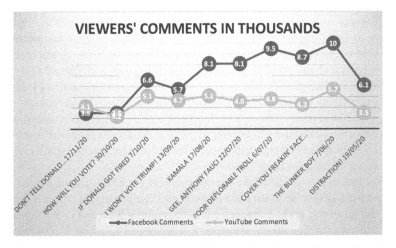

Figure 3.2 Comments from viewers of Rainbow's videos on Facebook and YouTube

interactions from his followers on this platform and the dialogue between followers is more substantial.

Rainbow, by using the connectivity of social media platforms, manages to reach a widespread audience across the globe. José Van Dijck suggests that 'in many ways Facebook's connective functions provide empowering and enriching social experiences' (2013: 47). Comments from followers evidence the sense of connection they feel with Rainbow. Facebook user Linda Smith-Lynch says, '*Truly great – just what we fellow sufferers need to brighten the day!*' and Donna Watkins expresses: '*Randy, please keep these coming! We need you right now!*' (comments, Randy Rainbow interviews Donald Trump part three).

Furthermore, although I shall discuss below the extensive negative and sometimes hostile remarks made by some users, a significant number of the comments indicate that they are politically aligned with him and support his work, not only for the artistic and comedic content but also, for the political messaging. On YouTube, TM says: '*Thank you for singing what we're all feeling! You are a welcome comic relief in these dark days*', Nesth Rodd comments: '*Randy R absolute genius, always impeccable editing, timing and political accuracy on point, acting and singing superb. A real treasure*' (comments, If You Ever Got Impeached 2018). Whether or not the same followers are also committed viewers of the mainstream news channels, or readers of the national press, can't be determined, but the strongest recognition in the comments and the 'Like' buttons is about the politics inherent in Rainbow's work. The way that the 'Like' button has become accepted across social media sites through the 'thumbs-up' icon is, as Van Dijck explains, '[T]he profound modification of a social norm' (2013: 49). As a user we respond to '[c]onnecting people, things, and ideas [this being] the principle behind the much-debated Like button' (2013: 49). Tero Karppi goes further by drawing attention to an empirical study by Facebook researchers in 2014, which focussed on emotional contagion: '[T]he researchers argued that Facebook manipulating the visibility of News Feed content could transfer users' emotional states from user to user … Emotional contagion happened without the users ever being aware of being subjected to a test' (2018: 114).

Jenkins's view is that the users of technology can determine the outcome of the way that we understand convergence. The participant is active, and this grassroots ethos empowers wider communities to engage with political and cultural movements, therefore, it is interesting to consider how both Rainbow and his followers, as well as those that are critical about the content of his work, take part in a form of political activism.

Rainbow and Trump

It was the Trump political campaign in 2016 that provided Rainbow with particularly evocative material to explore, arguably boosting Rainbow's profile to command a live tour. The performative elements of the US political rallies and presidential campaigns are ripe for Rainbow to satirize.[1] Rainbow realizes this early on in the Presidential campaign, and Trump becomes a key player in his videos from then on. There are a number of Rainbow's videos that focus on Trump's use of social media, such as 'TWEETS TWEETS & NOTHING BUT TWEETS' (uploaded 11 January 2017), which received 7.6 million views on Facebook and 314,000 views on YouTube. In this Rainbow adapts the 'Witch's Rap' from *Into the Woods* (Sondheim 1986), calling attention to Trump's overuse of Twitter, calling it '*hostile thoughtless, whiny and irreverent, exasperating, childish, intemperate and petty*'. *We said, 'no more!*' Then follows, 'BEFORE HE TWEETS'[2] (uploaded 5 July 2017) (Figure 3.3), 7 million views on Facebook and 611,000 views on YouTube: '*[H]e's dug himself into a hole, and he's acting like a basic cyber troll. Antagonizing almost everyone he meets.*' And then 'YOU CAN'T STOP HIS TWEETS' (9 April 2018)[3] with 1.8 million views on Facebook and 416,000 views on YouTube, Rainbow sings: '*You can't stop the arrogance of a racist off his pills, you can try to stop the sneaky right propaganda that he shills, and you can try and be a president with no competence or skills, but the worst is surely yet to come 'cause he just can't stop his tiny thumb*'.

The mocking of political leaders has come in many forms. *Spitting Image* (1984–96) created by Peter Fluck, Roger Law and Martin Lambie-Nairn in the UK used puppets as caricatures creating satirical political commentary as well as caricaturing celebrities, the Royal family and sports personalities. The programme attracted large audiences, up to 15 million viewers, and won a host of TV awards. The series returned to television after a twenty-four-year break, in Autumn 2020, with Trump amongst the new puppets. Many TV and live stand-up comedians focus on caricature and satire, perhaps some of the most well-known being from *Saturday Night Live* (1975 onwards), with Alec Baldwin's Trump impersonation winning an Emmy award in 2017. Political caricature and comedy have been used much earlier, going back centuries to Alexander Pope, John Dryden and Jonathan Swift, for example. Maurice Charney's edited collections, *Comedy: A Geographic and Historical Guide* (2005, volumes 1 and 2), give an in-depth analysis of comedy in relation to a range of themes including satire, farce and irony. The use of song in this context can be traced back to *The Beggars Opera* (1727), the work of Gilbert and Sullivan, and far more recently in US culture, to the series of political satires by George Gershwin; *Strike Up the Band* (1927), *Of Thee I Sing* (1931, which won the Pulitzer Prize) and *Let 'Em Eat Cake* (1933).

Roastings and send-ups have long been part of the dynamic of celebrity culture. As part of the *Kraft Music Hall* television series (1958–71), the Friars Club[4] roast lampooned individuals such as Jerry Lewis and Johnny Carson, and more recently *Comedy Central Roast* started in 2003 on American TV channel Comedy Central. The premise of a roast is when an individual is subjected to jokes at their expense to amuse the wider audience. It's interesting to consider the use of the word 'roast' in relation to the mocking of an individual. There is a suggestion that the audience slowly devour the humour and therefore the 'victim' of the roasting. Images of comedians being slowly turned over on a spit in front of an audience of laughing 'friends' wouldn't necessarily seem like an enjoyable experience. There is something quite heated and uncomfortable about the use of the 'roast'. Similarly, the expression to 'haul/rake someone over the coals' is sometimes used when someone has been angrily reprimanded. However, it was initially a form of torture used, in the middle ages, against individuals who spoke out against the church.

It's interesting to consider how we receive a mix of satire and parody as humour, and when this becomes something more sinister, potentially leading to a spread of hate or inciting hate in others. Comedian Kathy Griffin experienced the backlash of taking a joke too far, perhaps, when she posed with a 'Trump severed head' covered in ketchup for a photo shoot. In 2019 she released a film: *Kathy Griffin: A Hell of a Story*. Likewise, the creators of *Spitting Image* were used to getting complaints[5] in the newspapers or on TV shows such as *Points of View* (BBC 1961–). Now with parody such as Rainbow's appearing online to a wide audience, the comments are easy and instantaneous. The criticisms quickly traverse the realm of critiquing the object and move to personal and general political opinion.

'Randy Rainbow interviews Melania Trump' uploaded on 18 October 2016 has an incredible 18 million views on Facebook and 1 million views on YouTube. This is by far the highest number of views from any of his interview style videos, and indeed of all his Facebook video content (to date). This video is another sit-down interview. Rainbow opens with an insult about Melania Trump's 'emptiness'. He later says, '*[I]n your own words, what makes your husband qualified for the job?*' Melania Trump's edited response is '*because he did so many stuff in his life*', and this is inserted as a highlighted quote at the bottom of the screen referencing a news bulletin. It's not really clear why this video is so popular with Rainbow's followers, however, many of the comments criticize Rainbow for making fun of Melania Trump's use of the English language. Facebook user, Emine Dilek is one of those critics, firstly responding personally: '*As someone who came to this country as an adult and still have an accent, I don't find this funny at all*'. Dilek then moves to a reverse attack: '*I wonder how many languages the a-hole who thinks he is funny, speaks*'. Dilek then follows up with a generalized political statement that lumps all left-leaning politics together: '*Democrats are showing how disgusting they can also be when it comes to making fun of spouses ... I am so glad I am done with this corrupt party*' (comments, Randy Rainbow interviews Melania Trump, accessed November 2019). Thirty-one comments follow Dilek's thread, and these represent a back and forth of insults. It's not unusual to see followers make huge leaps in terms of logic within their responses, shoring up cognitive biases by viewing selectively. There is definitely a wave of Rainbow fans who also declare their political leaning, and unsurprisingly the most positive comments come from those who are inclined towards the Democratic party rather than the Republican. Although videos such as the one above tend to bring out the more nuanced conversations, including around the protection of women and migrants, the comments are dominated by angry responses towards Melania and her husband.

In fact, the use of personal mockery has been a characteristic tactic that Trump himself has used to belittle detractors. One of the most memorable instances was whilst he was campaigning in 2015 in South Carolina when he physically mocked a journalist with severe disabilities. In 2016, he tweeted about Stormy Daniels (an adult actress who supposedly had an affair with Trump): '*Great, now I can go after Horseface and her 3rd rate lawyer in the Great State of Texas*' (uploaded 16 October 2018, accessed 20 April 2020). So, to some extent, Rainbow's idiom and the tone of commenters are simply an extension of the same communicative discourse used by the President. Rainbow uses it as a tool to question power, whereas Trump's attacks have regularly pushed the boundaries of what is ethically and socially acceptable in terms of targeting minority or vulnerable groups. Trump also turns against those who question his authority, 'hauling them over the coals' with aggressive and provocative communications.

Sociologist Christian Fuchs explores Trump's use of Twitter and audiences' relationships with his Twitter account by using critical social media discourse analysis. He explains that 'Trump's followers do not have a rational, but an emotional relation with him' (2018: 198). Fuchs's analysis explains that the most retweeted of Trump's tweets are those highlighting the '"Us" versus "Them" logic ... The combination of nationalist ideology and the friend/enemy scheme seems to increase attention. Trump presents politics as a constant struggle between Americans on the one side and those whom he sees as enemies such as the liberal media, protesters, Fidel Castro, etc.' [*sic*] (2018: 205). Fuchs's further analysis of the positive and negative comments in Trump's tweets reveals that 'the number of negative references to persons and groups is twice as large as the positive ones, which shows that Trump's Twitter communication often operates by constructing scapegoats and enemies whom he attacks' (216). Additionally, the use of 'bots' on websites and social media platforms means that it is not always easy to identify whether it is a human interaction or an algorithmically generated response. Therefore, the propensity for social media to exacerbate divisive interpersonal discourse has been built into the mechanics of social media, regardless of human agency:

> Algorithms do not have morals, ethics, consciousness, identity or anticipatory thinking like humans. They can easily be programmed to insult and threaten humans and to communicate fascism and ideological violence. In (semi) automated politics, it becomes difficult to discern between what is communicated by humans and by machines. Algorithms can manipulate the public perception of politics and thereby undermine the validity claims of truth, truthfulness, rightness and understandability of political communication in the public sphere.
>
> (Fuchs 2018: 237)

Bradshaw et al. (2020) discuss the use of amplifying accounts that can 'include automated, semiautomated, and highly active human-curated accounts on social media' (186), which 'deliberately seek to increase the number of voices speaking about or the attention being paid to particular messages' (186). Their analysis includes a typology of what users have shared on social media, with particular reference to political conversations on *Twitter* between 2016 and 2018 (173). The concept of semi-automated politics is one that I consider to be a feature of the postdigital, where the intraconnections between machine and human are entangled.

In 2006, Jenkins said that 'the key battles are being fought now. If we focus on the technology, the battle will be lost before we even begin to fight. We need to confront the social, cultural, and political protocols that surround the technology and how it will get used' (212). Ten years after this statement, Trump became President of the United States and Facebook was embroiled in controversy concerning the Presidential elections. Jenkins's observation could be considered a forewarning of the way that the cynical and exploitative dynamics of social media platforms enable states to manoeuvre the apparently personal interactions of the platforms to suit their own ideological ends.

In 2017, Facebook produced a White Paper responding to questions around Russian interference with the American elections. Facebook reported that there had been approximately '3000 ads connected to about

470 inauthentic accounts'. They continued, '[T]he ads and accounts appeared to focus on amplifying divisive social and political messages across the ideological spectrum – touching on topics from LGBT matters to race issues to immigration to gun rights' (Weedon, Nuland and Stamos 2017). In 2018, Diraj Murthy introduces a collection of essays on 'social media, activism and organisations' expressing, '[A]lthough it is urgent for us to better understand social media use in social movements, it is particularly pressing for those understandings to include organizational constructions, perspectives, and theories' (2). What Murthy implies here is that the power of large organizations and the social media networks themselves have an agenda that we need to consider alongside individual use. The power to manipulate through user engagement has a significant impact on the way that social media is further used.

Entertainment or politics

In Rainbow's work, we hear a challenge to Trump's brand of populism, but if his work goes someway to constructing a counter-narrative, the comments from the mass audience often revert back to the problematic 'scapegoating and simplistic affective hatred' found in the voice of the right-wing propaganda machine (Fuchs 2018: 255). In the comments sections of Rainbow's video, 'An Interview with Donald Trump Part II (August 2016)', we see this at work. Maria Virginia Claudet says, '*[T]he interviewer looks too gay … … fortunately Trump is not homophobic*'. Samoht negdirp says, '*I'm mad gay people stole the fucking rainbow the rainbow should be for everyone … Why does the rainbow have to represent the lgbt community that alone is bullshit*'. Kaden Stahley says, '*This guys is just some gay democrat who could care less about the truth. I am so sick of the free-loading society the government has created*' [*sic*]. The video mocks Trump and his relationship with Vladimir Putin, as well as some of Trump's comments about Hillary Clinton. One can assume that the flurry of comments about rainbows and gay people are in response to Rainbow making fun of Trump and Putin's political relationship, which was brought in to question throughout the presidential campaign.

It's no surprise to hear the dominant right-wing voices being reiterated by a public on social media. Messages are expanding across social media sites, gathering a community of participants. Dhiraj Murthy explains this in terms of power: 'If Twitter helps promote ordinary people into well-known "opinion leaders" (from citizen scientists to citizen fashionistas), the medium may be challenging traditional media hierarchies or, at a minimum, generating new forms of influence and new types of "influencers"' (2013: 31). This would be an encouraging proposition in relation to grassroots activism, if there was a balance of political voices and opinions and a genuine democratic debate. But Murthy follows this statement with the comment, '[I]f most tweeting "opinion leaders" reflect influence already present in traditional broadcast media, Twitter does not represent a significant redress in systems of communicative power' (31). This is reminiscent of Jenkins's warning:

> contemporary media is being shaped by several contradictory and concurrent trends: at the same moment that cyberspace displaces some traditional information and cultural gatekeepers, there is also an unprecedented power within old media. A widening of the discursive environment coexists with a narrowing of the range of information being transmitted by the most readily available media channels.
>
> (Jenkins 2018: 211)

What becomes clear is that there is a constant battle between those wanting to expand the sociopolitical dialogue and those that want to control the messaging. What becomes increasingly complex is understanding who or what is in control of the messages. It's just as important to determine whose voices are seeking to expand the sociopolitical dialogue as it is to identify whose voices are seeking to peddle a particular ideology.

Rainbow ironically uses social media platforms to highlight Trump's use of social media, and the news narratives that surround him and his administration. The musical theatre style, satirically, explores the frivolous sentiment that can sometimes be presented in song, but reveals the statements that come from Trump's messages as nonsensical. This deliberate play between what is supposed to be taken seriously and what is often considered 'entertainment' exposes the absurdity present in contemporary politics. Rainbow becomes a political activist against the current administration: '[T]he new political culture – just like the new popular culture – reflects the pull and tug of these two media systems: one broadcast and commercial, the other narrowcast and grassroots' (Jenkins 2018: 211). Rainbow has a large following, and he is able to portray an alternative and satirical perspective on what is being broadcast on the major news channels and voiced through the dominant politicians. But there are followers who question the influence of his work. Facebook user Robert Leon Sanders comments: '*How many Republican/Independent minds have you changed? How many thousand dollars have you contributed to his un-election campaign?*' Sanders perhaps recognizes the limit of influence that Rainbow's work has if it is only recirculated amongst a fan base, or echo chamber of users who already share Rainbow's politics.

Jonathan P. Rossing explores the potential for humour to transverse issues of politics. However, he says responses that position humour in the realm of 'mere entertainment' diminish humour's power to 'traverse and contest rigid social orders' (2016: 61). Furthermore, he says that '[h]umor is relegated to something unreal, untruthful, and insincere while, by comparison, the serious work of Congress is maintained as pure and honest discourse' (2016: 71). Facebook user Jessie Hendrickson Nordvall says this in her own words when commenting on Rainbow's 'If You Ever Got Impeached' video: '*This is stupid. The office of the president is supposed to be respected. Regardless of personal opinion. Sad day, America. Bad form.*' If political leaders are supposed to 'tell the truth' and be held in high regard, then Rainbow's work, which is in opposition to the leadership, would represent mistruth and be disregarded. The apparently dismissible light entertainment format that Rossing refers to, which is seen in opposition to the voice of congress, risks creating even more polarized views for audiences whose political leanings are already entrenched.

In the comments for 'Randy Rainbow interviews Donald Trump', Facebook user, Ainsley Campbell says, '*I think Randy's production will not harm Trumps chances but rather improve them. He is preaching to a converted audience but swinging voters may find his editing to be in poor taste and feel sorry for Trump*' [*sic*]. Joe Staffieri protests, '*Randy, you just lost me as a fan. Hillary & Bernie have so much more, being Commies & un-American, to spoof on. You just screwed yourself.*' And Linda Traitz asks: '*I'm anxiously awaiting a #crookedhillary video? Any idea when we can expect that?.*' Interestingly, users able to balance political view with humour are Dixie Hoopes, who simply says: '*Lol I still love Mr. Trump!!!*' and Lisa Prosk comments: '*You are cray cray!!! But even I who happens to be a huge trump supporter find you hysterical. I'm sure President Trump does as well! He has a great sense of humor*' [*sic*].

Rossing suggests that 'it is vital for communication scholars and critics to uphold humor as a meaningful player in important sociopolitical debates and to continue exploring its unique contributions to public deliberation' (2016: 73). The work of Rainbow has the potential to contribute and change the way that we engage with the messages being sent by the political voices of power, because of the way that he plays with what is seen as entertainment, and what is supposed to be considered as serious. His attempts to obviously restructure the narrative enable a viewer to consciously explore and potentially reconsider messages. However, the commentary that runs alongside his online videos can often tap into the role of what Rossing would call tragic public political discourse, 'creating evil enemies, castigating scapegoats, and securing victories through the political "death" of the opposition' (2016: 72).

One Facebook user, Mary Gigliotti Katkic, says: '*I am so sick of FB being so liberal and shutting out all the conservatives!! Media should NOT be controlling the news and all views should have equal time. Sick of it!!*'

Some of the comments are because of the content of Rainbow's work, but others are from viewers who don't understand the way that the work is constructed. Facebook user Sarah Nickerson understands that Rainbow is using a playful montage of material but doesn't seem to realize that it is parody. She replies to the 'Randy Rainbow interviews Melania Trump' video, saying:

> *This is the kind of media that pisses me off. If you don't know already he had been green screened into this. As someone who knows a trick or to about editing and putting together a film I know that this is an actual interview that has been ripped apart by an editor to portray what they wish to. But not everyone can spot the details that make this so obviously fake. All I'm hear to say is don't put all your trust into everything you see because editors and people in the media have tons of ways of manipulating footage.*

There seems to be some confusion over the 'type' of work that Rainbow is producing, with users referring to him as a journalist and his work as media. There is also sometimes an assumption that 'Randy Rainbow' is a contrived stage name, it's his real name.[6] The fact that people assume that Randy Rainbow is a fictional name suggests that there is a political decision in his 'choice' of name and a distinction between the 'real' Randy and the 'performed' Randy. Furthermore, the combination of Rainbow's online and live show aesthetic enables him to converge his 'star' personality across media. Elizabeth Ellcessor calls attention to the convergence element in social media stars, noting that 'Internet-based fame depends on the authenticity of a star's self-representation and on the notion of intimacy, experienced through the possibility of interaction rather than through simple familiarity' (2012: 51). A sense of intimacy is created with the viewers through the use of the comments sections available on the apps. This paradoxically enables viewers to 'connect' with Rainbow as a 'real' person, someone they can be '*friends*' or 'enemies' with, depending on their response to his work.

The way that Rainbow dissects political and public commentary into a new form is confusing for some. They don't understand the parody of the form, the reinterpretation of the messages and therefore, for them, it also further confuses Randy Rainbow, the constructed social media personality with Randy Rainbow the person. Here we might connect this 'confusion' to what Liam Jarvis refers to as 'wrongness'. He discusses the way that fakes (deep and shallow) can be used for malevolence. Unlike failure, wrongness explains not only the technical success (or not) of deep- and shallowfakes, but also the moral dilemmas that are entangled. Rainbow's work isn't an attempt at creating a deepfake. It's a rather simple process of editing and parody; yet, some viewers of his work struggle to see the technological interventions, such as editing, instead they 'feel' that it's a trick, a sort of 'wrongness'. Facebook user Ronald Reed says: '*This video isn't real ... sad*', and Larry Burdick comments: '*For all the ignorant out there, this is a fake video. FAKE !!!*' (comments, 'Randy Rainbow interviews Donald Trump' accessed Nov 2019). Lisa D. Robinson states: '*Donald, you did GREAT keeping it together!!!. .... THIS JUST SHOWS YOU "WILL" BE A GREAT PRESIDENT!!!*' and in the comments for the video follow up 'Randy Rainbow interviews Donald Trump part II', Dave Davis says: '*I honestly didn't know he wasn't a real news anchor .... Hahaha why isn't he a real news anchor?? Why won't someone hire him .... I need this kind of reporting in my life.*'

By November 2020, Rainbow has uploaded 132 videos on his Facebook site (seventeen fewer than on his YouTube site). He has three playlists, categorized as 'Political Randy Rainbow' (twenty-four videos), 'Throwbacks' (ten videos), and 'GOP dropouts' (a pun on 'Beauty School Dropout' from the musical *Grease* – six videos). This means that ninety-two videos have not been archived in to a playlist. I draw attention to this because within this selection of archiving, there is a construction of the Facebook identity of Rainbow, and therefore an element of the construction of the social media star; for example, he chooses not to put some of his earlier work on Facebook. The Facebook details indicate that the 'Throwbacks' playlist was updated in 2015, as was the 'GOP dropouts' playlist. The 'Political Randy Rainbow' playlist was updated in 2018, with the most recent video, 'Just BE BEST – a Randy Rainbow song parody', uploaded on 15 October 2018. The earliest video in this playlist is 'Randy Rainbow performs at a Donald Trump rally', uploaded on 18 January 2016. The 'Throwbacks' playlist includes work from between 23 April 2015 and 3 May 2016. Four videos in the 'Throwbacks' playlist are uploaded after the earliest video from the 'Political Randy Rainbow' playlist. The 'GOP dropouts' playlist is a more defined archive in that 'Randy Rainbow serenades each of the 2016 GOP presidential hopefuls/losers' (Facebook). The videos here are from February to 5 May 2016. It's interesting to note that since October 2018 Rainbow hasn't archived any further videos into the 'Political Randy Rainbow' playlist, yet all of his videos have been politically themed.

Since Trump became president elect on 9 November 2016, there have been eighty-three videos. The first of these was uploaded on 10 November

2016 and is called 'Hillary Wins! Randy Rainbow's American Dream (a Musical)'. The end of this video is a voice-over from Rainbow saying 'it's only the beginning', with text that states, '4 more years of Rainbow'. Of the eighty-two videos that follow, six are publicity stunts for Rainbow's live tour or an album, one is about Jewishness and Christmas, and one called 'Kill the Release' is about gay characters causing controversy in Disney. The remaining seventy-four videos (as of the end of November 2020) are explicitly about the presidential administration.

It's clear to see that the presidential elections, the subsequent presidential administration, and then the 2020 elections, have supplied Rainbow with a wealth of material for his work, and the way that Rainbow has chosen to archive his videos indicates this thematic purpose in his material. The fact that his latest work is not archived is indicative that Rainbow's work is now well known and therefore viewers/followers know what to expect. The political satire is definitely a diversion from his earlier work which is much lighter in content, focusing on the humour of celebrity dating with faux telephone conversations. Rainbow really puts his flag in the sand from July 2016, and from hereon there are very few videos that are not related to American politics. With an awareness of the direction his work has taken he sings: '*If Donald got fired according to plan just think of the things I could do. I'd stop having nightmares about KellyAnn and fin'lly sing songs about somebody new*' ('IF DONALD GOT FIRED – Randy Rainbow Parody (featuring Patti LuPone!)' uploaded to YouTube on 7 October 2020).

Rainbow as chorus

The identity that Rainbow presents throughout his work is as a gay man – clearly supporting and fighting for LGBTQ+ rights. There is also the musical theatre performer, the comedian and the political satirist. Equally, Rainbow's work performs largely online as a social media presence and with this comes the multiplicity of social media identity, and the convergence of the star.

Rainbow as star becomes more playful in the way that he portrays the role of chorus in many of his videos. One Rainbow (edited as many Rainbows) against the dominant political voice and therefore visually and aurally is presented as a crowd. Technically he multiplies his image and layers his voice, and philosophically he uses his own position to create a political chorus for the 'left'. This chorus of Rainbows projects a clone-like nature to indicate that there are many more, like Rainbow, who want to express opposing views to the dominant administration. The 'GOP dropout' videos highlight the many voices amongst the hopefuls putting themselves forward

Figure 3.3 Rainbow as chorus in 'BEFORE HE TWEETS' (uploaded to Facebook 5 July 2017)

as the Republican presidential candidate. The multiple voices are heard again as the contentious leadership of Trump's administration causes fractious disagreements amongst members and voters. The questions that Rainbow puts to the edited news items of Trump, Melania or another member of Trump's administration become so comedic because the opposing view seems to either leave the administration speechless or change the original meaning of the conversation. This taking away of the dominant presidential voice is not only funny for the followers of Rainbow (and as previously suggested, therefore often politically aligned), but also symbolizes the power of the voice. It is here that we can view Rainbow's work as an attempt to subvert the mainstream dominant voice and switch the power play between who is heard and who is left without comment.

In terms of the cloned crowd, I am reminded of the Oompah Loompahs in *Charlie and the Chocolate Factory* (2005, dir. Tim Burton). Just after the greedy Augustus Gloop falls into the pool of chocolate and blocks the pipe, the Oompah Loompahs perform a song whilst rescuing him: '*Augustus Gloop, Augustus Gloop, a great big greedy nickenpoop, Augustus Gloop so big and vile. So greedy, foul and infantile*'. The Oompah Loompahs are all played by one actor (Deep Roy), and the voice work is recorded by one performer (Danny Elfman), overdubbing himself to create the chorus's polyvocality.

The hard-working Oompah Loompahs remind us of the impersonal and exploited identities of the masses. Rainbow's chorus also has this impact, as he voices opposition to power. However, there are also negative connotations of the clone, a type of identikit or someone perceived to be conformist with no view of their own, and as such Rainbow as cloned chorus is also rather symbolic of the way that social network services (SNS) are used by individuals but are coded by the business. Van Dijck refers to this as the 'double logic of connectedness versus connectivity, a logic that is mirrored by users' interests in mass-self-communication vis-à-vis the owners' interest in mass customization' (2013: 62). In a symbolic attempt, Rainbow creates more Rainbow not only across platforms, but also within one platform and within one work. This multiplication of Rainbow resonates with *The Matrix*'s Agent Smith (1999, dir. the Wachowskis), who creates more Smith to fight Neo as the personification of computational processes, in this case, a virus. However, the link here with online virality is infectious. This multitude of Rainbows within his work and across social media platforms creates a pervasiveness that highlights the entanglements between human users and technology. In the following sections I will discuss a triangulation that includes human and technological interactions.

Hijacking audiences

The video clip 'DONALD TRUMP, GROW UP! – Randy Rainbow HAMILTON Song Parody' (uploaded 22 November 2016) has had (as of November 2020) 2.2 million views on Facebook and 649,000 views on YouTube. The video comments on US Vice President Mike Pence's visit to the *Hamilton* show on Broadway, where his attendance caused the theatre audience to boo. This show is considered to be a particularly important musical because it has reinterpreted a white patriarchal history of America as a multicultural narrative. In this video, Rainbow 'interviews' Mike Pence and he edits a shot that is captured on an audience member's phone of Pence entering the auditorium to the sound of booing. The audience vocally express their resentment of Pence's presence at the show, perhaps in recognition of how the politics of the Trump administration jars with the theme of the musical that they are about to see. In Rainbow's video, he advises Pence not to 'go back' to Broadway, using the well-known tune from the show 'You'll be Back' (Miranda 2015).

Trump responds to the reception of Pence's visit to the theatre and in particular to the address made to Pence at the end of the *Hamilton* performance when actor Brandon Dixon says: '[W]e truly hope that this show has inspired you to uphold our American values and to work on behalf of all of us' (Mele and Healy 2016). Trump defensively and offensively tweets: '*The cast and producers of Hamilton, which I hear is highly overrated, should immediately apologize to Mike Pence for their terrible behavior*' (@ realDonaldTrump, 20 November 2016). Trump supporters then responded online by calling for a boycott of the *Hamilton* show. Twitter user Vic Freed said, '*#BoycottHamilton Boycott this Anti-American, Anti-White play whose cast verbally assault the audience who paid for a show not a lecture*'. Rainbow satirically weaves Trump's tweet in to his 'Donald Trump, Grow Up!' video and pushes back with '*Don't renounce a Broadway play, when you won't denounce the KKK*'.

In this example of live performance converging with social media platforms, there are multiple layers of audience reception and participation at play. The audience attending the performance on Broadway become participants (some boo, some cheer) in a political performance by Pence as he enters the theatre, and the live Broadway show is effectively hijacked by Pence's political 'show'. Pence waits until the audience is already seated (and captive) before making his own entrance with his entourage. The show's hijacking takes place in the theatre, and yet the event is subsequently given mass exposure through social media, with its audience members co-opted into the political drama of the event. The hijacking of the live event becomes a mediatized abduction of individuals whose complicity with one political side or another is used to amplify the politics.

It's interesting that Pence appears with a group of people, some of whom appear to be bodyguards protecting him from potential attacks. When this material is exposed on social media platforms, commentators adopt equivalent positions as (digital) bodyguards, to defend against hostile attacks from 'opposing' views. The social media abduction consequently enables a weaponizing of the mediatized audience reactions, further entrenching what Fuchs calls the 'Us versus Them Trumpian tactic of scapegoating', and highlighting how new modes of manipulating mediatized masses/crowds/audiences can be used for a particular agenda.

Such a hijacking of one scenario and its manipulation into a mediatized domain in order to magnify particular politics can also be seen in the way that Rainbow replicates his own image to create a chorus, creating a crowd voice, a copy of Rainbow, another Rainbow. Furthering the layering affect created by 'copy' and social media users, YouTube subscriber Dane Callstrom posted a video called 'I'll Be Back: A Trump Hamilton Parody' (November 2020), which crudely takes the technology for creating deepfakes to superimpose Trump on to the *Hamilton* stage with his mouth manipulated to sing the well-known song from the show, 'You'll be back', albeit with adjusted title and lyrics for parody. This is reminiscent of Randy Rainbow's parody version and further emphasizes the way that social media platforms can be influentially used, and create parody upon parody, or a further hijacking of ideas that appear as suggestions for me to view. As Patrick Lonergan says, 'the content that we receive has undeniably been framed by media, yet its creation continues to unfold before us; indeed, we may actually contribute to that creation by adding comments, by editing the original content, by sharing it onwards, by "liking" what we have seen, and so on' (2016: 33–4). YouTube user Garmr recognizes this connectivity when he comments on Rainbow's video 'If You Ever Got Impeached': '*[P]raise to the youtube algorithm! this showed up with perfect timing:D*'.

In a hijacking dynamic – using the abductor, hostage and bodyguard scenario – there is an entanglement related to protection and wrongdoing. In online scenarios, one person's bodyguard can be another person's abductor. In Liam Jarvis's chapter, this sense of wrongness is discussed at length in terms of ethical and moral problems. What is clear from the examples in this chapter is that the intraconnectivity between humans and social media is enabling in terms of creativity, but confusing in terms of identifying moral responsibility. This is not so problematic when the fakes are so shallow that we know they are fake, but as Jarvis's chapter explores it is morally significant when the fakes are more sophisticated. Parody and humour in this case can unknowingly slip in to treacherous territory.

Abductor, hostage and bodyguard

Rainbow's followers log on to see his latest video whilst critics check out his new work and often engage in some sort of commentary. Each engagement plays a part in representing the views on the politics that Rainbow is satirizing, contributing to the unfolding creation of the work. In Lonergan's view, 'whereas computer users had been like audience-members at a theatre, Web 2:0 and social media now allow them to be like actors, playwrights and directors too' (2016: 16). The functions of sites such as Facebook and YouTube enable the responses of audiences to be made public. This has been a popular tool for followers to feel that they are in contact with and can communicate with celebrities such as Rainbow. It can be an empowering tool for a community of people that might otherwise feel they can't reach the people they want to communicate with. Rainbow may not respond to individual comments, in fact he rarely does, but his followers pick up the conversations on his behalf. The responses continue to promote the video for Rainbow, and the fans of his work also act like 'bodyguards' in protecting Rainbow against negative comments. I appropriate the use of the word 'bodyguard' to explain how followers and supporters defend Rainbow and his work, whilst bodyguards for the 'other side' step in to support the target of his parody. The bodyguard is the third element to the hijack dynamic (abductor, hostage, bodyguard), and the triangulation can be fluid in the way that roles switch around; because of the ways that users engage with social media platforms these are not fixed positions. Facebook user Diane Guy says, '*To be fair and unbiased, we are expecting the same treatment for Democratic Candidates since you have satired all Republican Candidates*' [*sic*]. Facebook user AP Pigozzi plays the part of Rainbow's bodyguard when they say, '*Why does he have to be unbiased? He's a liberal comedian. He's not a politician, he's not a journalist, he's himself. He's not a "public figure" representing a corporation or institution*' ('Randy Rainbow Interviews Donald Trump' comments 2016). The first comment by Diane Guy attracted 180 likes. We might say that this small sign of approval for her comment comes from other individuals who feel that Rainbow's work has taken a particular bias towards ridiculing the Republican party. In return, the bodyguard, AP Pigozzi attracts 214 likes for their response. A back and forth between AP Pigozzi and Diane Guy encourages others to join in using the Facebook comments option and the 'political' commentary breaks down in to personal insults. AP Pigozzi comments: '*Fucking moron*', and Lindsay Kersey says: '*AP Pigozzi grow a brain. You are the legit ass crack of America. Any type of a public figure needs to at least try to be unbiased as to not offend. Unless of course he's only trying to attract dems*.'

Where Rainbow's work is about satire and parody, it's clear that the responses to his work are often much more aligned to a 'Them' and 'Us' hostile environment. In the 'Randy Rainbow Interviews Melania Trump' video, there are a number of 'bodyguarding' comments for the First Lady. For example, Facebook user Lisa Lis comments protectively of Melania against Rainbow's video and also asserts that she is probably a victim of her husband's abuse: '*As much vitriol that I have for Trump's ideas and actions, I do not agree with bullying and degrading his wife. I feel sorry for her and can imagine the many ways she has been a victim of his misogyny*'. Her comment highlights the adage that two wrongs don't make a right.

Rainbow's use of satire as a critical tool for expanding dialogue has in these cases just reinforced existing political views. The object of the ridicule is often misappropriated by both sides of the narrative, and therefore held as a hostage; the boundaries between protection and scapegoating are confused to the point that the friend/enemy scheme is blurred. In the responses to Rainbow's work it is no longer clear what the point is, who is making it, or why. The splurge of comments that litter many of Rainbow's videos are not only an opportunity for followers to evidence their appreciation of his work, but also for individuals to become tangled up with further scapegoating. This type of bodyguarding provokes comments and 'arguments' that then perpetuate the polarized views of the public on the political situation and create an echo chamber of noise for like-minded supporters. If work like Rainbow's is going to make any impact in changing the way that participants already view politics, then it needs to be considered beyond the form of 'entertainment', and the form of the work needs to be understood in the context of social media platforms, as a tool for expanding communication and dialogue. Jenny Edkins and Adrian Kear, in the introduction of their edited collection *International Politics and Performance: Critical Aesthetics and Creative Practice* (2013), consider 'performance and politics as "folded" in myriad and complex patterns inter-animating one another as domains of political subjectivation and creative practices undertaken by aesthetic subjects, a more conventional approach might be to see them as operating in dialogue' (2013: 8). Rainbow's use of social media goes someway to begin this inter-animated dialogic process, inherent in the way that he categorizes his video channel and intertextually embeds a number of motifs from the political rallies, mainstream media and musical theatre. However, the followers' engagement through comments alone is not proving to be a useful way of understanding the intertextual complexities of argument that are entangled in the work and the dissemination.

Social media at once becomes the abductor, hostage and bodyguard for Rainbow's work, as much as his videos also triangulate this dynamic. The entanglements of this dynamic become more complex with each sharing, each comment, and each like. Increasingly the role of bots also complicates the messaging, with these machines acting as 'digital abductors and/or bodyguards' in order to amplify particular narratives.

Rainbow's work though does seek to position another voice, the voice of many, whilst also rendering 'speechless' or changing the communication of the dominant, powerful voices. The body of Rainbow's work is an archive of challenges to the current political communications, providing a humorous and creative provocation to the Trump administration. The network of abductors, hostages and bodyguards adds a dynamic that takes control from the individuals that make the work, and this is further complicated when the abductors and bodyguards are not always human. Machines are used to hijack situations in order to dominate a message, and are often used to continue the friend/enemy regime that furthers divisive far-right propaganda. Human-to-human dialogue can be competitive but when machines, as digital abductors and bodyguards, contribute to the commentary it can very quickly become divisive, amplifying messages to suit the algorithm of control.

In 2020, Trump responded angrily to Twitter fact-checking one of his tweets about mail-in ballots for the 2020 presidential election campaign. He signed an executive order 'aimed at making it easier for people to sue Twitter and other social media platforms for what [he] and his allies have denounced as unconstitutional political censorship' (Tillman 2020). Meanwhile, Facebook decided against highlighting any issues with Trump's comments. Mark Zuckerberg commented, 'I just believe strongly that Facebook shouldn't be the arbiter of truth of everything that people say online' (Zuckerberg says Facebook won't be 'arbiters of truth' after Trump threat). The laws around the responsibilities of social media companies for hosting third speech material become further complicated when political leaders abuse their power. The line between freedom of speech and divisive rhetoric is one that Trump flaunts regularly, and Rainbow draws attention to this in his work. Ironically, in 2020, the advertisements that appear before many of Rainbow's videos are promoting Trump's campaign and re-election. In January 2021, Twitter and Facebook lock Trump out of his accounts after Trump protestors stormed Capitol Hill. The social media platforms took down some of his messages and accused Trump of having incited the violence. *The Washington Post* critically questions whether the social media platforms had responded 'swiftly and aggressively enough to rein in the dangerous rhetoric from Trump and his allies' (Romm, Dwoskin and Harwell 2021). The way that Trump supporters use the riots to further incite violence through online messaging escalates the divisive and dangerous rhetoric: 'As the mob of Trump supporters stormed the House and Senate, their compatriots online celebrated the chaos, cheering the violence across a wide array of social media sites and calling for bloodshed in the days ahead' (Romm, Dwoskin and Harwell 2021).

This appears to be more than an opportunity for opposing views to dialogue, and instead reinforces the power of the political and economically dominant voices, as well as the problems that social media platforms face in being partisan and fulfilling the criteria for connectivity.

Notes

1   Trump became known as the 'Twitter President' (prior to permanent suspension of his Twitter account in January 2021), and the marketing analysis firm, Tweetbinder, has done an analysis of Trump's tweets from 2009 until 2020 (https://www.tweetbinder.com/blog/trump-twitter/). He sent 51.5K tweets from his @realDonaldTrump account (as of May 2020). Trump regularly pushed his thoughts out in to the public domain, and this provided Rainbow with a wealth of material that he could access easily.

2   This song is a parody of Carrie Underwood's 2009 song 'Before He Cheats'.
3   Song parody from the 2007 movie *Hairspray*.
4   The Friars Club was aired on television (NBC) under the umbrella of the Kraft Music Hall (which had previously been on radio). However, the Friars Club started much earlier in a venue in NYC from 1904.
5   For more information about the recent return of the popular TV show *Spitting Image*, see Pelley (2020).
6   Media articles written about Rainbow often state 'yes, it's his given name', and we saw in the comments above that participants disliked the use of the rainbow being claimed as a gay metaphor.

References

Bradshaw S., P. N. Howard, B. Kollanyi, and L. M. Neudert (2020), 'Sourcing and Automation of Political News and Information over Social Media in the United States, 2016–2018', *Political Communication*, 37 (2): 173–93. doi: 10.1080/10584609.2019.1663322.

Charlie and the Chocolate Factory (2005), [Film] Dir. Tim Burton. USA: Warner Bros.

Charney, M. (2005), *Comedy: A Geographic and Historical Guide* (volumes 1 and 2), Westport: Praegart publishers.

Comedy Central Roast (2003–), [Television]. USA: Comedy Central.

Edkins, J. and Adrian Kear, eds (2013), *International Politics and Performance: Critical Aesthetics and Creative Practice*, Oxon: Routledge.

Ellcessor, E. (2012), 'Tweeting @feliciaday: Online Social Media, Convergence, and Subcultural Stardom', *Society for Cinema & Media Studies*, 51 (2) (Winter): 46–66.

Friars Club Roast (1904–), [Theatre/stand-up comedy]. New York City: Private Members Club.

Fuchs, C. (2018), *Digital Demagogue: Authoritarian Capitalism in the Age of Trump and Twitter*, London: Pluto Press.

Hamilton (2015), [Theatre]. Dir. M. Lin-Manuel.

If You Ever Got Impeached (August 2018), [online video] Creator. R. Rainbow. Available online: https://www.facebook.com/614736491961631/videos/165392017648614 and https://www.youtube.com/watch?v=sWTiFcl9OhU&t=4s (accessed September 2019).

Into the Woods (1986), Writer S. Sondheim.

Jenkins, H. (2018), *Convergence Culture: Where Old and New Media Collide*, New York: New York University Press.

Karppi, T. (2018), *Disconnect: Facebook's Affective Bonds*, Minnesota: University of Minnesota Press.

Kraft Music Hall Series (1958–71), [Television]. USA: NBC.

Let 'Em Eat Cake (1933), [Musical Theatre]. G. Gershwin, I. Gershwin, and G. S. Kaufman. USA: Broadway.

Lonergan, P. (2016), *Theatre & Social Media*, London: Palgrave.

McCarthy, T. (2020), 'Zuckerberg Says Facebook Won't Be "Arbiters of Truth" after Trump Threat', *Guardian*, 28 May. Available online: https://www. theguardian.com/technology/2020/may/28/zuckerberg-facebook-police-online-speech-trump. (accessed June 2020).

Mele, C. and P. Healy (2016), '"Hamilton" Had Some Unscripted Lines for Pence. Trump Wasn't Happy', *New York Times*, 19 November. Available online: https://www.nytimes.com/2016/11/19/us/mike-pence-hamilton.html (accessed October 2020).

Miranda, L. M. (2015), *You'll Be Back* [lyrics].

Murthy, D. (2013), *Twitter: Social Communication in the Twitter Age*, Hoboken, NJ: John Wiley & Sons.

Murthy, D. (2018), 'Introduction to Social Media, Activism, and Organizations', *Social Media + Society* 4 (January–March): 1–4.

Of Thee I Sing (1931), [Musical Theatre]. G. Gershwin, I. Gershwin, G. S. Kaufman, and M. Ryskind. USA: Broadway.

Pelley, Rich (2020), '"The More Complaints We Got, the Better – How Spitting Image Redefined Satire', *Guardian*, 1 October. Available online: https://www. theguardian.com/tv-and-radio/2020/ oct/01/spitting-image-satire-ian-hislop-roy-hattersley.

Randy Rainbow Interviews Donald Trump (May 2016), [online video] Creator. R. Rainbow. Available online: https://www.facebook.com/614736491961631/ videos/799534506815161 (accessed September 2019).

Randy Rainbow Interviews Donald Trump Part II (August 2016), [online video] Creator: R. Rainbow. Available online: https://www.facebook. com/614736491961631/videos/835886593179952

Randy Rainbow Interviews Melania Trump (October 2016), [online video] Creator. R. Rainbow. Available online: https://www.facebook.com/ 614736491961631/videos/891012107667400 (accessed November 2019).

Randy Rainbow Interviews Donald Trump Part Three (December 2016), [online video] Creator. R. Rainbow. Available online: https://www.facebook. com/614736491961631/videos/943346169100660 (accessed September 2019).

Randy Rainbow Is Dating Mel Gibson (July 2010), [online video] Creator. R. Rainbow. Available online: https://www.youtube.com/ watch?v=guU7EGkl98g (accessed September 2019).

Romm, T., E. Dwoskin, and D. Harwell (2021), 'Twitter, Facebook Lock Trump's Accounts Amid D.C Riots', *The Washington Post*, 6 January. Available online: https://www.washingtonpost.com/technology/2021/01/06/trump-tweet-violence/ (accessed 8 January 2021).

Rossing, J. P. (2016), 'Humor's Role in Political Discourse: Examining Border Patrol in Colbert Nation', in B. Couture and P. Wojahn (eds), *Crossing Borders, Drawing Boundaries: The Rhetoric of Lines across America*, 60–75,

University Press of Colorado. Available online: www.jstor.org/stable/j.
cttlb18vhw (accessed 17 April 2020).

Saturday Night Live (1975–), [Television] Creator. Lorne Michaels. USA: NBC.

Spitting Image (1984–96), [Television] Creators. Peter Fluck, Roger Law, and
Martin Lambie-Nairn.

Strike Up the Band (1927), [Musical Theatre]. G. Gershwin, I. Gershwin, and
G. S. Kaufman. USA: Broadway.

The Beggars Opera (1727), [Opera] Writer John Gay.

Tillman, Zoe (2020), 'Trump Wants to Help Conservatives Sue Twitter for
Censorship, But He'll Face an Obstacle: Justice Brett Kavanaugh', *Buzzfeed
News*, 28 May. Available online: https://www.buzzfeednews.com/article/
zoetillman/trump-twitter-executive-order-230-brett-kavanaugh (accessed
2 June 2020).

Van Dijck, J. (2013), *The Culture of Connectivity: A Critical History of Social
Media*. New York: Oxford University Press.

Weedon J., W. Nuland, and A. Stamos (2017), *Information Operations and
Facebook*. Available online: https://about.fb.com/news/2017/09/information-
operations-update/ (accessed 17 April 2020).

4

Deepfake-ification: A Postdigital Aesthetics of Wrongness in Deepfakes and Theatrical Shallowfakes

Liam Jarvis

Introduction: Franken-Cages and other reprogrammable body images

In 2018, an online trend emerged among users of social news platform Reddit (or 'Redditors') in which facial images of Hollywood actor Nicolas Cage were inserted onto the bodies of other actors in a peculiar quest to edit him into 'every movie ever made'. Using a deep learning application called FakeApp, internet users could remix new edits of popular movies, recasting Cage into films in which he had never appeared. Users created mash-ups of Nicolas Cage as James Bond, as Indiana Jones, as Lois Lane (see Figure 4.1) and so on, ad infinitum.

None of these AI-assisted 'deepfake' videos were meant to fool anyone. Incongruous assemblages of Cage's facial images on the digitized shoulders

Figure 4.1 Screengrab from YouTube. Nicolas Cage as Lois Lane in *Man of Steel* (2013)

of other well-known actors were intended as humorously uncanny Franken-Cages – a portmanteau term I use throughout this chapter that amalgamates Frankenstein's Creature as a fictionalized assemblage of body parts with 'Nicolas Cage' as a manipulatable series of online likenesses of the Hollywood actor. The Franken-Cages were a pervasively copied visual gag spread across an ever-multiplying series of user-generated online memes. This joke may be an allusion to one of Cage's previous roles as Castor Troy, a character that undergoes a face transplant in American science fiction film *Face/Off* (1997). But the interception and manipulation of others' images online is raising urgent new concerns in relation to less benevolent acts of online cutting and pasting using machine learning algorithms.

In 2017, researchers at the University of Washington used recurrent neural network artificial intelligence (AI) to model how Barack Obama moves his mouth when he speaks (Suwajanakorn et al. 2017). Using AI learnt lip-synching, which advanced from antecedent techniques of dubbing such as 'video rewrites' (Bregler et al. 1997), they were able to create a photorealistic synthetic 'Obama', putting words into his mouth that were taken from another audio track. A year later in 2018, American actor and comedian Jordan Peele used the same downloadable AI face-swapping tool used to fashion the Franken-Cages to create his own 'Obama'. This obscenity-laced YouTube video of the former President speaking switches to split screen in order to reveal the true actor behind 'Obama's' words (Peele) (see Figure 4.2), urging people to be 'more vigilant' with what they trust on the internet and signing off with the expression 'stay woke bitches'

Figure 4.2 Screenshot of Barack Obama Deepfake, YouTube: BuzzFeedVideo

('You Won't Believe What Obama Says ... ' 2018). This video was intended to enter into virulent circulation online and raise awareness about the spread of disinformation associated with the much-abused term 'fake news', which should mean 'news that is factually false or contains misleading content' (Guo and Vargo 2018), but has increasingly been hijacked by political leaders such as Donald Trump to discredit his critics, or unfavourable real news. These are just a few examples of online viral videos produced by deepfake technologies, with many further techniques of redubbing from facial images emerging in the field of computer science (Chung et al. 2017). 'Shallowfakes' (sometimes called 'cheapfakes') is another term that has been coined by human rights campaigner Sam Gregory to describe more low-tech techniques of video manipulation used with malicious intent (Johnson 2019), for example, the slowing down and pitch-correcting of a 2019 video of Nancy Pelosi, Speaker of the United States House of Representatives, to create the false impression that she was inebriated (CBS This Morning 2019). This doctored video was shared on Twitter by her political rival, Donald Trump, on 23 May 2019. Notably, both Twitter and Facebook had refused to delete it, instead attaching a link to a third-party factchecking site that pointed out that the clip was misleading.

More recent apps such as Zao, FaceApp and Reface (rebranded from its original name, Doublicat) have enabled the rapid creation of deepfake images, GIFs and videos that implant a user's facial image from selfies via their smartphone's live camera/camera roll onto celebrities' body representations with all the novelty of bodily distortions associated with a funfair hall of mirrors. The fabrication of the deepfake 'Obamas' are premised on their veracity and ability to mislead as the 'real' thing, while I argue that the user-generated Franken-Cages correspond more closely with the postdigital as a crowdsourced 'aesthetics of failure' (Cascone 2000: 13). For American composer Kim Cascone, the term 'post-digital', which he coined in the context of digital music, had emphasized the end of the revolutionary period of digital information age (392–3). For Cascone, 'failures' marked a distinctive style in music that emphasized the hidden aspects of digital technologies, from application errors to system crashes. Technological errors that were typically controlled or suppressed were instead being intentionally brought into sharper focus by artists. This emphasized the 'background' elements of technical systems in which artists were embedded, surfacing data that day-to-day would often be hidden in a listener's 'perceptual "blindspot"' (394). But this emphasis was by no means confined to music, extending to various forms of 'glitch art'. And arguably, in the Franken-Cages something of the computational intervention that underlies these curious images is brought to the fore. For Matthew Causey, postdigital works 'think digitally' in the sense that they embody an 'activist strategy of critique' against ideological strategies of 'control, alienation, and self-commodification' (2016: 432). Deep- and shallow-fakes provide an interesting conceptual site where users wrestle for control over their self-images and are afforded a tool with which to hijack and distort the images of others. Unlike Cascone's focus on music, I question in this chapter what is being resurfaced within the images and texts where machine learning is used by artists or in artworks that express 'digital thinking' akin to AI networks? Unlike 'failure' – a benevolent term bound up in notions of 'lack of success in doing or achieving something' ('Failure') – I contend that deepfakes such as the Franken-Cages stage their 'wrongness' as partially synthetic images that *intentionally* fall short of traversing the 'uncanny valley' (Mori 1970). Conversely, when aligned with 'disinformation' tactics, it is the overcoming of the valley that is the basic requirement of a truly seamless deepfake video of a human subject.[1] 'Wrongness' as a noun carries the ambiguous dual meaning of being both not quite 'correct' but also not 'morally right or honest' ('Wrongness'). Unlike the benevolence of 'failure', 'wrongness' can be not quite 'right' in two distinct ways that are aesthetic and/or moral, always carrying the underlying possibility of malevolence. Deepfakes can embody these two distinct meanings of wrongness as either visibly uncanny or undetectably false.

Much as the Franken-Cages perform their wrongness by signposting the machine learning that underlies their provenance, my interest in this chapter is on examining eclectic cultural phenomena from films and television programmes to participatory theatre works as techno-feedback loops that intentionally or unintentionally deconstruct computational processes, surfacing the role of hardware and software in contrast to virtual simulation, for example, which denies 'bits, pixels and binary codes' (Ryan 2015: 43). The works I discuss capture traces of either their performers' or spectators' data as reprogrammable digital artefacts that are run through the mangle of either machine learning or machine-learning-like processes. In turn, the outputs of such processes confront spectators and users with urgent questions of trust in key aspects of post-truth networked society.

I will first examine the etymologies and suspect origins of the blended term 'deepfakes', identifying correspondences between what I will call 'deepfake-ification' and a postdigital 'aesthetics of wrongness'. I will discuss different manifestations of deepfakes and machine learning, including proto-deepfake CGI performances that reanimate deceased actors in *Star Wars: Rogue One* (2016) and AI-assisted re-assemblages of internet users as avatars *postmortum* through their online data on *eterni.me*. I will then consider acts of semi-automated playwriting that deploy machine learning in order to critique the logic of algorithms underlying everyday predictive text apps in Roslyn Helper's *Lifestyle of the Richard and Family* (2018). It will also be important to explore how technology associated with deepfakes and non-consensual acts of online body-jacking have been used for comedy, for example, to insert controversial comedian Chris Lilley's face onto the body of an adult film actress in Netflix mockumentary *Lunatics* (2019). While what I term as the Franken-Cage memes have prompted a cottage industry of further replications by internet users, Lilley's series has been much derided for its layering of his face onto the identities of different kinds of marginalized others. Finally, I will discuss Ontroerend Goed's (OG) *A Game of You* (2010–), a circuitous 'one-on-oneself' theatre piece in which a spectator's secretly recorded webcam footage becomes input training data for another audience member to construct a new virtual identity for them with an imagined life of its own. I argue that this performance's theatrical form places the spectator within the mechanics of low-fi shallowfake-construction. While predating deepfakes, this work has correspondences with online AI generative adversarial networks (GAN). I argue that it provides a framework to think through computational processes of image manipulation that use post-industrial 'apparatus' in Vilém Flusser's use of the term, the defining feature of which are technologies that seek to turn all aspects of the world into manipulatable objects. OG's participants are offered a dual perspective, fabricating another spectator's identity and having their own identity manipulated, in turn. In this respect, its spectatorial position is akin to the 'generative' and 'discriminatory' networks involved in manufacturing deepfakes. Throughout this chapter I will question what is it that we might recognize in different manifestations of a deepfake/shallowfake in varying presentational contexts? And what might more low-fi theatre works that implicate spectators in a process of misinformation-creation help to surface from the background hum of our perceptual blind spots? The case studies I discuss, while diverse in form/medium, all share the commonality of objectifying either their participants, performers or authors as either mediatized body images, auto-corrected texts or fabricated identities. The case studies all connect with the two distinctions of wrongness I have outlined in this introduction, enabling spectators to see manipulated images as either 'not quite right' or highlighting the intervention of disinformation-producing technologies as morally dubious. In relation to the latter, apparatuses are used as a self-reflexive tool to highlight possibilities for resistance in the process of mutating and replaying our data back to us, encouraging us to take a position on our becoming reprogrammable objects.

Deepfake-ification and postdigital aesthetics of wrongness

Recent developments in theatre scholarship have attended to deepfakes as symptomatic of a wider 'paradigm shift' that is problematizing assumptions about representation and verification online and beyond (Fletcher 2018). It is my contention that in the context of this discussion, an 'aesthetics of wrongness' becomes particularly bound up in the disclosure of computational processes involved in the creation and distribution of a subset of 'misinformation', a term that means misleading information based on error or ignorance (Bittman 1985: 49); namely, *disinformation*. The word 'disinformation' derives from the Russian *дезинформация*, which was defined in *The Great Soviet Encyclopaedia* (1952) as 'false information with the intention to deceive public opinion' (49). Prior to examining different manifestations of deepfakery, it is necessary to first unpack the definition of both 'deepfakes' and the concept of 'deepfake-ification' that I will carry forward into my analysis.

'Deepfake' is a portmanteau word that combines the machine learning technique known as 'deep learning' with the late eighteenth-century word of uncertain origin 'fake', meaning a 'counterfeit' or 'imitation'. 'Fake' is commonly understood to relate to slang derived from the German *fegen*, meaning to 'sweep' or 'plunder' ('Fake'). As a blend of these words' meanings, 'deepfake' is analogous in some respects to the blended outputs of computer processes that combine images or other kinds of data from multiple online sources. Like the illicit act of plundering from which the word 'fake' derives, the deepfake algorithm plunders vast amounts of online facial images as training data; an apprehension that resonates with the 'hijacking' of mediatized audiences discussed in Karen Savage's chapter. But deepfakes pose a serious threat of 'plundering' selfhood as a tool for cybercrimes, such as synthetic identity theft. This involves leveraging the trust of another in order to commit fraud by posing as a synthetic double of a legitimate person. The first such case was reported in 2019, in which the CEO of a UK-based energy company was defrauded out of €220,000 in an AI-assisted voice-spoofing attack.[2] The very word 'deepfake' has a particularly dubious past. As a username, 'deepfake' originates from a Reddit user that posted under this pseudonym, using AI tools to insert actors' faces into pornographic videos in 2017. This user was eventually banned, but due to the popularity of the phenomenon, a dedicated subreddit (a niche forum) called 'deepfakes' was created to host thousands of user-generated videos.

Data scientist Siraj Raval offers a general overview of how the deepfakes algorithm works for the lay user, which forms the backbone of my explanation here (Raval 2018). I illustrate this explanation with a deepfake I created,

Figure 4.3 (Left) Nicolas Cage GIF on *Reface* app, (centre) Liam Jarvis photograph, (right) Nicolas Cage/Liam Jarvis deepfake result on *Reface* app

blending an image of Nicolas Cage (face A) with an image of my own face (face B) using the RefaceAI GAN (see Figure 4.3). The deepfake algorithm gathers training data such as images of Nicolas Cage and the intended actor with whom his face will be swapped (which is myself in Figure 4.3). The FaceSwap repository on GitHub – a service that enables users to track changes in source code during software development – has scripts to automatically download large amounts of images from online sources to a home directory where they are stored. Face detection is performed on each of these images in the OpenCV library using a method called Histogram of Oriented Gradients (HOG), which removes the colour data and replaces pixels with arrows that show the flow from light to darkness across the image, capturing a basic representation of the face. This HOG face pattern is then compared to others and if it is close enough by a small margin of error, the system considers the face 'detected'. But the aim of the deepfake algorithm is not just to classify faces, but rather to learn a representation of two faces and morph face A (Nicolas Cage) to look like face B (Liam Jarvis). An autoencoder is used, which is a convolutional network that tries to reconstruct the input image. The deepfakes algorithm trains two different networks, both share an encoder but have different decoders. The autoencoder transforms an image into a base vector (a set of numbers that identify the important features of a face), while decoder A transforms that vector back to an image. There's an error function that measures the quality of the transformation, lowering the overall errors within training. The first network is only trained on image A (Nicolas Cage) and the second is only trained on image B (Liam Jarvis). Decoder A learns how to convert a base vector to image A, while decoder B learns how to convert a base vector to image B. After this network training, the user can subsequently feed the network a video (a collection of image frames), cropping out the target face and then performing a face swap on it. Image A (Nicolas Cage) is fed to the encoder creating a base vector that is then fed to decoder B. This results in a face that looks like B (Liam Jarvis) that can be overlaid onto the original frame, concatenating all of the images together. This is the computational process that underpins the Franken-Cages discussed in my introduction, and which results in the crudely blended screenshot of an animated GIF that can be seen on the right of Figure 4.3.

In online common parlance, the word 'deepfake' has become an umbrella term for a range of outputs including face-swaps, audio deepfakes, deepfake puppetry/full-body deepfakes (Esser et al. 2019) and deepfake lip-synching. This suggests that the term doesn't have strongly demarcated boundaries in relation to the specific technical methods that underlie the different kinds of outputs propagated online. However, there is broad consensus that it predominantly refers to a 'subset of fake video that leverages deep learning [...] to make the faking process easier' (Brundage qtd in Vincent 2018a). 'Deepfakes', as I will suggest, is a usefully paradoxical term because its very meaning draws attention to the underlying computational processes of synthetically created videos/images. The irony is that a truly successful deep 'fake' stages the disappearance of these machinic processes. Put differently, a successful deepfake would not be received in the order of a 'deepfake' at all. *Thispersondoesnotexist.com* is a website that curates multiple cases in point, using an algorithm to create and display AI-generated faces every time the user refreshes the webpage, none of whom exist offline (see Figure 4.4). Unlike the face-swap manifestation of a deepfake, these photorealistic representations are highly convincing fabrications of non-existent humans. The image's AI-assisted construction is belied only by the title of the website's uniform resource locator (URL) 'Thispersondoesnotexist' and a text box in the bottom right corner of the screen containing hyperlinks to information about how these images were created. Deepfakes of this order could quite easily be read by the casual or uninformed viewer as photographs of 'real' people. They do not perform their wrongness and incongruity in the way that the Franken-Cages do and are not easily readable as 'deepfakes'. The term 'deepfake-ification' that I will use throughout this chapter carries forwards the paradox embedded within the word 'deepfake' as a verb, referring more broadly to the concept of aesthetic experiences that either reveal themselves to be machine-made through their execution (e.g. the uncanny Franken-Cages) or within the context in which they are displayed. Deepfake-ification then, like René Magritte's painting *The Treachery of Images* (1929) – which denies its painted pipe's status as a real pipe with the accompanying sentence

Figure 4.4 Screenshot of a photorealistic human image created by an AI generative adversarial network (GAN) from the https://thispersondoesnotexist. com website

'*Ceci n'est pas une pipe*' – disallows the counterfeit to enter into circulation before signifying the computational involvement in its creation.

In relation to photography, Vilém Flusser's *Post-History* (2013) made the case that Western culture has been an ongoing project to make an 'apparatus' of existence. Photographic apparatus operates in 'opaque black boxes' that obscure their inner workings to their operators while fundamentally reprogramming the experience of looking. More detrimentally, for Flusser, apparatuses turn all aspects of the world into manipulatable objects (2013: 9). He cites the Nazi extermination camps as an extreme prototypical example of humans reduced to 'objects' but contends that increasingly less brutal developments such as the 'robotization of society' are presenting new affordances to objectify mankind (2013: 10). Face-swap deepfakes offer a further example, reducing individuals to mediatized interchangeable body parts through computational processes.

Synthetic replications: *Reanimating dead actors, semi-automated playwriting and deepfake body-jacking on Netflix*

Digital automation and the use of machine learning to generate synthetic replications that impersonate others online are presenting distinct ethical, political and legal problems in relation to ownership of one's likeness, commonly termed in law as 'personality rights'. But simulating humans is nothing new. The first attempt that used computer software code was Joseph Weizenbaum's 'ELIZA' (Weizenbaum 1966), a precursor to chatterbots and virtual assistants such as ActivBuddy's SmarterChild, Siri, Alexa and Google Assistant. However, the synthetic 'Obamas' discussed in the introduction of this chapter raise new concerns about increasingly simple ways to manipulate political discourse by hijacking the body-image of a politician to potentially sway public opinion through social media channels, much as Karen Savage has identified (in Chapter 3) that audience reactions to Mike Pence's presence at the musical *Hamilton* were hijacked and repurposed towards online anti-Trump videos that extended the political play-off in the theatre auditorium onto social media platforms. The kinds of mimetic deceptions in online deepfake videos are also occurring in parallel with the creation of bots acting as human users that publish fake trends on Twitter; a phenomenon that Savage in the previous chapter linked to Christian Fuchs's notion of '(semi) automated politics'. On the day of the US election in 2016, automated Twitter accounts linked to Russian electoral interference sent out the hashtag #WarAgainstDemocrats more than 1,700 times (Shane 2017). The weaponizing of AI has also led to the harvesting of personal information in order to 'micro-target' individual voters with propaganda to influence their voting behaviour (Anderson and Horvath 2017). For example, Cambridge Analytica – the now defunct British political consulting firm – leveraged its alliance with Facebook to access the personal data of over 87 million users to similarly influence the result of the 2016 presidential election by creating political advertisements based on their psychological profiles, in turn, exposing US privacy laws as 'deficient' (Isaak and Hanna 2018).

AI is also prompting urgent questions in film and theatre practice in relation to a range of phenomena, such as the 'reanimation' of dead actors using digital avatars (Goering et al. 2018), the impact of automated computational processes on playwriting, or online misuses of another's body image without permission. While not AI-generated, the posthumous appearance of 'Peter Cushing' as Grand Moff Tarkin in *Rogue One* (2016) is one example that has set a precedent for the digital revivification of deceased actors.[3] Cushing died in 1994 and his likeness appeared in the *Star Wars* spin-off with the permission of his estate. In actuality, Tarkin was played by living actor Guy Henry through his vocal and motion capture performance. But behind the scenes, Tarkin was also being played by Industrial Light and Magic's (ILM) *re*animators using the 'facial pipeline' technologies/techniques developed by Kiran Bhat and Michael Koperwas, who had previously collaborated to solve the problem of faces on the computer-animated martial arts action film, *Teenage Mutant Ninja Turtles* (2007) (discussed in Cantwell et al. 2016). During the filming for *Rogue One*, actor Guy Henry wore a facial performance rig with the location of the motion capture dots on his face remapped onto a digital 3D model. Meanwhile, Cushing had previously had a plaster lifecast of his face moulded decades earlier during the filming of *Top Secret* (1984), which Industrial Light and Magic (ILM) 3D-scanned to render an accurate digital Tarkin as a completely synthetic character. In postproduction, ILM's *re*animators intervened to deliver a Tarkin with Cushing's performance and *not* Henry's by adjusting the way that Tarkin's lips enunciated and which parts of the face created the 'visemes', which refers to 'distinctive speech movements of the visual speech articulators' (Disney Research qtd in Seymour 2017). And yet, like Jordan Peele lurking behind a deepfake Obama, underlying *Rogue One*'s Tarkin is a highly complex layering of Henry-playing-Cushing-playing-Tarkin, Cushing's digitized face from a mould taken in the mid-1980s and an accrued pipeline of technical know-how that can be traced to the development of CGI tools to animate the faces of entirely fictional mutant turtles in the mid-2000s. The macabre connotations of Cushing's synthetic *re*animation accrue further unintended resonances given his background in Hammer Horror films. Perhaps most pertinently as Baron Victor Frankenstein in *The Curse of Frankenstein* (1957), who scavenges human remains that he reanimates as his Creature; a fleshy proto-deepfake assemblage of body parts.

The appearance of 'Cushing' (or something akin to him) prompted highly varied responses, from Twitter users who commented that his appearance was so convincing that they didn't realize he wasn't real until reading online reviews (Ironfield 2016), to technology websites complaining that there is 'something not quite right about Cushing's zombie avatar' (Firth-Godbehere 2016). The authorized reanimation of Cushing, elides with the notion of wrongness as aesthetically 'not quite right', more so than the malevolent disinformation associated with the deep- and shallow-fakes of politicians that I discussed earlier in this chapter. Furthermore, the CGI techniques used on *Rogue One* are not a direct equivalence with deepfakes' use of machine learning. However, digital post-death legacies are taking on new AI-assisted forms via tech start-ups such as *eterni.me*, who repurpose their client's online data to enable grieving relatives to converse with an algorithmically generated impression of their deceased relative with the promise of living 'forever' as a digital avatar. Marius Ursache proposed to develop this site partly in response to questioning what happens to a person's avatar in the virtual game *Second Life* (2003–) after they die. Was there a '*Second Life* purgatory where abandoned avatars lived on in a zombie-like state, long after their human operators had passed away? What would happen if one tried to interact with these avatars?' (Ursache in Dormehl 2016: 194). This hypothetical scenario of evacuated avatars is not akin to Cascone's 'aesthetics of failure'. They are not a system malfunction brought to the fore by an artist, nor does this represent an activist gesture, glitching a gaming structure through transgressive acts of play, but rather the offline death of a player simultaneously manifesting in an online zombie-avatar left in virtual limbo. Ursache's vision involves programming an artificial agent to convincingly mimic the behaviour of the avatar's deceased human counterpart.

Beyond this techno-utopian (or dystopian, depending on one's view) promise of AI as a means of 'skyping with the dead' (as Ursache had described it), playwrights such as Roslyn Helper have used automated computational processes in their playwriting to critique the way in which predictive functions can 'limit our access to language, ideas and diverse perspectives' (Helper 2018). Helper used an app that incorporates a predictive text program called SwiftKey Note to write *Lifestyle of the Richard and Family* (2018). SwiftKey uses a blend of artificial intelligence technologies that enable it to learn the writer's writing style and predict the next word/phrase that the user intends to type. This leads to a playwriting logic in which the characters' speech follows the AI's predictions from the author's previous inputs. Correspondingly, one reviewer of *Lifestyle* noted that 'the characters on stage are barely people anymore, rather figures expressing the needs of the algorithms that drive their daily lives' (Ball 2018). Embedded in this AI-assisted expression of creative writing, I would identify a wider postdigital disenchantment with the algorithms that pervade our daily lives. For example, Amazon's A9 algorithm that decides what product recommendations to make using data from past purchases as well as big data. Pre-internet, Flusser had contended that human beings struggle against automatic programming, 'attempting to create a space for human intention in a world dominated by apparatuses. However, the apparatuses themselves automatically assimilate these attempts at liberation and enrich their programs with them' (Flusser [1983] 1984: 74–5). Apparatuses for Flusser *intend* to be automatic, meaning 'independent of future human intervention', resulting in progressive human exclusion from their functions. The way to re-establish freedom in a programmed world for Flusser is to free ourselves from being mere functions of apparatuses. While Flusser's discourse predates the 'postdigital turn' (Berry and Dieter 2015: 6), in many respects it anticipates its inherently activist backlash towards new media's myth of progress. The post-death puppeteering of a user's online data as a reanimated avatar is an extreme variant of assimilation to a program. In contrast, Helper's outsourcing of part of the writing task onto an autocorrect programme offers an aestheticizing of a programme's wrongness. In *Lifestyle*, characters become ciphers for AI's predictions of what the author *may* write next, which manifests not as seamlessly human-authored dialogue, but as a 'consumerist doublespeak' in a play that excavates its character's pressures to comply with the demands of social networking and market success.

Deep learning has also been used to multiply the face of a comedian as a technologically assisted extension of character comedy. Netflix's *Lunatics* (2019) by Australian comedian Chris Lilley is a ten-part mockumentary that has been described as like 'scrolling through Instagram at 3am' (Grey Ellis 2019). It follows the lives of six 'misfits' all played by Lilley. The characters span different ages, genders and ethnicities, which has prompted fierce criticism when such a diverse range of identities are represented by a cisgender white male comedian. In particular, Lilley's perceived use of blackface, cross-dressing, shtick that 'punches down' at marginalized individuals and his perceived re-inscribing of dominant stereotypes have led some critics to review the series as 'nasty and grotesque' (Heritage 2019). Some of the characters represented by Lilley include a college student and non-identical twin that is 7' 3" tall (Becky Douglas), a South African lesbian pet psychic (Jana Melhoopen-Jonks) and an ex-porn star hoarder called Joyce Jeffries, all of whom recognizably sport Lilley's face, much as Nicolas Cage's face has digitally colonized a range of different bodies.

The comedian's face is also multiplied in another respect using AI machine learning. Fictional character Joyce Jeffries's past as a glamour model and subsequently a porn star is recounted through flashbacks in Episode 1, which is accompanied by doctored photographs with the face of Lilley-as-Joyce edited onto different naked women's bodies on the covers of adult film VHS cases. Lilley's face is also swapped onto an adult film actress in a deepfake porn video where we see a Lilley-Joyce porn star blend being undressed, stopping just short of presenting more graphic sexualized acts. This use of deepfake face-swaps in *Lunatics* recalls the original application of machine learning on Reddit to create digitally altered face-swap porn, in which the likeness of a celebrity is stitched onto an adult film actor's body with variable levels of fidelity and *without* consent. The episode uses Lilley's own facial image, so the act is not unconsented in this context. Nonetheless, the moral ugliness that some commentators have identified in Lilley's work might, in part, be a recognition of the moral ugliness we might observe more broadly in the hijacking of other's body-images online. Some have argued that deepfakes represent a troublingly misogynistic trend through which to vicariously 'own' women's bodies as a digitized commodity (Cole 2018).

The disproportionate weaponization of synthetic media against women in particular is given credence through a report conducted by cybersecurity firm Deeptrace, which discovered that of the 14,678 deepfake videos it found online in September 2019, 96 per cent were pornographic and 100 per cent of mapped faces from female celebrities onto porn stars were women (Ajder et al. 2019). Unlike the mutual transactions of virtualized body-swapping in applied VR performance practices that I have examined elsewhere in my scholarship (Jarvis 2019), face-swapping of this order often represents acts of online abuse, exploiting another's likeness for economic imperatives or with malicious intent (e.g. revenge porn). Of particular concern has been the fact that in countries such as the United States, legislation of non-consensual pornography has been premised on a violation of privacy. However, face-swap deepfakes were not viewed as a privacy issue in the eyes of the law because the body exposed is not one's 'own', even if a convincing deepfake in circulation online might mislead users into believing otherwise (Grey Ellis 2018). Layered online identities created through machine learning have escaped jurisdiction, but legislation in this area is changing rapidly as policymakers wrestle with emerging deepfake-related threats, with a range of new protective laws introduced in 2019.[4]

Even those characters that sport Lilley's face in *Lunatics* without the assistance of machine learning might be thought to mirror deepfake's morphing of multiple facial images in online acts of misogynistic abuse. For example, in one sketch, Lilley – a 44-year-old man – plays a 12-year-old male character called Gavin McGregor, who sexually harasses a preteen girl on her way home from school. Lilley's sketches not only smuggle in AI-tools directly, using them in a context that resonates with the ethically problematic provenance of non-consensual face swap porn, but they also stage another kind of wrongness; the mismatch between Lilley's middle-aged face and the 'twelve-year-old' character he is playing. Some have argued that putting Lilley's face on these wildly different characters carries within it a social commentary, that we 'all contain multiple selves, and those selves, especially when refracted through social media, become both stranger and more similar' (Grey Ellis 2019). This positioning of Lilley's work and the apparent defence of the representations it offers are untenable when the humour still derives from the single viewpoint of a white misogynist male. *Lunatics* re-facing of Lilley onto countless others only serves to buttress its style of 'punch down' comedy. Wrongness in this context slips from uncanny grotesquery to the morally dubious, when the cultural power of the joke is unevenly weighted, afflicting the afflicted or marginal rather than the comfortable or culturally dominant.

Deepfake-ification and Ontroerend Goed's
A Game of You (2010–)

Belgian theatre performance group Ontroerend Goed's *A Game of You* (2010–) is the third part of the company's 'personal trilogy', which followed *The Smile Off Your Face* (2003) and *Internal* (2007). While their work doesn't directly integrate technologies associated with machine learning in the way that the previous examples I have discussed do, I argue that it has correspondences because it provides the low-fi-ness of a shallowfake with an offline theatrical form that is akin to online generative adversarial networks (GANs). The show enacts a machinic logic that fictionalizes a virtual double of each audience member from covertly filmed video footage captured within the performance on a webcam. The hijacking of the spectator's video image – which resonates with the hijacking of audience images in Randy Rainbow's videos towards ideological ends in Karen Savage's chapter (see Chapter 3) – and their subsequent replication into a new self-identity constructed by another spectator and an 'Avatar' (the name given to the performers in OG's script), provide a useful framework to think through computational apparatuses associated with deepfakes. It also provides a playful space to critically reflect on ownership of one's distributed identity online and participants as the 'exploited object of others' attention and curiosity' (Lonergan 2016: 50).

In *A Game of You*, the space is configured as a circuit-like labyrinth of mirrored rooms. The spectator begins by sitting in a waiting room, where they are secretly filmed and observed by a member of the company called 'Avatar 1' from behind a two-way mirror. Avatar 2 enters and sits beside the spectator, revealing information about 'themselves' that gradually becomes understood as a mismatch for the body that is recounting the information. The spectator then exits into a red curtain-lined corridor, coming face to face with Avatar 1 for the first time who mimics their every movement before taking the audience member to the 'copy room' – an identical simulacrum of the first waiting room. Avatar 1 recreates this spectator's gestures from their observations behind the two-way mirror. A curtain is then opened, playing the webcam footage of the spectator back to themselves and providing a comparator through which to verify the accuracy of Avatar 1's imitation. The audience member is invited to scrutinize their onscreen bodily behaviours, before being guided behind the screen where they view new webcam footage of another audience member in the performance's loop. The audience member is invited to invent a life for this unknown onscreen identity through answering a series of open-ended prompt questions. The audience then moves to a room where they receive a phone call from Avatar 1 as the very 'character' they had just created. They are then ushered to the central 'nerve centre' of the operation, where they receive a CD with 'About You' written on it, containing an audio file of another spectator who has invented a life for them. The spectator completes the circuit by arriving back in the waiting room, but this time on the reverse side of the two-way mirror, seated beside an Avatar who is learning yet another new visitor's movements on the hidden side of the two-way glass. Without any agency to intervene, the spectator looks on as Avatar 1 re-enters the waiting room and performs the fabricated version of them, akin to a live performance variant of a deepfake, but one generated by the intelligence of human avatars, nonetheless acting out an uncannily computational logic. The earlier 'mismatch' in the very first encounter between the Avatar's incongruous performed identity and the body performing it becomes clear in this moment; the Avatars in *A Game of You* can be understood as multiply morphed layers of accrued identity that resonate with the incongruity that I have articulated as 'deepfake-ification'. I argue that this work, in the tradition of post-internet art, encourages spectators to 'think in the fashion of the network' (Archey and Peckham 2014), raising timely questions about manipulation and control over one's distributed self-identity that are becoming increasingly urgent in light of AI's ability to construct synthetic replicants.

The replicative system of *A Game of You* parallels the kinds of technological processes of machine learning associated with the production of deepfakes such as generative adversarial networks (GAN) (of the kind I had used to create the deepfake in Figure 4.3), which are enabling non-human acts of imagining. GAN's involve two artificial neural networks – a *generator* network and a *discriminator* network (Goodfellow et al. 2014) – which are pitted against one another. The generator network uses a sample image input to create new fake images while the discriminator is trained to examine the content that the generator produces, estimating whether it is authentic. Computer scientist Ian Goodfellow describes this adversarial relationship as akin to 'counterfeiters' and 'police' (Goodfellow 2016) – the counterfeiters want to create credible fake money, while the police want to allow people to spend money without being punished but would also like to remove counterfeit money from circulation. These networks learn from one another and the generative model produces evermore convincing fake images until the counterfeits are indistinguishable from the 'real' images. Moral 'wrongness' is embedded in this very analogy, since the 'police' (the discriminator network) ultimately only functions to aid the perfecting of the crime.

In *A Game of You*, the spectator's recorded and monitored body language in the waiting room provides the equivalent of sample input data that feeds the performance's low-fi 'generative network'. Avatar 1 uses this sample data to produce a counterfeit of the spectator, which is then presented back to them followed by the original dataset; namely, the spectator's video image. I argue that the spectator in these moments is situated as a 'discriminator' assessing their fake identity, which is both mimicked by Avatar 1 and later reimagined as a character on an audio recording created by another spectator, against the mediatized 'real' counterpart recorded in the waiting room – itself, another kind of reproduction. The spectator is also invited to participate in the work's generative network by artificially fabricating an identity for another. The spectators' assimilation within the performance's 'generative' and 'discriminatory' networks enables them to occupy dual positions on their constructed virtual identities, examining the extent to which their fake is discrepant with their own internalized self-image.

For Flusser, power is not possessed by the owner of an object but by its programmers and 'information imperialism' marks a shift of power from the object to the symbol (Flusser [1983] 1984: 12). Much as automated processes can place words in a likenesses mouth (e.g. a synthetic Obama) or constitute a digital Franken-self from other's mediatized body-parts, *A Game of You* provides a generative network that separates a spectator's mediatized self-image from their subjective experience, reprogramming it in ways that are beyond their control. Simultaneously, the show's network affords each spectator the agency to enact a similar reprogramming of another based on mediatized bodily cues and inferences. Online platforms such as *Instagram*, *Skype* and *FaceTime* are prompting the self-capturing of our images/video to large data storage services. This places heightened emphasis on the self as an externally constructed image in a world of 'networked individualism' (Wellman 2000; Rainie and Wellman 2012) in which fashioning unique identities becomes a process of active and persistent self-construction. *A Game of You's* spatial dynamics are organized in such a way that audience members never come into direct contact with one another during the experience, except through mediatized relays or encounters obscured by the two-way mirror partition that affords awareness of another spectator's presence in only one direction. In the reverse direction, the spectator entering the performance's circuit sees only a 'selfie', a mirror image of themselves. In this respect, Ontroerend Goed stages a solipsistic model of performance in which other visitors are only ever a surface to be virtualized on the basis of interpretations from exterior bodily signifiers. The 'self+' presented back to each participant post-performance on their CDs – a self that is imagined/imposed through others' interpretations of their recorded image and captured as an audio file – is akin to the kinds of identities produced by GAN networks, a distorted reflection migrating across different mediums. The unknowing capture and dispersal of participants' body-images as a source of manipulation by other parties provide a good model for what I have termed as deepfake-ification in performance, since it raises critical questions in an offline theatrical experience about our agency over the usage of our selfies online. This is especially crucial when the terms and conditions of deepfake apps such as Russian-based FaceApp – which the FBI are reported to have identified as a 'potential counterintelligence threat' (Reuters Staff 2019) – have caused significant alarm. Usage of this app in 2017 had granted the company a 'perpetual, irrevocable, nonexclusive, royalty-free, worldwide, fully-paid, transferable sub-licensable license to use, reproduce, modify, adapt, publish, translate, create derivative works from, distribute, publicly perform and display your User Content [...] without compensation to you' ('Terms and Conditions' 2017).[5] This permits a user's private selfies to be used in potentially very public ways at a later point, rendering users as passive as OG's audience member, unable to intervene while watching 'themselves' performed by an Avatar as a kind of live-action deepfake on the other side of the two-way mirror.

Conclusion

What might different internet users recognize in a deepfake video? A face-swap deepfake may identifiably stage the wrongness of placing a recognizable face on an incongruous body. But that face, as I have discussed in relation to the FaceSwap repository, is not singular but a concatenated multiplicity of faces. For example, a vast library of different Nicolas Cage facial images collapsed into a moving video sequence. When Peele speaks through Obama's mouth, it *is* Obama's mouth. Or more precisely, a computer-generated chorus of multiply mediatized Obama mouths sourced from a vast online image pool. Like Karen Savage's analysis of Randy Rainbow, who duplicates his face into a chorus of himself in home-made satirical musical numbers, deepfake faces are always already a 'chorus' of sorts, multiplied through machinic processes, but to different ends. As I have contended, different manifestations of machine learning's human likenesses are presenting both meanings of the word 'wrongness', from the not-quite correctness of uncanny posthumously reanimated avatars, to the morally dubious 'wrongness' that manifests in varying ways, from the undetectable deepfake to the complex layering of identities in Chris Lilley's comedy that both resurfaces the dubious moral past of deepfake porn and refaces other's visages with Lilley's to enact a 'punch down' comedy. In the other theatre works I have analysed, the use of machine learning to create plays/performances or low-fi theatrical forms that mirror GAN-like systems provide theatre audiences with a postdigital critical position on computational processes of replication. From predictive functions on smart devices repurposed from their intended function to correct user-errors and self-reflexively expose the failings of computer algorithm-aided character development in Roslyn Helper's *Lifestyle of the Richard and Family*, to the manipulation of participants' self-image in Ontroerend Goed's *A Game of You*. The latter might be thought of as a metaphor through which to productively examine and critique other kinds of automated apparatus of mediatized replication. Its specific mode of analogue, offline spectatorship oscillates participants between generative and discriminatory networks and in doing so, provides a dual position to explore both a loss of control over one's active self-constructed identity and agency to generate a new identity for another as features of networked individualism in postdigital culture. The performance recreates discrepancies that occur in between offline 'adversarial networks' by producing altered and ambiguous identities for the audience member that raise questions about control and possible abuses of an objectified self-image that exists 'out there', independent of its physical body.

In each of these works, people become a virtual object, a trace of their own bodily information. N. Katherine Hayles has argued that ownership of oneself predates market relations and owes nothing to them, although self-ownership simultaneously lays the foundations on which those relations can be built (Hayles 1999: 3). But an increasing plasticity of selfhood means that these foundations are ever shifting. Whereas what C. B. Macpherson referred to as 'possessive individualism' concerned the notion of an individual as the 'proprietor of his [or her] own person or capacities' who owes nothing to society for them (Macpherson 1962), the complex entanglements of networked interactions in the work discussed raise questions about the limits of our freedom from the wills of others and self-determination over our virtualized identities arising from our mediatized likeness or quantified selves. That which is observable as a deepfake, which I have sought to encompass through the verb 'deepfake-ification', also has the capacity to draw attention to a user's vulnerability to exploitation by different pre-programmable apparatus. In post-industrial society, Flusser contended that the 'programmers' have the power, not the owner of objects. An apparatus is programmed to produce a particular output, and every output is the realization of one of the virtualities contained in that program. In works such as *A Game of You*, the spectators' data become a virtuality of the programme of the performance, which in turn makes use of the pre-programmed apparatus of webcams. I have sought to correspond a postdigital 'aesthetics of wrongness' with the paradoxical concept of deepfake-ification. Wrongness in this respect concerns still being able to identify the fakeness of an image. The uncanny valley, a landscape where disinformation can be viewed in sharp relief, might be the last refuge before technical advancements render it wholly out of sight, enabling wrongness in the morally dubious sense to flourish.

Notes

1 Some commentators have even argued that photoreal deep-learning-generated content may signal the 'end of the Uncanny Valley' altogether (Upson 2017), though I would note that this technical achievement cannot be the only marker of a deepfake video's verisimilitude, since they do not only represent human forms. For example, NVIDIA Research's *GauGAN* system can leverage machine learning to transform on-screen doodles into photorealistic images of landscapes that don't exist in the real world; 'GauGAN' as portmanteau combines Post-Impressionist painter Paul Gauguin's name with the acronym for Generative Adversarial Networks (GAN), which generate synthetic data.

2 *The Wall Street Journal* reported the first noted instance of an artificial intelligence-generated voice deepfake used in a scam in 2019; 'Criminals used artificial intelligence-based software to impersonate a chief executive's voice and demand a fraudulent transfer of €220,000 ($243,000) in March in what cybercrime experts described as an unusual case of artificial intelligence being used in hacking' (Stupp 2019).

3 This is a phenomenon that has been touched upon in Ralph Remshardt's chapter with the digital reanimation of the late Laurence Olivier (et al.).

4 According to David Fink and Sarah Diamond in 2019, 'Virginia was the first state to impose criminal penalties on the distribution of non-consensual deepfake pornography. Texas was the first state to prohibit the creation and distribution of deepfake videos intended to harm candidates for public office or influence elections. In October 2019, California Governor Gavin Newsom signed two deepfake bills into state law: AB 730 makes it illegal to circulate deepfake videos, images or audio of politicians within 60 days of an election, and AB 602 allows a victim of non-consensual deepfake pornography to sue for damages' (Fink and Diamond 2019).

5 Though I would note that the wording of *FaceApp*'s terms and conditions was revised on 3 December 2019 to link this clause to user 'feedback' rather than 'user content' ('Terms of Use Agreement' 2019).

References

Ajder, Henry, Giorgio Patrini, Francesco Cavalli, and Laurence Cullen (2019), 'The State of Deepfakes: Landscape, Threats, and Impact', *Deeptrace*, September. Available online: https://regmedia.co.uk/2019/10/08/deepfake_report.pdf (accessed 20 November 2020).

Anderson, Berit and Brett Horvath (2017), 'The Rise of the Weaponized AI Propaganda Machine', *Medium*, 13 February. Available online: https://medium.com/join-scout/the-rise-of-the-weaponized-ai-propaganda-machine-86dac61668b (accessed 9 May 2019).

Archey, Karen and Robin Peckham (2014), 'Art Post-Internet', *Exhibition Catalog, Ullens Center for Contemporary Art*. Available online: http://ucca.org.cn/wp-content/uploads/2014/07/PAI_booklet_en.pdf

Ball, Tori (2018), 'Lifestyle of the Richard and Family', *Theatre People*, 6 May 2019. Available online: http://www.theatrepeople.com.au/lifestyle-of-the-richard-and-family/ (accessed 6 May 2019).

Berry, D. and M. Dieter (2015), *Postdigital Aesthetics: Art, Computation and Design*, UK: Palgrave Macmillan.

Bittman, L. (1985), *The KGB and Soviet Disinformation: An Insider's View*, Washington, DC: Pergamon-Brassey's. Available online: https://archive.org/details/sovietdisinformation2

Bregler, Christoph, Michele Covell, and Malcolm Slaney (1997), 'Video Rewrite: Driving Visual Speech with Audio', in *Proceedings of the 24th Annual Conference on Computer Graphics and Interactive Techniques*, 353–60, ACM Press and Addison-Wesley Publishing Co.

Brundage, Miles, Shahar Avin, Jack Clark, Helen Toner, Peter Eckersley, Ben Garfinkel, Allan Dafoe, Paul Scharre, Thomas Zeitzoff, Bobby Filar, Hyrum Anderson, Heather Roff, Gregory C. Allen, Jacob Steinhardt, Carrick Flynn, Sebastian Farquhar, Clare Lyle, Rebecca Crootof, Owain Evans, Michael Page, Joanna Bryson, Roman Yampolskiy, and Dario Amodei (2018), 'The Malicious Use of Artificial Intelligence: Forecasting, Prevention, and Mitigation', Future of Humanity Institute, University of Oxford, Centre for the Study of Existential Risk University of Cambridge, Center for a New American Security, Electronic Frontier Foundation and OpenAI. Available online: https://img1.wsimg.com/blobby/go/3d82daa4-97fe-4096-9c6b-376b92c619de/downloads/1c6q2kc4v_50335.pdf

Campaign Against Sex Robots (CASR) (2018), 'An Open Letter on the Dangers of Normalizing Sex Dolls & Sex Robots', *Feminist Current*, 27 August. Available online: https://www.feministcurrent.com/2018/08/27/open-letter-dangers-normalizing-sex-dolls-sex-robots/ (accessed 18 April 2019).

Cantwell, Brian, Paige Warner, Michael Koperwas, and Kiran Bhat (2016), 'ILM Facial Performance Capture', *ACM SIGGRAPH 2016* Talks 26: 1–2.

Cascone, Kim (2000), 'The Aesthetics of Failure: "Post-Digital" Tendencies in Contemporary Computer Music', *Computer Music Journal*, 24 (4): 12–18.

Causey, Matthew (2016), 'Postdigital Performance', *Theatre Journal*, 68 (3): 427–41.

CBS This Morning (2019), 'Doctored Pelosi Video Highlights the Threat of Deepfake Tech', 25 May. Available online: https://www.youtube.com/watch?v=EfREntgxmDs (accessed 1 June 2019).

Chung, Joon Son, Amir Jamaludin, and Andrew Zisserman (2017), 'You Said That?' *British Machine Vision Conference (BMVC)*, Cornell University. Submitted 8 May. Last revised 18 July. Available online: https://arxiv.org/pdf/1705.02966.pdf (accessed 16 August 2018).

Cole, Samantha (2018), 'Deepfakes Were Created as a Way to Own Women's Bodies – We Can't Forget That', *Vice*, 18 June. Available online: https://broadly.vice.com/en_us/article/nekqmd/deepfake-porn-origins-sexism-reddit-v25n2 (accessed 11 August 2018).

Dormehl, Luke (2016), *Thinking Machines: The Inside Story of Artificial Intelligence and Our Race to Build the Future*, Great Britain: WH Allen.

Esser, Patrick, Johannes Haux, Timo Milbich, and Björn Ommer (2019), 'Towards Learning a Realistic Rendering of Human Behavior', *Github*. Available online: https://compvis.github.io/hbugen2018/images/rerender.pdf (accessed 9 March 2019).

'Failure', *Oxford Learner's Dictionary*. Available online: https://www.oxfordlearnersdictionaries.com/definition/english/failure?q=failure (accessed 17 November 2020).

'Fake', *Oxford Dictionaries*. Available online: https://en.oxforddictionaries.com/definition/fake (accessed 10 August 2018).

Fink, David and Sarah Diamond (2019), 'Deepfakes: 2020 and Beyond', *Law.com*, 3 September 2020. Available online: https://www.law.com/therecorder/2020/09/03/deepfakes-2020-and-beyond/?slreturn=20201020155637 (accessed 20 November 2020).

Firth-Godbehere, Rich (2016), 'Rogue One: Digging Up the Dead in the Uncanny Valley', *Gizmodo*, 19 December. Available online: https://www.gizmodo.co.uk/2016/12/rogue-one-digging-up-the-dead-in-the-uncanny-valley (accessed 4 May 2019).

Fletcher, John (2018), 'Deepfakes, Artificial Intelligence, and Some Kind of Dystopia: The New Faces of Online Post-Fact Performance', *Theatre Journal*, 70 (4): 455–71.

Flusser, Vilém ([1983] 1984), *Towards a Philosophy of Photography*, trans. Vilém Flusser, Göttingen: European Photography.

Flusser, Vilém (2013), *Post-History*, trans. Rodrigo Maltez Novaes, Minneapolis: Univocal Publishing.

Goering, Kevin, Justin Hughes, Mary LaFrance, Jennifer Rothman, Nathan Siegel, Nancy Wolff, and Jeremy Sheff (2018), *New York Right of Publicity Law: Panel Discussion, 36 Cardozo Arts & Ent. L.J.* 22 February, 601.

Goodfellow, Ian J. (2016), 'NIPS 2016 Tutorial: Generative Adversarial Networks', *arXiv*, 3 April. Available online: https://arxiv.org/pdf/1701.00160.pdf (accessed 10 August 2018).

Goodfellow, Ian J., Jean Pouget-Abadie, Mehdi Mirza, Bing Xu, David Warde-Farley, Sherjil Ozair, Aaron Courville, and Yoshua Bengio (2014), 'Generative Adversarial Networks', in Z. Ghahramani, M. Welling, C. Cortes, N. D. Lawrence, and K. Q. Weinberger (eds), *Advances in Neural Information Processing Systems 27*, 2672–80, Red Hook, NY: Curran.

Grey Ellis, Emma (2018), 'People Can Put Your Face on Porn – and the Law Can't Help You', *WIRED*, 26 January 2018. Available online: https://www.wired.com/story/face-swap-porn-legal-limbo/ (accessed 7 August 2018).

Grey Ellis, Emma (2019), 'Netflix's New Comedy Lunatics Is Dizzying, Tone Deaf', *Wired: Culture*, 19 April. Available online: https://www.wired.com/story/netflix-comedy-lunatics-is-dizzying-tone-deaf/ (accessed 27 April 2019).

Guo, Lei and Chris Vargo (2018), '"Fake News" and Emerging Online Media Ecosystem: An Integrated Intermedia Agenda-Setting Analysis of the 2016 U.S. Presidential Election', *Communication Research*, 4 June.

Hayles, N. Katherine (1999), *How We Became Posthuman: Virtual Bodies in Cybernetics, Literature, and Informatics*, Chicago, IL: University of Chicago Press.

Helper, Roslyn (2018), 'Lifestyle of the Richard and Family', *Roslyn Helper*. Available online: https://www.roslynhelper.com/lifestyle-of-the-richard-and-family (accessed 16 August 2018).

Heritage, S. (2019). 'Lunatics Is Nasty and Grotesque. Chris Lilley's Career Is Shot'. *The Guardian*, 23 April. Available online: https://www.theguardian.com/tv-and-radio/2019/apr/23/lunatics-is-nasty-and-grotesque-chris-lilleys-career-is-shot-surely (accessed 2 May 2021).

Ironfield, Ross (2016), '#RogueOne Is Absolutely Brilliant. The CGI Peter Cushing Is So Convincing I Didn't Even Realise He Wasn't Real until I Saw Online Reviews!' *Twitter*, 16 December. Available online: https://twitter.com/RossIronfield (accessed 5 May 2019).

Isaak, Jim and Mina J. Hanna (2018), 'User Data Privacy: Facebook, Cambridge Analytica, and Privacy Protection', *Computer*, 51 (8): 56–9.

Jarvis, Liam (2019), *Immersive Embodiment: Theatres of Mislocalized Sensation*, Switzerland: Palgrave Macmillan (Palgrave Studies in Performance and Technology Series).

Johnson, Bobbie (2019), 'Deepfakes Are Solvable – but Don't Forget That "Shallowfakes" Are Already Pervasive', *MIT Technology Review*, 25 March. Available online: https://www.technologyreview.com/2019/03/25/136460/deepfakes-shallowfakes-human-rights/ (accessed 20 November 2020).

Lonergan, Patrick (2016), *Theatre and Social Media*, Basingstoke: Palgrave Macmillan.

Macpherson, Crawford Brough (1962), *The Political Theory of Possessive Individualism: Hobbes to Locke*, Oxford: Oxford University Press.

Mori, Masahiro (1970), 'Bukimi no tani' ('The Uncanny Valley'), *Energy*, 7: 33–5.

'NEW JAMES BOND IS NOT BLACK, ITS NIC CAGE (deepfakes)', *Nick Cage DeepFakes* [*sic*], 29 January 2018. Available online: https://www.youtube.com/watch?v=peFE-OBFrpA (accessed 21 April 2019).

'Nic Cage Is the New Indiana JONES (Confirmed) (Deepfakes)', *Nick Cage DeepFakes* [*sic*], 29 January 2018. Available online: https://www.youtube.com/watch?v=v0zFR0ElRd4 (accessed 21 April 2019).

Ontroerend Goed (2014), *All Work and No Plays: Blueprints for 9 Theatre Performances*, London: Oberon Books.

Rainie, Lee and Barry Wellman (2012), *Networked: The New Social Operating System*, Cambridge, MA and London: MIT Press.

Raval, Siraj (2018), 'DeepFakes Explained', *YouTube*, 2 February. Available online: https://www.youtube.com/watch?v=7XchCsYtYMQ (accessed 5 May 2019).

Reuters Staff (2019), 'FBI Says Russian *FaceApp* Is "Potential Counterintelligence Threat"', 2 December. Available online: https://www.reuters.com/article/us-usa-tech-russia-idUSKBN1Y62D4 (accessed 21 November 2020).

Ryan, Marie-Laure (2015), *Narrative as Virtual Reality 2: Revisiting Immersion and Interactivity in Literature and Electronic Media*, Baltimore: Johns Hopkins University Press.

Seymour, Mike (2017), 'Part 3: Rogue One, ILM's Digital Humans Sci-Tech Award Winning Pipeline', *fxguide*, 2 February. Available online: https://www.fxguide.com/featured/part-3-rogue-one-digital-humans (accessed 27 April 2019).

Shane, Scott (2017), 'The Fake Americans Russia Created to Influence the Election', *The New York Times*, 7 September. Available online: https://www.nytimes.com/2017/09/07/us/politics/russia-facebook-twitter-election.html (accessed 20 April 2019).

Stupp, Catherine (2019), 'Fraudsters Used AI to Mimic CEO's Voice in Unusual Cybercrime Case', *The Wall Street Journal*, 30 August. Available online: https://www.wsj.com/articles/fraudsters-use-ai-to-mimic-ceos-voice-in-unusual-cybercrime-case-11567157402 (accessed 20 November 2020).

'Superman and Lois Lane Deep Fake Nicolas Cage Meme', *Rage*, 5 February 2018. Available online: https://www.youtube.com/watch?v=UwiagqaX4fA (accessed 21 April 2019).

Suwajanakorn, Supasorn, Steven Seitz, and Ira Kemelmacher-Shlizerman (2017), 'Synthesizing Obama: Learning Lip Sync from Audio', *ACM Transactions on Graphics (TOG)*, 36 (4): 1–13.

'Terms of Use Agreement' (2017), *FaceApp*, 8 March. Available online: https://www.faceapp.com/terms-20170803.html

'Terms of Use Agreement' (2019), *FaceApp*, 3 December. Available online: https://www.faceapp.com/terms-en.html *thispersondoesnotexist.com* (accessed 20 April 2019).

Upson, Sandra (2017), 'Artificial Intelligence Is Killing the Uncanny Valley and Our Grasp on Reality', *Wired: Backchannel*, 16 December. Available online: https://www.wired.com/story/future-of-artificial-intelligence-2018/?mbid=social_twitter_onsiteshare (accessed 4 May 2019).

Vincent, James (2018a), 'Why We Need a Better Definition of "Deepfake": Let's Not Make Deepfakes the Next Fake News', *The Verge*, 22 May. Available online: https://www.theverge.com/2018/5/22/17380306/deepfake-definition-ai-manipulation-fake-news (accessed 8 August 2018).

Vincent, James (2018b), 'How Three Students Used Borrowed Code to Put the First AI Portrait in Christie's', *The Verge*, 23 October. Available online: https://www.theverge.com/2018/10/23/18013190/ai-art-portrait-auction-christies-belamy-obvious-robbie-barrat-gans (accessed 29 April 2020).

Weizenbaum, Joseph (1966), 'ELIZA – A Computer Program for the Study of Natural Language Communication between Man and Machine', *Communications of the ACM*, 9 (1): 36–45.

Wellman, Barry (2000), 'Living Wired in a Networked World: The Rise of Networked Individualism', Keynote address, Founding Conference, Association of Internet Researchers, Lawrence, KS, September.

'Wrongness', *Oxford Learner's Dictionary*. Available online: https://www.oxfordlearnersdictionaries.com/definition/english/wrongness (accessed 17 November 2020).

'You Won't Believe What Obama Says in This Video!' *YouTube: BuzzFeedVideo*, 17 April 2018. Available online: https://www.youtube.com/watch?v=cQ54GDm1eL0 (accessed 7 August 2018).

5

The Glitch, the Diva, and Coming Back Out: Aging and Postdigital Identity

Asher Warren

The opening episode of Tony Ayres and Louise Fox's 2017 Australian television drama *Glitch* begins with a sequence of shots that survey the dark streets of a fictional country town. The streetlights flicker and the stuttering zap of electrical activity is audible. The sequence ends in the town cemetery, where several bodies have emerged from their graves. Covered with dirt, and with only fragments of memory, the dead return in seemingly perfect health. The 'glitch' in this opening moment that extends from electrical fault to biological resurrection serves as a starting point for this chapter. This glitch connects technology to control over life and death, and indeed, to a literary genealogy. Shelley's *Frankenstein* springs readily to mind, with the novel's subtitle, *The Modern Prometheus,* pointing us even further back to the Titan of Greek mythology who created humans, and then gave them fire stolen from the gods. The subtitle, however, draws on a phrase first coined by Immanuel Kant, who refers to Benjamin Franklin – the man who stole lightning from the sky – as the 'Prometheus of modern times' (see Rogers and Stevens 2012: 127). Similar prophetic warnings have been made of our more contemporary 'digital revolution' with its techno-libertarian visions of cyberspaces populated with online identities and avatars, with the titans of technology (Steve Jobs or Mark Zuckerberg) playing an updated role of Prometheus. In the Greek myth, Zeus punished Prometheus chaining him to a rock, where his liver was pecked out only to regrow again each day, forced to endure a glitch of his own immortality. In this chapter, I wish to consider *glitching* as both an aesthetic and a method that offers insights into the relationships between technologies, bodies and the experience of aging. To do so, I examine how glitching has been taken up in three recent Australian performances to flesh out, quite literally, the more complex precarities experienced by older bodies, through a sensibility that I would argue we might understand as *postdigital.*

The three works explored in this chapter all raise and nuance the expressions of LGBTI+ identities in this postdigital milieu. The first, *Aeon* (2017), is a participatory performance developed through collaboration between lead artist and performer Lz Dunn, sound artist Laurence English, choreographer Shian Law and dramaturg Lara Thoms. Taking the flocking behaviours of birds as a starting point, *Aeon* challenges assumptions about natural ecological 'laws', exploring how individual behaviours and group dynamics can be shaped. I argue that by dramaturgically incorporating the glitch, *Aeon* exemplifies key aspects of postdigital performance, and through the development of a postdigital 'flock', raises the complex issue of inclusion, particularly of older bodies. The second work, *Calpurnia Descending* (2014) by Sisters Grimm, takes up age related discrimination more directly, by focusing on the film and television 'diva'. Through a highly mediated stage production, *Calpurnia Descending* adopts the glitch as a means of collapsing temporalities, playfully exploring the relationship between the aging diva, media technologies, drag performance and diva worship. Finally, I trace the issues framed by these two works to examine the *Coming Back Out Ball* (2018–) by All the Queen's Men, a large-scale performative gala ball. Through this celebration of LGBTI elders and the deliberate, inclusive engagement with actual bodies, the gala ball performs a layered identity activism, both within the event and through a strategic campaign to increase the visibility of these bodies more broadly. Taken together, I argue that these works 'glitch' in ways that draw audiences, participants and the broader public to engage with identities that are not seamless, but spread out and altered by differing access to real and virtual spaces, and differing levels of both desire and ability to 'keep up' with change over time.

While these three performances are markedly different, they each engage with the intersecting forms of discrimination and marginalization experienced by LGBTI elders, including ageism (within and beyond the LGBTI community) as well as homophobia, transphobia and importantly, legislative inequality. Gerontologist Maria T. Brown argues that LGBTI elders are silenced and rendered invisible in the fields of both gerontology (the study of aging and the effects of aging) and queer theory. Brown asserts that while not necessarily intentional, 'this silencing is an extension of homophobia and heterosexism in gerontology and ageism in queer theory' (Brown 2009: 66). Indeed, the issue of this marginalization and silencing raises an important issue for expressions of LGBTI identity in a postdigital milieu: what space is available for those who are not 'digital natives'? Through exploiting the glitch, I argue these performances also offer insights into an underdeveloped dimension of the postdigital: its relation to *aging bodies*.

Aeon: A walk in the park

As the product of multi-disciplinary collaboration, *Aeon* is a difficult work to categorize. It was programmed as part of the 2017 Melbourne Dance Massive Festival, which frames the performance as dance, while the structure of the work – which set the audience loose to wander within a large, open grassland – suggests it might also be framed as interactive or participatory. Moreover, the small wireless speakers participants were given and the immersive sonic experience at the conclusion of the performance suggest it might also be framed as an audio work. This interdisciplinarity is given some clarity by lead artist Lz Dunn, who writes in the production program, '*Aeon* is a question about interactions and intersections; an attempt to activate encounters and shift perception; to assemble a group of moving bodies and hover briefly, dilate slightly, unfix a little' (Dunn 2017). The dramaturgy of the work similarly resists fixed form by withholding explicit audience instruction, with participants 'primed with cue cards that spoke about birds and given little bluetooth speakers' (McGregor 2017), then sent off into the parkland. As reviewer John Bailey writes, there is no speaking during the work, and 'little literal explanation of what's going on' (2017). In both form and content, *Aeon* picks up threads explored in Dunn's earlier work *Flyway,* an audio led urban walking tour, exploring avian migratory routes and drawing from fieldwork with conservationists. The movement of birds is a key component of *Aeon,* but rather than migration, this work explores the dynamics and science of *flocking.* As a press release for the work explains, 'scientists have used computer modelling to illustrate the three simple rules that enable the synchronized movement of bird flocks' ('Aeon' n.d.). Those rules, set out by Craig Reynolds in a 1987 conference paper and employed in his 1986 modelling program *Boids,* are separation, alignment and cohesion.[1]

Aeon draws on the dynamics that emerge from the complex, cascading interactions of individuals following simple rules within a flock, developing an altogether different modelling technique through its own set of rules (the cue cards, no speaking, instructions to 'head over there'), leaving the audience to figure out the rest. Bailey writes that his initial uncertainty in the work was 'quickly overrun by the equally startling sense of animal group dynamics. Some members of the crowd wander off but never too far, while the mass itself seems to follow an instinct larger than any of its members' (2017). As Dunn notes in an interview with online magazine *Scenestr,* the reverse engineering of a computational model back into embodied – analogue – sensation and experience was a deliberate choice, intending to have the audience '[t]rusting in and communicating through their various bodily intelligences. I think as humans we've become less and less attuned to our own bodily intelligences, quite disembodied in many ways' ('Aeon: A Sonic Walk' 2017). To this end, the work embeds several dancers, who provide 'inputs' to the flock, testing who might follow. As reviewer Cleo Mees's vivid description suggests, this is both *effective* and *affective*:

> In this slowly churning mix, something starts to shift: individuals break into sprints, running for their lives in great, swooping arcs, and then return to walking. The running feels urgent, and looks delicious to do. Questions thump in my chest: 'What is happening? What will we all do? Also, what will I do? Will I run? Should I run? I really, really want to run'.
>
> (Mees 2017)

These accounts all assert the embodied experience of *Aeon*, which paradoxically structures this embodiment around the 'disembodied' digital code of modelling software. By connecting the two, I argue *Aeon* exemplifies a postdigital sensibility or aesthetic. Scholar of art, media and religion, Mel Alexenberg gives one definition of 'postdigital' in the preface to his 2011 monograph *The Future of Art in the Postdigital Age*.[2] Alexenberg defines the term as an adjective 'of or pertaining to art forms that address the humanization of digital technologies through interplay between digital, biological, cultural, and spiritual systems' (2011: 10). Clearly, *Aeon* fits into such a category, with its interplay of ecological, computational and social systems, but equally, this definition is broad enough to describe a great many works. To better identify the shift in relation to digital media that might warrant the 'post', we might turn to the origin of the term, and Laurence English's sound design for *Aeon*.

The small speaker that each participant is given to cup to their ear in *Aeon* provides a soundscape that operates as more than simply a sonic texture. Different rhythms slip in and out, as fragments of sound loop, delay, shimmer and decay. There are snatches of sound recognizable as 'natural', and as urban, but that emerge only for a moment before being cut up or fractured, glitching from familiar to foreign. The score is *glitchy*, which is to suggest it might be placed in the *genre* of glitch composition, or as musician Kim Cascone prefers, 'post-digital composition' (2000: 12).[3] Prior to its adoption in electronic music, glitch traces its etymology from the Yiddish *glitshn* (to slip, slide or glide) and emerged as a term used by Astronauts in the 1960s to describe faults, surges or otherwise rogue behaviour in electrical systems of NASA spacecraft (see Gurney 1965: 86). It is now commonly used to describe any fault in a digital technology, and particularly associated with the sonic artefacts produced as a by-product of these faults.

Many identify Japanese-American sound artist Yasunao Toné's 1985 *Music for 2 CDs,* as the first glitch composition, created by selectively damaging and obscuring the surface of two compact disks, which resulted in playback that randomly mixed fragments of recorded music with the sound of the CD player glitching. Throughout the 1990s, electronic musicians took up the glitch as a sonic texture and began to 'construct music out of the clicks, squeaks and fragments' (Sangild 2004: 201). Bates describes it as 'a meta-discursive practice: rather than writing new music inspired by older recordings, it constructs new music inspired by the technological conditions and limitations in which those recordings emerged' (2004: 222). Cascone, as both practitioner and theorist of glitch, posits the genre is

> characterized by its use of artifacts or detritus/failure/bugs found in digital audio. These artifacts form a critique of the perceived perfection of digital audio in that it exposes the flaws and illusion of 'perfect reproduction.'
>
> (Cascone 2001)

This *critique* of digital technology, built from the *failures* of digital technology, is the aspect of a postdigital art that Alexenberg's definition lacks: the utilization of digital technologies in a way that allows a simultaneous scepticism of these technologies and the ideologies that surround them.

The postdigital critique of 'perfect reproduction' is built upon by *Aeon*, through an overlapping of digital and biological systems. Indeed, while the glitch aesthetic undermines the 'perfect reproduction' of digital information, *Aeon* more pointedly seeks to unsettle assumptions regarding biological reproduction. As the artistic team note, the work is also informed by 'queer ecological thinking that questions established ideas of what is valued as "natural"' ('Aeon' n.d.). The work brings glitch and queer ecology into dialogue, the former with its critique of perfect digital reproduction, and the latter extending on ecofeminist critiques of 'pristine' landscapes and 'natural' ecology and pointing towards adaptations and reconfigurations that exceed or unsettle these terms. As Mortimer-Sandilands argues, evolutionary theory was particularly influential in establishing distinct categories of sexual practice, as

> [h]eterosexual reproduction was the only form of sexual activity leading directly to the continuation of a species from one generation to the next; thus, logically, other sexual activities must be either aberrant or, at best, indirectly part of the heterosexual reproductive process.
>
> (Mortimer-Sandilands 2005)

Anything else, this model suggests, is a *glitch*: malfunction, error or flaw. In fact, there are many correspondences between the postdigital glitch and queer ecology. Timothy Morton goes so far as to suggest queer ecology could extend to both non-human and non-organic, 'embracing silicon as well as carbon' (Morton 2010: 279). Sangild traces a connection back the other way, noting that 'genetic "glitches" occur when the copying of genes from one generation to the next is imperfect', which means that 'evolution *depends* on errors and imperfections' (Sangild 2004: 207, emphasis added). By deploying the bodies of participants as active 'de-coders' that engage and respond to a range of sensory data, *Aeon* opens up spaces of indeterminacy that un-fixes assumptions across both digital and biological realms.

Through the creation of a queer, postdigital 'flock' in performance, *Aeon* links the biological, cultural and technological, where a diverse collective of bodies might, through their participation, explore alternative models of relation to the other bodies around them. The flock becomes an inclusive space where bodies might engage and experience more fluid, performative expressions of identity, but also, I suggest, raises a set of challenges for participants who might be excluded from the flock. If we take Dunn's statement that '[m]ovement and sound unfix a body' and focus on the significant amount of walking and listening involved, we might ask how bodies which are less mobile, or less able to hear, can be part of the flock. For these bodies, the flock may be difficult to join, or difficult keep up with. While this speaks to questions of inclusion and ability broadly, mobility and hearing are notable as these often diminish as bodies age. The biological process of aging changes the body, but aging also reorients relations to culture, nature and technology. Indeed, this question of aging and the 'queer flock' is doubly challenged by the preference amongst elders to identify as LGBTI, rather than LGTBIQ, as the term 'queer', which is viewed negatively by those who have experienced it as an abusive label, intended to humiliate or shame. However, rather than older bodies being left behind or excluded from the postdigital, I want to focus on ways that the postdigital might incorporate these bodies and challenge the way age can work to 'fix' identities. As this discussion of *Aeon* illuminates, 'fixing' and 'unfixing' might occur in a number of ways, from physical limitations, to preferences that emerge from cultural and generational experience. The glitch, I will argue, as it reappraises fragments, artefacts and processes of material degeneration, provides fertile ground for artists to take up this challenge.

Keeping up: *Calpurnia Descending*

The issue of trying to 'keep up' with culture and technology is explored with considerable complexity in the 2014 production *Calpurnia Descending*.

A co-production by Sisters Grimm (Ash Flanders and Declan Greene), with the Sydney Theatre Company and Malthouse Theatre (Melbourne), *Calpurnia* was a high camp, intermedial, drag remediation of the Hollywood 'backstage melodrama', epitomized by Joseph L. Mankiewicz's 1950 classic *All About Eve*. Central to *Calpurnia* is the figure of the diva, as both populist idol and object of camp affection, emulation and ridicule. The production cleverly entangled the diva with the technologies that facilitate her fame, tracing a media genealogy that overlays a pivotal issue at the heart of the backstage melodrama – *aging* – and transposes this conflation of biology and technology onto diva worship and camp performance.

Founded in 2006, Sisters Grimm have made a name for themselves as subversive, irreverent theatre makers with productions that have pushed the acceptable limits of good taste, while re-evaluating and queering norms in popular culture. A continuing focus across their body of work has been an engagement with cinematic genre, from which familiar narratives, stereotypes and clichés are subverted on stage through cross-gender and cross-race casting, queering these caricatures to expose their construction. Staged in an underground carpark, their 2008 production *Cellblock Booty* was a raucous and exuberant take on the 1970s 'women in prison' genre film (more often known as 'sexploitation' films) epitomized by producer Roger Corman's *Women in Cages* and *The Big Dolls House* (both 1971). In 2010, they took on the 'evil child' genre with *Little Mercy* (2010) and in 2012 they presented *Summertime in the Garden of Eden*, inspired in equal parts by *Gone with the Wind* and the theatrical legacy of Tennessee Williams. The latter was described by reviewer Allison Croggon as 'melodrama on amyl nitrate', a production 'underpinned by a deftly intelligent subtext that skewers the binary world of white heteronormativity' (Croggon 2013). The dialogue between the cinematic and the theatrical that animates these productions might be understood using Jay David Bolter and Richard Grusin's definition of the term 'remediation', as they represent or recreate one type of media in another (2000: 39). As Steve Dixon notes, however, the term remediation has been adopted elsewhere, and has 'been common coinage in the waste disposal and recycling industries for some years' (2007: 136). The use of the term across media theory and waste management is curiously fitting in this instance, as it brings us to a sensibility Flanders and Green employ with abundance: camp.

Camp traces its etymology to the French verb, *se camper*, 'to pose in an exaggerated fashion', and while practiced at least since the late nineteenth century, became the subject of academic analysis in Susan Sontag's seminal 1964 essay 'Notes on Camp'. Sontag describes camp as a sensibility that delights in artifice: 'the essence of Camp is its love of the unnatural: of artifice and exaggeration' (1999: 53). It is an aesthetic mode of experience that sees everything in quotation marks, as role play. Immensely theatrical, '[t]he whole point of Camp is to dethrone the serious. Camp is playful, anti-serious' (62). As David M. Halperin notes in *How to be Gay*, '[c]amp is not only a mode of cultural appropriation, a way of recycling bits of mainstream culture; it is also productive, a creative impulse in its own right, a strategy for dealing with social domination' (2012: 203). In *Calpurnia*, this playful, anti-serious, recycling aesthetic is at work both within the play, but also in a more meta-theatrical matter. To make this argument, it is necessary to examine how camp has historically engaged with the body and aging, and how *Calpurnia Descending* connects this history to glitch and the postdigital.

The plot of *Calpurnia Descending* echoes *All About Eve,* as it traces the young and (seemingly) naive Violet St. Clair as she befriends reclusive star Beverly Dumont, who becomes inspired to make her Broadway comeback in a production of *Julius Caesar*, where she – naturally – will play Calpurnia. The unfolding drama follows the scheming and manipulation of both characters as one tries to resurrect her career, and the other to launch it. Both are played in camp drag, but the two leads take up differing inflections. The young St. Clair is played in a *naive* camp (in a blonde wig) by Ash Flanders, while the aging Dumont is played in an *acerbic* camp (with and without wig) by actor and singer Paul Capsis. By casting Capsis and Flanders as the 'old star' and the 'starlet', we see a doubling down of the diva-feud: both in its populist incarnation, and a more subcultural key, of drag-divas. Capsis has a long and glittering history as a drag performer, from his 1992 solo show *THE LADY IS A CAMP*, performed as part the Sydney Gay and Lesbian Mardi Gras, to playing his Grandmother in the critically acclaimed *Angela's Kitchen* (co-written and directed by Julian Meyrick), Capsis has arguably blazed a trail in Australia, which Flanders has gone on to follow – building his own career in large part by playing women. Through this meta-theatrical layering, *Calpurnia* creates a platform to examine attitudes towards aging amongst gay men, while also allowing the Sisters Grimm to reflect on a foundation of their theatrical practice: the logic of camp.

In her ethnography of US drag queens, *Mother Camp*, Esther Newton observes the role of camp performance as a method of negotiating stigma within the gay male community, embracing it and making it an object of ridicule. 'Camp humor', Newton writes, 'is a system of laughing at one's incongruous position instead of crying' (1979: 109). Before it was adopted as an adjective, 'Camp' was used as a noun, with *the* camp a particular role that was played at parties and performances. The camp was opposed to the 'beauty', the object of desire and sexual attraction. As Newton writes:

The camp, both on and off stage, tends to be a person who is, by group criteria, less sexually attractive, whether by virtue of advancing age or fewer physical charms or, frequently, both. Whatever the camp's 'objective' physical appearance, his most successful joke is on himself.

(Newton 1979: 56)

Newton's observation shows a rather complex relationship between a camp aesthetic and 'advancing age'. As Caryl Flinn notes, Sontag's famous essay was originally going to be titled 'Notes of Death' (Flinn 1995: 54), and as Flinn herself suggests, '[c]amp has always been fascinated with, and has fashioned itself on, the outmoded, the out of date, the artifact past its time' (Flinn 1995: 55). In their programme note, Flanders and Greene observe that this outmoded artefact is often the diva herself, writing:

As the diva ages, as she loses her desirability as a figure of identification, her gay audience is as quick to 'turn' as any cartoon Broadway producer. The logic of camp marks the aged diva as an object of fond ridicule – placing her in a space somewhere between revulsion and idolatry.

(Flanders and Greene 2014)

As Flinn argues somewhat forcefully, this 'turn' away from the diva is implicitly tied up with her body, as 'the imperative to breed – which is culturally forced upon bodies of heterosexual women like a straightjacket and wrenched from lesbians with equal force – is indispensable to the grotesque tradition of which camp partakes' (1995: 73). Indeed, the historical construction of, and fixation with, the female celebrity (built on youth and beauty as markers of reproductive fitness) brings us back to the Darwinian influence on cultural values and assumptions about 'natural' bodies and desire raised by *Aeon*, and the way that 'camp doesn't just mock what is outmoded, but what – and who – is old' (1995: 65).

The problematic association between misogyny and camp is only reinforced by the debates regarding the 'ownership' of camp, and the widespread assumption that 'the only authentic form of camp is gay and generally misogynist' (Robertson 1996: 57). However, as Robertson, and more recently, Crosby and Lynn argue, such a position 'overlooks how much of camp is and has been appropriative of women' who have 'historically been producers of camp' (2017: 48). Taking Dolly Parton as their case study, Crosby and Lynn observe how the unnatural and artificial can be deployed against the 'imperative to breed', noting that 'through camp, women can play with the *un*natural and thus challenge these assumptions that limit women and uphold patriarchal domination' (2017: 51). Turning back to *All About*

Eve, we might read Bette Davis's performance as Margo as decidedly campy, in the way it asserts an alternative identity to the youthful, natural (and of course, fertile) Eve.

However, there is a brief exchange in the penultimate scene of *All About Eve* that offers another perspective. Eve, accepting the Sarah Siddons Award for Distinguished Achievement, finishes her speech by remarking, 'Although I am going to Hollywood next week to make a film – do not think for a moment that I am leaving you. How could I? For my heart is here in the theater – and three thousand miles are too far to be away from one's heart' (Mankiewicz 1950). A short time later, an arch Margo responds, '[N]ice speech, Eve. But I wouldn't worry too much about your heart. You can always put that award where your heart ought to be.' We might read beyond the personal hostility in this scene to a broader fight playing out between Broadway and Hollywood, an old and a new media. The theatre, as Eve alludes, is characterized as the place where the heart resides, and Hollywood a place *without* a heart. The metaphor flows through a range of layers: live theatre opposed to 'dead' film, the theatre as an organic, living body and the cinema as a technological machine. When Margo suggests Eve's heart can be replaced by the award, she prefigures an *unnatural* being animated by a prosthetic heart: the cyborg diva.

This repositioning of the diva in relation to a new media form brings us to the second notable feature of *Calpurnia Descending,* which is its performance of a media genealogy that cannily connects to the diva and camp diva-worship. After the first scene of *Calpurnia,* a huge projection screen descends, completely hiding the stage. The unfolding backstage melodrama plays out on the screen, created live for cameras *behind* the screen. This mediated, multi-camera, live-cinema spectacle, designed by Matthew Gingold, is ambitious, complex, and also very camp. Cheesy dialogue is matched with equally cheesy cinematography that playfully acknowledges the audience's gaze, and works through an array of stock cinematic shots, including dialogue cross-cutting, the point of view, the dramatic zoom and exposition. The humour relies on a knowledge of these filmic conventions, but also, the reciprocal relationship between the theatre and screen media, which, as Philip Auslander has shown, constructs our very understanding of liveness (2008). As the performance progresses, we move through the history of screen media, from black and white cinema, to colour, and finally, as the melodrama winds up its pace, we accelerate towards an aesthetic of video games and contemporary networked technologies. In Scene 14, we find Dumont/Calpurnia in a vision of the underworld, approached by a shadowy figure.

————Script Excerpt————
from Scene 14: THE UNDERWORLD

BEVERLY
   Who are you?
NECROMANCER
   I am the one that blessed you with your visions
BEVERLY
   Are you a God or a man?
NECROMANCER
   I am neither. I am a Belkin N600 Wireless N+ Router
BEVERLY
   Are you single band, or double band?
NECROMANCER
   Double band

Dramatic music. Under the cowl, the two glowing eyes flare into a line of small green eyes: all of them blinking. It's a modem.

NECROMANCER
   You were a fool to release Cleopatra. It shall be your undoing, daughter of Rome
BEVERLY
   No. She warned me of Brutus' treachery. She –
NECROMANCER
   It is not Brutus who seeks Caesar's death. But she herself. The Queen of Snakes
BEVERLY
   No. I will stop her!
NECROMANCER
   It is too late, daughter of Rome. The Gods have spoken – Caesar shall die this hour
BEVERLY
   I can outrun them!
NECROMANCER
   Hubris! Hubris! Nothing can outrun fate, not even I with my speeds of over 300MB per second – allowing you to stream content in glittering HD!
BEVERLY
   Tell me more about Belkin!

A banner scrolls across the screen: FACEBOOK.COM/BELKIN ... ...
TWITTER: (???) ... ... WWW.BELKIN.COM ... . BELKIN, MAKE
YOUR INTERNET SAFE
NECROMANCER
> You have not the time, daughter of Rome. Why not simply 'Like' us
> on Facebook.

BEVERLY
> Thank you, Belkin. You are a noble sage – and an inexpensive solution
> for my home and office! Now .... To kill Cleopatra!

Her dagger raised, BEVERLY/CALPURNIA runs from the
NECROMANCER. As soon as she is gone, the NECROMANCER cackles
evilly. It pulls back its hood: underneath it is Cleopatra. She laughs and
laughs. Her face splits open like a broken.GIF image. From the rift,
thousands of smiling 'Cleopatras' pour out.
————end excerpt————

The visual explosion described takes the form of a wild, glitching cacophony
of images and digital animations, full of internet memes, references to
1990s era technologies and software, and quite specifically referencing the
pop-camp music-video of Katy Perry's 2013 'Dark Horse'. It is telling that
this collision of glitch with camp occurs at the moment of shape-shifting
between diva and router-modem and results in an explosion of reproductive
excess. The dense layering reveals a tight relationship between the diva and
the media technologies that facilitate her fame, and the insistent, demanding
churn to constantly *produce* in order to keep up as these technologies and
networks move faster and faster. These scenes, I argue, perform a type of
'diva dromology', drawing on Paul Virilio's neologism for 'that body of
knowledge concerned specifically with the phenomenon of speed, or more
precisely, with the way speed determines or limits the manner in which
phenomena appear to us' (James 2007: 29). In *Speed and Politics*, Virilio
writes of the automotive technological developments that create a 'body able
to annihilate time and space through its dynamic performances' (2006: 84),
and we see the same annihilation through audio visual technologies, as the
diva expands beyond a single body, proliferating across the network evoked
by the glitching GIF.

In following the figure of the diva into the twenty-first century, it is not
surprising that the Sisters Grimm single out Perry as their target of ridicule
in this scene, as her career has been defined by 'pop-camp', a mainstream,
marketable appropriation of camp designed to traverse the network at high
speed, largely *without* subversive or acerbic edge. Most telling, however, was a

tweet issued during the Melbourne season, by none other than Perry herself, who happened to be on tour in Australia at the time. She posts, 'Fantastic 1st day in Melb! Got 2 deliver a check 2 a girls school, pop in on my pop up & see the HIGHlarious new play Calpurnia Descending' [*sic*)] (Perry 2014). Deftly absorbing *Calpurnia* by redistributing it within her own social media sphere, Perry is quick to laugh along, and just as quickly illustrates the next iteration of the cyborg diva, unceasingly connected so as to better perform across contemporary mediated networks.

How, though, does the intermedial examination of the diva in *Calpurnia* bring us back to the question of LGTBI identity? We might begin by taking up Chris Philpot's suggestion that 'queers engage in community-building around female divas because of an identification with the divas' performance of excess and waste' (Philpot 2017: 68). This links us back again to the deployment of camp, which as Andrew Ross argues, involves 'a rediscovery of history's waste', remediating it (in the sense of waste management) as a '*re-creation of surplus value*' (1989: 151). In *Calpurnia,* the young Cleopatra/ St Claire/Flanders navigates, and then is figured *as* the changing media landscape, while Calpurnia/Dumont/Capsis struggles to keep up, frantically responding to sudden shifts in the glitching camp aesthetic, as it steamrolls through a visual barrage of video games, corporate branding and 1990s net culture. This camping-of-glitch/glitching-of-camp dredges up historical waste, gesturing towards obsolescence and death. However, it also revives and remediates this waste, staving off obsolescence by breathing life into a new assemblage built from the old parts.

After the glitching crescendo, the theatre falls dark and silent. The screen is raised. The aftermath of the frenzied work required to execute this last scene in real time is made visible, and provides a glimpse into the backstage machinations. Calpurnia/Dumont/Capsis is posed atop a ladder, required for the green-screen trickery, and exhausted. Slowly, s/he descends, and layers of green fabric, costume and wig come off. Finally, it is just Capsis, stripped to his underwear, standing centre stage. This moment might be read as one of pathos that distances itself from camp, but as Flinn notes, 'camp strenuously insists *on* the body and its materiality' (1995: 77). I suggest that this moment retains a playful sensibility but adopts a slightly different game. It plays with the entwined challenges, anxieties and indeed, the *ethics* of camp identity across broader cultural and technological changes, drawing attention to an older body, the stereotypes and perceptions of aging in a broad sense, but particularly for gay men. Notably, research shows that gay men have an especially negative view of aging, with the late 1930s perceived as 'old' – much earlier than perceptions among heterosexual men and lesbians (Schope 2005). This perception has been theorized as *accelerated aging*, drawing another parallel to the accelerations experienced by the diva. Through the glitch-camp aesthetic, *Calpurnia Descending* explores a way to laugh *with*, rather than *at* women and gay elders. By framing the experience of aging alongside the aging of media technologies (and media content) in this particular context, Flanders and Greene highlight that experiences of, and attitudes towards aging are diverse, informed by identities, communities, histories and experiences. Which brings us to the final performance I wish to discuss, the *Coming Back Out Ball*.

Coming back out and futurity

On 7 October 2017, All the Queen's Men (ATQM) hosted the *Coming Back Out Ball* (*CBOB* hereafter) in the Melbourne Town Hall, a flagship event of the Victorian Seniors Festival, held in association with the National LGBTI Aging and Aged Care conference. Over 550 LGBTI seniors (65+), sixty volunteers, and 100 artists, performers and crew took part in the lavish gala comprising several acts and entertainments, dinner and of course, dancing. ATQM (Tristan Meecham and Bec Reid) described the ball as a gift to honour the elders in attendance, and those in the broader community. As Melanie Joosten writes for *The Guardian*:

Figure 5.1 *The Coming Back Out Ball* by All the Queen's Men (2017) © Photographer: Bryony Jackson. www.comingbackoutball.com

The *Coming Back Out Ball* is so named because one of the biggest challenges faced by many older people within the LGBTI community is whether to be out and proud in late life, or keep this aspect of themselves hidden.

(Joosten 2017)

As Joosten points out, many LGBTI elders keep their sexuality or gender identity hidden to avoid social, material and policy-based discrimination, with an Australian study showing a 'distressing fear for participants was that they would have to "straightenup" their lives, or hide their sexual orientation if they required residential aged care' (Barrett et al. 2015: 139). The emphasis on coming back out draws attention to the importance of thinking about temporal change, acknowledging the fight for acceptance, and how sociocultural attitudes surrounding the act of disclosing sexual or gender identity have changed remarkably within the span of a generation, while also identifying the more individual aspects of what the process of 'coming out' means for different people at different stages of their lives. With the *CBOB,* ATQM appropriates and refigures the gala ball as form of activism, first by reclaiming a significant public, civic space for older LGTBI bodies, and second by insisting on the presence of these bodies by mediating them for a larger audience. To unpack the latter, however, we must begin with the former, and consider the Ball as *embodied* event.

In 2016, prior to the extravagant scale of the gala ball, Meecham, Reid and Andrew Westle created the *LGBTI Elders Dance Club*, an ongoing, monthly event held at the Fitzroy Town Hall for rainbow elders and allies. Inspired by UK group Duckie, the dance club was envisioned as a consistent, ongoing event, which allowed ATQM to build relationships in the community, negotiate differing mobilities and develop strategies to maintain inclusion. The dance club has continued since 2016, with numerous 'chapters' also starting up across Australia, often in partnership with local councils and community groups, and even internationally in Scotland, through partnership with the National Theatre of Scotland, Eden Court and Luminate. In 2020, due to the Covid-19 pandemic, in-person gatherings were postponed, but regular events shifted online with a *Digital Dance Club.*

In coming together and affirming the importance of regular meeting, the *LGTBI Elders Dance Club* and the *CBOB* also draw attention to cultural change. For decades, LGBTI venues and events served an important role as community hubs, yet in recent years, a number of factors have led to their decline (Nunn 2019). One of these factors is a growing social acceptance of diversity, yet as noted earlier, this has proven somewhat uneven, with aged care homes and medical services slower to implement more inclusive policies and practices. Another factor is the rise of social networking apps and online spaces where people can socialize, make friends, and find sexual partners. These new networked spaces, however, can also present barriers for older users, with their distinct cultures of use, and the literacies required to navigate these devices and online environments. The dance club and gala ball both create spaces for bodies to come together, eat, drink and dance, while also paying homage to the significance of the gay and lesbian balls held in Melbourne throughout the 1970s and 1980s, as events that created safe spaces to gather, socialize and express gender and sexual diversity.

With these issues in mind, it is clear why ATQM invested considerable time and attention addressing accessibility in the two-year lead-up to the gala ball, and remain invested in an ongoing process of listening. An example of this is the production of a report commissioned about the *CBOB*, where several interesting observations were collected. Perhaps unsurprisingly, many elders affirmed a strong desire to move and interact, surmised by the succinct advice: '[L]ess entertainment, more time for dancing & talking' (Badham, Bourke and Meecham 2018: 15). One particular comment in the report, however, captures the entwining threads of bodily change and cultural change that I have sought to explore in this chapter, with the advice that 'shorter bursts of dancing take less toll on the aging joints. Perhaps consult with some older people about dance music. Some of it was OK but extended play 90s disco was not so much' (2018: 15). The request for shorter bursts is notable as it draws attention away from the simplistic binary of bodies being able/unable, to more nuanced consideration that includes duration and frequency. Similarly, the request for less 1990s disco might point towards generational differences in taste, but may simply be an individual preference. Interestingly, the comment illuminates how sound and movement can also work to *affix* bodies with identity in this instance.

The entertainment at the gala ball included a wide variety of acts – as well as the sharing of stories and experiences of LGBTI elders, which sought to recognize past pain and suffering, but also celebrate the rights and privileges hard won. While the gala was an affirming and inclusive embodied event, it was also extended beyond the guests, quite deliberately, as a mediatized event in order to draw attention to and affirm LGBTI elders in the wider community. A publicity campaign for the gala led to national, and international coverage in newspapers, on radio, television and online outlets. Many of these articles involved profiles of LGBTI elders, such as Judith Slade, who forged a career in the male-dominated world of sheep shearing, and was sentenced to a month in prison because of her sexuality (Byrne 2017), and David Morrison's coming out at age seventy-six (Webb 2017), or trans woman Michelle, who also came out later in life, explaining, 'I knew from my earliest memories that

I was trans, but there was no word for it then' (Russell 2017). These profiles ranged across a diverse spectrum, often drawing attention to historical and contemporary experiences of homophobia and the challenges of aging, but also offering perspectives on contemporary debates regarding equality.

The mediated activism of the *CBOB* also fell within a larger national context, as the gala ball took place at the height of a prolonged and polarizing campaign to legalize same-sex marriage in Australia. The campaign faced considerable resistance from many conservatives and religious groups, and political machinations meant the issue of marriage equality was not put to a referendum, or even a non-binding plebiscite, rather, it was decided that a voluntary national postal survey was administered between September and November – and the *CBOB* landed, quite unexpectedly, right in the middle of this period. This unanticipated scheduling meant the *CBOB* media campaign could not only address the marginalization of LGBTI elders, but incorporate their voices into the campaign for LGBTI rights in the future. The voluntary survey results were announced on 17 November 2017, with 61.6 per cent of respondents in favour of legalizing same-sex marriage, and a private members bill amending the marriage act was passed by the Australian parliament on 7 December 2017.

The issue of futurity, I argue, is the oft-unmentioned subtext that brings together these various works and the complex issue of aging for the postdigital LGBTIQ identity. The horizon of the future has been an issue explored by several queer theorists, perhaps most notably by Lee Edelman in *No Future: Queer Theory and the Death Drive* (2004). Edelman observes how the future is overwhelmingly imagined in biologically reproductive terms, through the figure of the 'Child', which excludes this future from all who are unable to reproduce. Moreover, this figurative child is frequently called up and deployed in arguments against sex and gender equality (such as same-sex marriage or reproductive rights). For these reasons, Edelman proposes instead a radical model of anti-oppositionality: 'a refusal of the coercive belief in the paramount value of futurity' (2004: 6). However, I want to suggest that *Aeon, Calpurnia Descending* and the *Coming Back Out Ball* all imagine a different future – one that is not built around a figural child, but rather, the body and its materiality.

This queer future is different to that of 'reproductive futurism', and offers what I suggest is a postdigital modality of 'queer time', extending the concept originally formulated by Judith Halberstam, which resists 'the temporal frames of bourgeois reproduction and family, longevity, risk/safety, and inheritance' (2005: 6), with an original 'emphasis on the here, the present, the now' (2). Halberstam suggests queer time is most apparent 'within those gay communities whose horizons of possibility have been severely diminished by the AIDS epidemic' (2) and the uncertainty of the future led to a focus on the present. However, as Brown argues, this conception 'encourages the queer community, whether intentionally or not, to look away from aging as a potential for a given individual's future and to look away from individuals in the LGBT community who are aging or who are old' (2009: 71). The performances analysed in this chapter each formulate a 'postdigital queer time', that centres on the body, and its materiality, while simultaneously drawing attention to digital mediation. This modality, I suggest, contemplates a very different horizon of the future, entangled with the 'digital revolution', but also detached from it. On one hand, it points to the unfulfilled promises of this revolution: of the body made obsolete, or at the very least to make aging a thing of the past. Similarly, it speaks to the unfinished work of gay liberation, of lingering homophobia, transphobia, ageism and many other forms of discrimination and marginalization faced by the LGBTI elders. On the other, it embraces advances made: of progressive changes to policy and law, of greater representation of diversity in media, and of course, medical advances, such as the increasingly effective (and available) treatments for HIV/AIDS. It is also to recognize the increasing cultural change that has come about through the development of social media, exemplified by the success of the campaign to legalize same-sex marriage in Australia, but also the awareness that these platforms are not always egalitarian or accessible, and the acceleration towards their widespread use also has a host of unintended consequences.

To conclude, I wish to return to the television series *Glitch*, and the fictional scenario of a technological glitch bringing the dead back to life which served as a starting point for this chapter. The source of the glitch in *Glitch*, however, was decidedly *industrial*, a product of experiments carried out by the fictional Noregard laboratory. The glitches examined in *Aeon, Calpurnia Descending* and the *Coming Back Out Ball* are decidedly more post-industrial and postdigital, focused not on the crossing between life and death, but on a more nuanced exploration of the faults, surges and rogue behaviours that emerge in the use of bodies and technologies over time. The postdigital glitch here does not imagine bodies reborn as avatars in cyberspace, nor a bioscientific promise to eradicate aging; but rather, like camp, appropriates and recycles – but unlike camp, moves *away* from artifice and ridicule, moving instead quite earnestly to bring bodies back into focus in an accelerating digital-media landscape, and resist an evolutionary futurism of 'perfect reproduction', and imagine other models of support and community. *Aeon, Calpurnia Descending* and the *Coming Back Out Ball* each offer a glitch to the futurity imagined by the 'digital revolution', directing us to think seriously about how a contemporary 'flock' might include the bodies, voices and perspectives of LGBTI elders.

Notes

1   Reynolds was also involved in programming scenes for the ground-breaking 1982 film *Tron,* which was influential in its visualization of digital technologies and cyberspace.
2   The book itself was an updated edition of his earlier work, *The Future of Art in the Digital Age* (2006).
3   Cascone is generally recognized as the first to coin the term 'post-digital' in this 2000 essay.

References

'Aeon: A Sonic Walk, A Queer Nature In Perth' (2017), *Scenestr,* 6 October. Available online: https://scenestr.com.au/arts/aeon-a-sonic-walk-a-queer-nature-in-perth (accessed 15 September 2019).

'Aeon by Lz Dunn & Collaborators' (n.d.), *Performing Lines.* Available online: https://www.performinglines.org.au/projects/aeon/ (accessed 15 September 2019).

Alexenberg, M. (2011), *The Future of Art in a Postdigital Age: From Hellenistic to Hebraic Consciousness,* Bristol: Intellect.

All About Eve (1950), [Film] Dir. J. L. Mankiewicz, USA: 20th Century Fox.

Auslander, P. (2008), *Liveness: Performance in a Mediatized Culture,* 2nd edn, London and New York: Routledge.

Badham, D. M., L. Bourke, and T. Meecham (2018), *Reflections on The Coming Back Out Ball: A Dialogic Evaluation,* All The Queens Men. Available online: http://www.comingbackoutball.com/cms/wp-content/uploads/2018/02/cbob_evaluation.pdf (accessed 13 June 2019).

Bailey, J. (2017), 'The Audience on the Inside', *RealTime.* Available online: http://www.realtimearts.net/article/issue138/12567 (accessed 15 September 2019).

Barrett, C., C. Whyte, J. Comfort, A. Lyons, and P. Cramer (2015), 'Social Connection, Relationships and Older Lesbian and Gay People', *Sexual and Relationship Therapy,* 30: 131–42.

Bates, E. (2004), 'Glitches, Bugs, and Hisses: The Degeneration of Musical Recordings and the Contemporary Musical Work', in C. Washburne and M. Derno (eds), *Bad Music: The Music We Love to Hate,* 212–25, New York: Routledge.

Bolter, J. D. and R. Grusin (2000), *Remediation: Understanding New Media,* Cambridge, MA: MIT Press.

Brown, M. T. (2009), 'LGBT Aging and Hetorical Silence', *Sexuality Research and Social Policy,* 6: 65–78.

Byrne, A. (2017), 'Shear Delight', *Herald Sun*: 130.

Cascone, K. (2000), 'The Aesthetics of Failure: "Post-Digital" Tendencies in Contemporary Computer Music', *Computer Music Journal,* 24: 12–18.

Cascone, K. (2001), 'Deleuze and Contemporary Electronic Music', *Intersects: Between the Disciplines*, December. Available online: https://web.archive.org/web/20030119183118/ and http://www.iisgp.ubc.ca/whatsnew/intersects/issues/dec01/cascone.htm (accessed 16 September 2019).

Croggon, A. (2013), 'Summertime in the Garden of Eden, Sisters Grimm – Review', *The Guardian Australia*, 11 November. Available online: https://www.theguardian.com/culture/australia-culture-blog/2013/nov/10/summertime-garden-eden-sisters-grimm-review

Crosby, E. D. and H. Lynn (2017), 'Authentic Artifice: Dolly Parton's Negotiations of Sontag's Camp', in B. E. Drushel and B. M. Peters (eds), *Sontag and the Camp Aesthetic: Advancing New Perspectives*, 47–62, Lanham: Lexington Books.

Dixon, S. (2007), *Digital Performance: A History of New Media in Theater, Dance, Performance Art, and Installation*, Cambridge, MA: MIT Press.

Dunn, L. (2017), *Aeon [Program]*. Available online: http://www.artshouse.com.au/wp-content/uploads/2017/08/Aeon-by-Lz-Dunn-Show-Program.pdf (accessed 15 September 2019).

Edelman, L. (2004), *No Future: Queer Theory and the Death Drive*, Durham, NC and London: Duke University Press.

Flanders, A. and D. Greene (2014), 'A Note from the Creators', *Calpurnia Descending* [Program]. Malthouse Theatre.

Flinn, C. (1995), 'The Deaths of Camp', *Camera Obscura: Feminism, Culture, and Media Studies*, 12: 52–84.

Glitch (2015), [TV Programme] Australian Broadcasting Corporation (ABC), 9 July, 20.30.

Gurney, Gene (1965), *Americans into Orbit: The Story of Project Mercury*, New York: Random House.

Halberstam, J. (2005), *In a Queer Time and Place: Transgender Bodies, Subcultural Lives*, New York: New York University Press.

Halperin, D. M. (2012), *How to Be Gay*, Cambridge, MA: Belknap Press of Harvard University Press.

Joosten, M. (2017), 'The Coming Back Out Ball: Being Out and Proud and Older in Australia', *The Guardian*, 25 March. Available online: https://www.theguardian.com/world/2017/mar/25/the-coming-back-out-ball-how-the-older-gay-community-is (accessed 29 September 2019).

McGregor, F. (2017), 'Liveworks in Review: Ambitious, Engrossing', *The Monthly*, 7 November. Available online: https://www.themonthly.com.au/blog/fiona-mcgregor/2017/07/2017/1510014638/liveworks-review-ambitious-engrossing (accessed 20 September 2019).

Mees, C. (2017), 'Liveworks: AEON, a Desiring Flock', *RealTime*, 1 November. Available online: https://www.realtime.org.au/liveworks-aeon-a-desiring-flock/ (accessed 15 September 2019).

Mortimer-Sandilands, C. (2005), 'Unnatural Passions?: Notes toward a Queer Ecology', *Invisible Culture: An Electronic Journal for Visual Culture*, 9. Available online: https://www.rochester.edu/in_visible_culture/Issue_9/sandilands.html

Morton, T. (2010), 'Guest Column: Queer Ecology', *PMLA*, 125 (2): 273–82.

Newton, Esther (1979), *Mother Camp: Female Impersonators in America*, Chicago and London: The University of Chicago Press.

Nunn, G. (2019), 'Gay Clubs Are Closing at an Alarming Rate Worldwide – Here's Why', *ABC News*, 21 September. Available online: https://www.abc. net.au/news/2019-09-21/nsw-lockout-laws-going-development-threat-sydney-lgbtqi-scene/11524200 (accessed 27 September 2019).

Perry, K. (2014), 'Fantastic 1st Day in Melb! Got 2 Deliver a Check 2 a Girls School, Pop in to My Pop Up & See the HIGHlarious New Play Calpurnia Descending!', *Twitter*, 13 November. Available online: https://twitter.com/ katyperry/status/532843628352512001 (accessed 13 April 2016).

Philpot, C. (2017), 'Diva Worship as a Queer Poetics of Waste in D. Gilson's *Brit Lit*', in B. E. Drushel and B. M. Peters (eds), *Sontag and the Camp Aesthetic: Advancing New Perspectives*, 63–76, Lanham: Lexington Books.

Robertson, Pamela (1996), *Guilty Pleasures: Feminist Camp from Mae West to Madonna*, Durham: Duke University Press.

Rogers, B. M. and B. Stevens (2012), 'Classical Receptions in Science Fiction', *Classical Receptions Journal*, 4 (1): 127–47.

Ross, A. (1989), *No Respect: Intellectuals & Popular Culture*, New York: Routledge.

Russell, S. A. (2017), 'The Coming Back Out Ball: A Celebration of Pride, Visibility and Strength', *SBS Topics*, 6 October. Available online: https://www. sbs.com.au/topics/sexuality/fast-lane/article/2017/10/06/coming-back-out-ball-celebration-pride-visibility-and-strength (accessed 29 September 2019).

Sangild, T. (2004), 'Glitch: The Beauty of Malfunction', in C. Washburne and M. Derno (eds), *Bad Music: The Music We Love to Hate*, 198–211, New York: Routledge.

Schope, R. D. (2005), 'Who's Afraid of Growing Old?: Gay and Lesbian Perceptions of Aging', *Journal of Gerontological Social Work*, 45 (4): 23–39.

Sontag, S. (1999), 'Notes on "Camp"', in F. Cleto (ed.), *Camp: Queer Aesthetics and the Performing Subject: A Reader*, 53–65, Edinburgh: Edinburgh University Press.

Virilio, P. (2006 [1977]), *Speed and Politics*, trans. Marc Polizzotti, Los Angeles, CA: Semiotext(e).

Webb, C. (2017), 'I'm Coming Out: Gay Elders Embrace New Dance Club', *The Age*, 6 August. Available online: https://www.theage.com.au/national/ victoria/im-coming-out-gay-elders-embrace-new-dance-club-20170806-gxqep4.html (accessed 29 September 2019).

6

Voicing Identity: Theatre Sound and Precarious Subjectivities

Lynne Kendrick and Yaron Shyldkrot

I'll just be a voice in your head

(*Chekhov's First Play*; Dead Centre 2016)

Introduction

Writing about voice is a seemingly contradictory act. Here are voices to be read, sans speech, sans grain, sans sound. How can voices manifest through writing? In the introduction to *Listening and Voice* (2007), Don Ihde reflects on the phenomenology of sound in the visual form of the written word; a 'book is read and its words are seen rather than heard' (2007: xx). For him, the slippage into visuality, which was a gradual yet 'momentous gestalt shift' (1986: 41), was not so much a loss of sonic content but a destabilizing of the voice as it was 'submerged' in writing (1986). Ihde identifies a kind of vocal precarity in this shift; the voice is not so easily confined in the visual sphere, and nor is the origin of it – the speaker. His submerged voice has an ally in the aural sphere, something which the silenced acoustic act of reading can unleash. Ihde finds that 'sometimes there is a "singing" of voice *in* writing. I have often been shocked at "hearing" a friend's voice on reading his or her latest article or book' (2007: xx, original emphasis). I have often thought about this quote, how I cannot read a certain sound studies scholar without hearing her accent, or how I've sometimes attributed phantom voices to writers – hearing, for instance, a certain performance studies scholar all shouty, then being mildly surprised, when I met him, by his gentle Northern English tones. I wonder if those of you that know us may be able to navigate your way through this chapter by hearing our respective voices throughout? And for those of you that do not, how do you hear us?

- *Sorry to intervene but I don't I'm afraid. When I read your work, I don't hear your voice.*

- *Really? I can't not hear you when I read yours.*
- *Isn't the voice the first thing you forget about a person?*
- *Isn't hearing the first sense to awaken, and the voice often the first thing heard? The parent's or the anaesthetist's? Like Ihde, I hear voices that seem to buffer the text; sometimes I think the voice isn't so far removed, it's always already there – and can burst through.*

The written word is a kind of avatar. These words stand for voices, they are icons of speech which can be fashioned to forge certain identities. These words are voices at large, roaming free until they are 'heard' through reading, when they can be re-awakened in the aural sphere. As avatars, words reveal the precarity of voices, their feral and fragile nature: they may be represented or not; heard, or not; 'given a voice' or 'spoken for'. In the case of the precariat, words without certain voices can be avatars of power which listening needs to circumvent, and theatre has long been considered the place whereby the words of other voices can be heard.

In theatre, written words are unleashed into the acoustic realm. It is the art form where voices can gain new speakers as well as new audiences. The itinerant voice at large – also known as the acousmatic, or ventriloquist voice – has emerged as an important tactic for contemporary theatre that presents subjectivities in their making – such as the telephonic and telepathic identities of Complicité's *The Encounter* (2015), or the unseen characters of Darkfield's *Séance* (2016), *Flight* (2018) and *Coma* (2019). Whether in shipping containers, in complete darkness or in more conventional auditoria, these landmark productions and immersive experiences are significant because they were created through the relocation of the voice to the ears through headphones (see Klich 2017). More widely, this relocation takes place through other forms of amplification which act as a mediator between mouth and ear: the voice travels from the actor's body and moves through the loudspeaker into my ear. While my perception might reunite voice and body, giving the impression that the voice is coming/returning to the physical body emitting it, this voice is heard through another mediating source. Other theatrical tactics, such as voice-overs or pre-recorded voices, lip-syncs and glitches demonstrate the creative use of this relocation of voice, body and ear. These are playful sonic strategies that make apparent this mediation that often goes unnoticed.

In light of the current neoliberal crisis, which Marissia Fragkou describes as 'a social ecology of precarity that firmly connects issues of dispossessions, intolerance, fear, xenophobia, uncertainty and disillusionment for the future humans and the planet' (2019: 2–3), we would like to propose that vocal intermedial identities are also aural avatars, which bring forth particular precarities of the subjects (and sometimes the creators) of the work and capture these uncertain perceptions and conceptions of identity, subjectivity and belonging. These avatars are created through the performance of dislocated voices, a conscious destabilization of the voice for the ear in ways that trouble the understanding of who is speaking: how do you know it is I that you hear? This is why, in this chapter, to continue to unsettle the 'I', we merge and perform Lynne and Yaron, through a joint I, an avatar standing for voices not held securely in position.

- *I think that's a good idea.*
- *Thanks.*

This chapter thus lends an ear to voice(s) as a sonic entity, in order to explore precarious subjectivities in sound-led theatre. These voices, I argue, manifest the performance of precarity and, significantly, they attest for identity in peril, troubling vocal location by confounding the ear and thus questioning whose identity they might bring forth. Within the broader and ubiquitous digitized culture that this volume studies, one is continuously confronted by a cacophony of voices: on mobile phones, in public announcements and self-checkouts, through voice operators and social media, whether commuting or at home; I am surrounded by mediated voices. Whether human or machine-generated, recorded or transmitted, disembodied or de-located in space and time, these aural avatars are not simply floating in the newly reformed digital soundscape. Critically, they underscore how voices are – or have become – unstable; unpredictable entities in exile. The growing presence of disembodied voices within the acoustic world can be understood as part of the wider postdigital shift in the ways in which sociality, identity and subjectivity are mediated and performed by means of and as a result of media technologies (Berry and Dieter 2015). To continue and explore this shift and its effects on identity and subjectivity, I use voice as an entry point, asking: what does the dislocation of the voice from body offer to the performance of precarity? What does this separation from the body afford, risk or lead to? How does the precarity of voice reconfigure the relationship between voices and bodies? And, how does the *return* of the voice to the body invite a resounding of identity – and whose?

To explore these questions, I turn to two works by Dublin- and London-based company, Dead Centre: *Lippy* (2013) and *Chekhov's First Play* (2015). Formed in 2012 by Bush Moukarzel and Ben Kidd, the company experiments with creative sound design and layer the visual and the aural as a way of exploring voices *out of sync* – literally and metaphorically. Through these works, I will explore the potential – and even the need – for new, more plural forms of listening. As an errant operation, this sound-led approach to theatre demonstrates how voice can rupture 'fantasies of normality and security' (Fragkou 2019: 5) and might unsettle, problematize and resist different structures of power that demand listening to certain things, in a certain way. In other words, this chapter considers how different voices in Dead Centre's productions *perform,* and how sound and sonic manipulations trouble (the appearance of) 'stable' identities. Listening to the voice beyond mere sematic vocal exchanges, I attune to theatrical strategies that 'unshackle the body from its appearance in the scopic sphere' (Kendrick 2017: 43), so as to trace performative tactics, tropes or dramaturgies of precarity which can generate aural engagements and performances that are not easily fixed because they demand 'more mutable experiences that are relational, changeable and sometimes constitutive of the theatre experience' (Kendrick 2017).

> – *Thanks for the reference.*
> – *You're not collapsing the I.*
> – *Ah, yes, sorry about that – just a glitch.*

Precarity in theatre – vocal delocation in Dead Centre's *Chekhov's First Play*

In the dominant theatre tradition of the well-made play, it is a truth universally acknowledged that if a gun appears in the first act, it will most likely go off in the third. But if the director walks on stage holding a pistol in the prologue, what happens then? It may well be fired earlier, perhaps unpredictably, he could have a pot shot at the cast, or take out the whole audience? In *Chekhov's First Play,* Dead Centre raise the game of the gun by destroying the entire production in the third act with a wrecking ball, but not before they have picked apart the theatrical form that Chekhov's plays inaugurated. *Chekhov's First Play* commences in a traditional 'realist' style – with characters in period dress gathered outside their grand abode, assembled and awaiting the arrival of 'Platanov' (the ostensibly 'titular' figure of Chekhov's first play without title). Yet, from the outset this production places the entire audience on headphones so that all that is seen on the vast stage is heard in close proximity. This intimate aurality is a deliberate tactic to unveil the full workings of the production. This is not just a case of listening to what the actors' say in auditory close-up, more importantly, it is a device that gives exclusive access to the director. Unheard by the actors on stage, but revealed through the headphones, his voice is for the audience's ears only.

Figure 6.1 Dead Centre's *Chekhov's First Play*. Photographer: José Miguel Jiménez

For the prologue the audience meets the Director (with a capital 'D', played by Bush Moukarzel), who enters the stage alone to tell the audience how the show is going to work (see Figure 6.1). He explains that 'I did a version of this show last year and it went OK, but, talking to people afterwards, it became clear that they didn't really get it, they didn't really understand what I was trying to do [...] so I thought I'd set up a Director's commentary to explain what's going on' (Dead Centre 2016: 11). Disappearing to the wings, his performance continues as a comic counterpoint to what is seen on stage: the Director sniggers through the text – 'a rare cock joke from Chekhov there' (16) – remarks on terrible performances, confesses he's slept with one of the actors and soon enough loses patience with how the show is going – 'I think it's best if I just talk over this or I'll never get around to explaining everything' (23). In undercutting the production in this way – 'I *could* just let them speak' (22, original emphasis) – Dead Centre draw on all the clichés' of poor directorial practice; 'it's more the *subtext* I want to tell you about', because 'this play's getting in the way of me explaining it' (21, original emphasis), indicating the infamous authorial tension between the writer's and director's voice that has beset twentieth- and twenty-first-century traditional theatre practice and began with the notorious spats between Chekhov and Stanislavski.[1]

Precariousness is certainly the subject of this production. Dead Centre's choice of text not only sheds light on the vast differences between Chekhov's portrayal of early twentieth-century idle rich/middle class and the inequalities and uncertainties of contemporary precarity, but also draws attention to a futility of recourse to history in neoliberal times. This is in part because neoliberalism has claimed culture for its own, as cultural economy, market regeneration, or entrepreneurial endeavour, and in this mix the theatre is either a benign heritage industry or just 'not work'. But also because neoliberalist precarity works by annexing the individual, it notoriously aligns the 'I' with economy and, in doing so, severs the subject from history in favour of capitalism's promise of progress and bogus growth. Precarity troubles the presence of history. As Nicholas Ridout and Rebecca Schneider point out, 'if precarity is life lived in relation to "someone else's hands," it is also newly experienced by many as life lived in relation to a future that cannot be propped up securely upon the past' (2012: 5). Dead Centre stage an attempt to produce theatrical history in order to draw attention to contemporary anxieties about theatrical labour, of 'acting' but particularly that of 'directing'. The directorial de(con)struction of *Chekhov's First Play* at first serves to foreground the significant irrelevances between Chekhov's world and the twenty-first-century precariat. The director's commentary contains a number of disparaging gripes about these 'wealthy people moaning about their mansions' (2016: 31); the precariat, also known as 'generation rent', and the UK/Ireland's housing crisis are clearly the reference point here. As the production descends into chaos, it becomes clear that it is the precarious nature of the director's authority, his lack of 'hold' on the text, his disgruntled vexation with the labour of his cast, which suggests that this is a production about the state of precarity, typified by anxieties about the labour of performing, the denigration of its value and ultimately, the dislocation of the artists from the work. This is not only achieved by the words of the director's commentary, it is the displacement of the Director's voice that performs this precarity. The director's voice is always already one that defies location in theatre, it is (more often than not) an unseen, yet omnipresent entity not attributable to any one 'body' or 'object'. The presence of this 'artist of the theatre' is akin to the cinematic *acousmêtre*, that notorious cinematic unseen voice which has the power to direct all that one sees and hears.

The acousmatized voice – the Director's voice

While, according to Ihde, voices may sometimes be heard in the visual form of writing, the more dominant theories of vocality – particularly of *acousmatisation* – assert the voice's non-visual presence. In *La Voix au Cinema* (1982), theorist and composer, Michel Chion, traces the emergence of this disembodied, un-see-able voice from silent movies to the talkies. Drawing on Pierre Schaeffer's use of the term *acousmatic* – which refers to the engagement in sounds without the visual presence of their source – Chion articulates the development of the cinematic *acousmêtre*, a voice-being who is yet to be seen but may appear at any time. The *acousmêtre* is a kind of cinematic shadow, such as a narrator, or the 'man behind the curtain' – a *potentially* visualized sound (and a reversal of Schaeffer's *musique concrete*). According to Chion, silent movies were akin to theatre productions, whereas the talkies owed more to early moving image art forms, such as the magic-lantern show, a narrated demonstration of projected images in which the voice occupied a place just outside of the visual frame.

However, in describing the difference between silent movies and sonified cinema, Chion was wrong to say that the theatre is the place of the 'synchronous voice' (1982: 4). From the Ancient Greek amphitheatres to the clumsy acoustics of some nineteenth-century auditoria, the theatrical voice has not always been at one with its emitter and has often struggled to relate to its producing body. However, Chion was not wrong when he pointed out that the elision of voice and body is very much a theatrical construct, and a sophisticated one at that. If theatre's very ontology is based on the circulation of voice, then its aesthetics are articulated by different approaches to its embodiment. The voice leaves bodies and, as twentieth-century psychologists and philosophers have often said, it is impossible for it to return to the hapless entities that emitted it, let alone be authored in its production. Chion argues that it is not possible for the *acousmêtre* to appear in theatre, because the theatre voice is always locatable *somewhere*, whereas the cinematic version is 'at once inside and outside' (1982: 23) of the visual production. However, the introduction of sonic technologies, such as headphones, to the theatre have made the mutable constructs of the theatre voice more apparent; the theatre voice can now, more than ever, occupy the slippery spaces of the cinematic. The separation and layering of the aural and visual have produced a similar liminal sonic space, these are not so much cleaved, but their potential relation is heightened and the voice is their bridge. Dead Centre use this to great effect, employing the performance of acousmatized voices, voices at large that seek 'a place to settle' (1982) as Chion put it. As such, the theatre they make manifests the contemporary crisis of who is speaking on behalf of whom and what kind of listening this demands.

If precarity is the subject of *Chekhov's First Play*, the performance of precariousness in it takes place through the dislocation of the voice. Transmitted entirely through headphones, the director's voice is positioned away from the body that emitted or expressed it. This deliberate staging of the production's voice challenges the stable boundaries of the speaking body; the voice is neither entirely of it nor entirely apart from it. But in the case of the director's voice, a more complex dislocation between the voice and the body is at play. The director's voice is theatre's ultimate acousmatic voice. It is a theatrical version of Chion's 'I voice' – it stands *for* the work, supposedly it is its author, its creator, and the means by which the audience might understand the work. In this sense the voice is also *delocated*, not just dislocated – as in moved slightly out of joint – it is undone from its position. *Chekhov's First Play* hinges on the shifting acousmatic relations of the director's voice that see this move from one of authority to eventual demise. Moving from prologue (addressing the audience as a group), through dialogue (with audience 'individually'), to confessional monologue (soliloquized thoughts 'exclusively' for the audience's ear), this director's voice enacts a range of theatrical tactics, from the comedy of disparaging commentary on the actors' performances, to the futile search for meaning. Dead Centre's Director ultimately loses control of the production.

– But I think Dead Centre's Director is more than an in joke. His directorial descent is not just ineptitude, not just a consequence of finding himself on the circumference of the production. It's not just because it's all going to shit and he can't do anything about it, but because his is a role that ostensibly controls the whole thing – to ensure the cohesion of a unified vision of a single ...
– Collective?
– Voice.

Once the director's commentary drifts into a personal subtext it plays on its proximity to the audience – 'I'll just be a voice in your head' he coos, 'unless, like me, you already have a voice in your head, in which case you'll have two' (Dead Centre 2016: 12). At this collapse of directorial authority the production is punctuated by the 'real world' – delivery pizza, road works – other labouring bodies appear and draw attention to the precarity of performing as, on neoliberalist terms, not work. Eventually the production employs audience participation. After the director has dispensed with his actors, he resorts to audience members to play the long awaited Platonov. The text of the production describes it thus:

> A spotlight appears on a single audience member. The audience member slowly rises from their seat and moves forward onto the stage. They are hearing a different track from everyone else. They are receiving private instructions. They are Platonov.

From here on whatever the seated audience hear will be almost as if they were Platonov. i.e. if someone whispers in to Platonov's right ear, the audience will hear a voice whispering into their right ear. (Dead Centre 2016: 38, original emphasis)

This moment of participation – whether through listening and/or performing – suggests a culmination of the acousmatization of *Chekhov's First Play*. When the audience listens *as* Platonov they are being subjected to the character's acoustic world. In the same vein, as the audience member speaks, they lend their body to the words of the play. These interventions can be understood as an example of Chion's deacousmatization (1982: 27), which is the return of the voice either by the revelation of its 'source' – the speaking body of the voice at large – or by underscoring its absence and instability, by lending of another body to it, albeit temporarily.[2] But this is by no means a resolution of the acousmatic operation. Rather, in this production, the listener is being *subjected to* the voice. At this moment, the Director's voice has interpolated the listener and, considering the type of director that Moukarzel is playing, there is a difficulty in this. As it occupies, this rather insipid, self-obsessed voice takes up residence in the audience's ears in ways perhaps they would rather he did not. In this way, the delocation is somewhat different to Chion's deacousmatization. Dead Centre's delocation is not a return to the body of the director, rather it is a revelation of the reach of the voice's power. Therefore, *Chekhov's First Play* not only offers a clever critique of the precariousness of an art form on the cusp of the hostile takeover of 'director's theatre', they are staging another, more ominous vocal precarity. As he accidently fires the gun, the Director continues to speak to the participant through their headphones, but at this moment the rest of the audience are no longer privy to his voice – it has moved away from us, and settled, like a sound in another ear.

Voice as sound

The voice, as Adrianna Cavarero (2005) and Mladen Dolar (2006) remind us, is sound not speech. And in order to fully explore the reach of voice in staging precarious identities, it is necessary to consider the voice *as sound*. The material, vibrational properties of sound provide a useful model for the movement of the acousmatic voice. Likewise, theories of sonority, vibration and resonance are integral to understanding engagement in it (see, for instance, Nancy 2007; Fiumara 1990; Kendrick 2017). More recently, new materialism has demonstrated ways in which sonic bodies – voicing and listening bodies – are not just affected but are altered, even constituted through vibrational force. In *Sonic Agency* (2018), Brandon LaBelle draws out a politics of sound, stressing how politics does not occur solely within the 'arena of visibility' (2018: 155). For LaBelle, sound's political force is predicated on the subversive power of the non-visual, taking advantage or 'enabling one to skirt the logic of visual capture' (2018: 17), so that the emancipatory potential of the voice is released from the visible presence of the speaking subject. Thus, LaBelle offers a kind of 'ethics *beyond the face*' (2018). Drawing on new materialism, in particular Jane Bennett's *Vibrant Matter* (2010) and Suely Rolnik's 'vibratile body' (1998), he explores the impact of vibrational sound on voicing bodies. For Rolnik, and her exploration of 'today's subjectivities' (what she refers to as 'vibratile body') 'estrangement takes charge of the scene' (Rolnik in LaBelle 2018: 62). Rolnik continues:

> […] destabilized, displaced, discomforted, disoriented, lost in time and space – it's as if we were all 'homeless': Not without a concrete home […], but without the 'at home' of a feeling of oneself, a subjective, palpable consistency familiarity of certain relationships with the world, certain ways of life, certain shared meanings, a certain belief.
>
> (Rolnik in LaBelle 2018)

LaBelle reads Rolnik to inform an understanding of the vibrancy that Bennett speaks of, where vibrant matters are not only the basis for alliances and assemblages between different bodies, but also act as a condition of loss, fragmentation and indeed, estrangement. He concludes that 'adrift in time and space, untethered from any grounded logic, subjectivities are cast into a globalized "homelessness"' (LaBelle 2018: 62). In doing so, the acousmatic voice becomes not so much unshackled from the body, but a sound which *distributes the body* – and by extension identity, and expressions of subjectivity – in its wake. As LaBelle notes:

> The potential of a sounded, voiced, and vibratile subject extends what I can do by also breaking my body apart; in extending this body that acts, that expresses my subjectivity as an intensity of fragments and vectors, I am also made vulnerable to conditions of being *overheard*. In articulating a body in pieces, *unhomed from identity,* one is potentially captured in so many ways – in short, one is picked up, tracked and hacked, monitored and registered, followed and arrested through conditions of vibratility.
>
> (2018: 63, original emphasis)

In other words, the vibrational force of sound is not automatically emancipatory, rather it is in a risky state. However, LaBelle posits an agency of the sounding body, one which becomes possible with attention to the sonic in relation to speech and action. As he attunes to experiences of sound and listening that reverberate through in social and political struggles, his sonic agency attempts to confront conditions of loss and powerlessness (2018: 155). When enacted, this sonic agency brings sound back to speech (and, by extension, I might say voice back to writing).

Crucially, while LaBelle's sounding body is precarious and in peril – it also has potential. Just as Jo Scott in the chapter that follows finds opportunities for plurality through place-mixing and the 'wild' discoveries that might erupt as a consequence of the mix, the uncertainties surrounding the *unhomed* or fragmented sonic body can reveal a range of (often muted) possibilities for listening and being heard. Similarly, Marissia Fragkou conceives material precarity as a social ecology that cuts across a broad spectrum of spaces, people and sociopolitical conditions (2019: 6), featuring in these uncertain times not only as disturbing, or disconcerting but as enabling. This is because this particular ecology 'also implies interdependency and relationality and offers the opportunity for resignifying the tropes of responsibility, solidarity, value and care. In other words, precarity carries the promise to reinvent social relationships through the perception of human life as relational rather than autonomous and sovereign' (2019: 7). When manifested in theatre sound, precarity, as a condition of uncertainty and relationality can mobilize affects which have the potential to trouble ideologies of normality, identity and subjectivity (2019: 183). Therefore, following LaBelle and Fragkou, I ask: how are these 'affects' manifested in theatre practice? Rather than representing its destructive potential, how does sound stage precarity in productive ways, to reveal its possibilities?

One of the techniques adapted by Dead Centre is the setup of one sonic aesthetic that is interrupted by another. The 'sound of theatre', by this I mean the usual sounds made up of voices – audience hubbub, actors' dialogue, direct audience address – often prologue their work. These appear acoustically innocuous, a normative sonic ecology of theatre production. Here I'm drawing on Barry Truax's notion of an 'acoustic ecology' which elucidates the relationship(s) between 'the individual listener and communities of listeners to their environment as mediated by sound', suggesting that the perception of the acoustic space plays a fundamental role in forming these encounters (2017: 258). Truax argues that

[t]he habitual sounds we experience daily both reflect and confirm our sense of physical space, as well as our place within it. Individuals and communities have a definite sense of 'what belongs' in their acoustic space, and what kinds of noise are 'invasions' of that space.

(2017)

- *So what I mean by this is that Dead Centre set up an acoustic ecology, and then continuously reform it.*
- *And the voice?*
- *It becomes one of the invasions.*
- *But in Dead Centre's work, sounds are not always discernible as voice; because these are voices of precarious speakers, those at risk – in risk – and so they manifest as intruders, they arrive as sounds, noises, glitches, not-yet-voices.*

Voice-as-sound-as-glitch

I will now explore how glitches and voices out of sync (as a possible glitch), are ways in which the voice-as-sound stages precarity. Thus far in this chapter, I have shown that precarious subjectivities and authorial power are staged through the cleaving and delocation of the voice. But what of voices that are so precarious that they are unperformable? What of subjectivities that have been absented? Voice-as-glitch is a staging of voice-as-sound that troubles the apparent fixity of theatre's acoustic ecology. These are not manifestations of voice, *but are voices* that demand or facilitate (to echo LaBelle) listening across different, diverse meanings and possible interpretations. Instead of an annoying, overbearing and unwanted disturbance, I want to emphasize the generative and enabling (to echo Fragkou) potential uttered through voices out of sync. Like the acousmatized, these are voices at large but they do not easily find a destination – their resolution to a body (the speaker or the listener's) is troubled by their manifestation as sound. They do not always arrive as semantic meaning – as language or semantic expression – rather, a faulty deacousmatization takes place. Any arrival of the voice-as-glitch to one's ear is as interference, intrusion, interruption because these voices were already in risk at their origin. For those who are accustomed to listening to noise this will probably sound familiar. However, within the growing exploration of the political possibilities and capabilities of sound, I would like to shift or expand the understating of glitches from accidental errors in the system, to intentional interventions in the aural sphere. As theatrical tactics, and performances of precarity, these sonic invasions, I suggest, can resist, unsettle or problematize different structures of power that demand attention to certain voices, in a certain way. Consequently, from the perspective of the ear, I build on LaBelle's notion of 'itinerant listening' (2018), and propose a listening modality that shifts between different possible interpretations. From the perspective of the mouth, I want to emphasize the creative opportunities embedded in the staging of precarious identities, and the potential that glitches and disruptions hold in sonic performances and beyond.

Figure 6.2 Dead Centre's *Lippy*. Photographer: Jeremy Abrahams

If *Chekhov's First Play* stages precarity via proximity of voice to ear, *Lippy* is about their distance. In *Lippy*, Dead Centre attempt to hear the voices of four women who died in a mysterious suicide pact. These women are not present in the 'real time' of the production, nor, arguably, in the (re-)telling of their story. *Lippy* is a production that attempts to evoke these missing voices, continuously on the lookout for 'what they said' (Dead Centre 2014: 24) (see Figure 6.2). In staging this effort, Dead Centre meticulously layer the aural and the visual and harness imaginative sound design to explore voices out of sync – literally and metaphorically. Experimenting with failed lip-reading as well as glitches, noises and out-of-sync lip-syncs as some of its creative compositions, the performance constantly opens a gap between what is said, who is saying it, how things are told and crucially how things are understood or *could be* understood. It is a sonic performance that shifts and travels between different bodies and meanings and as a result reforms or agitates the acoustic ecology within which it reverberates.

Precarity through sound – vocal intervention in *Lippy*

Lippy begins at the end with a post-show discussion following a 'play' the audience has not seen, telling a story they did not hear. This post-show 'talk' is mostly a conversation between the interviewer – Bush Moukarzel (also the playwright and co-creator of the show, together with director Ben Kidd) and the lip-reader, one of the actors in the unseen show. The latter – at least in the fictional world – previously collaborated with Ben (the director) trying to make a show about the daunting story of the Mulrooneys – an aunt (Frances) and her three nieces (Josephine, Catherine and Bridg-Ruth) who starved themselves to death in mysterious circumstances. As they enthuse about the production, they discuss their initial ideas for making a show about lip-reading. Mark O'Halaran, it transpires, earns a real living lip-reading for the Gardee (the Irish police) and he invites Moukarzel to take part in a demonstration of this to reveal how (in)accurate it can be. Donning headphones to block out any acoustic content, O'Halaran proceeds to read what Moukarzel says to the audience, initially to much comic effect. It is this pivotal moment in the show, the separation of listener from speaker, which introduces the subject of *Lippy*. O'Halaran was employed to view the last seen footage of two of the Mulrooney sisters as they were caught on CCTV on their final visit to town. Not long after, the family was found surrounded by mountains of shredded documents, attempts at an erased existence for no discernible reason. The only possible witness to the reason why they began their end is O'Halaran, who did not hear their voices but 'saw what they said' (Dead Centre 2014: 27). Also on stage is Adam, the sound designer who, having seemingly finished his technical duties for the evening, is catching up on email. The sound of the outlook 'sent' notification is one of a series of hitches, noises, feedbacks, buzzes and faults that are woven throughout this conversation and the entire performance, which continuously destabilize the sonic-world of the show.

Lippy interrupts definitiveness, generating an acoustic ecology which, unlike Truax's version, defies clear-cut distinctions between what fits and what does not: a sonic world formed or defined by its glitches. Listening to *Lippy* brings about an interesting tension. On the one hand, the performance problematizes what belongs or does not belong within the acoustic space, especially if one attends the performance with the expectation of clearly following a plot, listening to text spoken by actors and being able to understand the semantic meaning of what is said. These ongoing disruptions appear to not belong as they stand in the way of 'conventional' theatrical performances where sound 'supports' text and story. On the other hand, a continuous incoherent soundscape forms (or reforms) an acoustic ecology where eventually, glitch becomes the new flow, an aural sphere where glitches and disruption are the expected sonic 'norm'. Either way, I argue, these acoustic entities are not simply sonic objects out of place. Rather, through the performance of sound and voice *Lippy* changes habitual sonic patterns which can encourage listeners to become attuned to more destabilized acoustic ecologies, not only directing attention to what largely remains unheard or ignored, but critically inviting a reconsideration of 'what fits' and why.

Dead Centre's destabilized acoustic ecology creates the sonic conditions ripe for LaBelle's sonic agency. This agency is activated by what LaBelle terms 'itinerant listening', a listening modality through which I want to conceptualize the potential of glitches in sonic performances not only to present, but to reveal the *enabling* potential of precarity to reconsider and reconfigure seemingly stable identities and acoustic ecologies. To explore how listening as an intervention is manifested, LaBelle elaborates on several sonic 'figures' and/or listening modalities, which he conceives both as 'bodies of knowledge as well as constructs from which to suggest potential tactics and ways of *being political*' through sound (2018: 16–17, original emphasis). As noisy, quiet or unstable sonic actants, these gestures – namely, the invisible, the overheard, the itinerant, and the weak – resist, expand, unsettle or threaten constructs of political dominance, social order and systems of power (2018). For LaBelle, each sonic figure or listening mode can, in its way, become a force, a 'vector of power' (63) nodding towards the potential for 'creative resistance' (104). In this vein, 'an unfamiliar or muted voice' might demand greater consideration (155); the voice of 'the marginal and the different' (69) can reverberate and create affects, and a strange body of sound can move so that it is 'dizzying the certainty of any singular perspective' (102). Thus, itinerant (or *shifting*) listening – as in, shifting between meanings, or reforming what is perceived – allows one to listen across a concurrent 'what is that sound' and 'what else it could be'.

This is useful for understanding the potency of glitches and voices out of sync as well as the political work manifested in *Lippy*. LaBelle theorizes itinerant listening as a strategy for public life, 'by which identities and communities figure in and amongst the crowd' (2017: 285). However, if sociality is understood as a collection of encounters, these relations are also 'prone to being formed through interruptions and agitations' (LaBelle 2018: 61). In that sense, to embrace sound's inherent restlessness allows one to 'unsettle and problematize directives of control and domination, searching instead for ways of being and doing that push at the seams of particular systems' (LaBelle 2018: 21). By demanding a less fixed listening experience – fixity here could be attached to meaning, to source, to space, to a body, to language, etc. – glitch can upset the expectation of a singular permanent meaning, rendering the auditory precarious. It is not that glitches erase individual perspectives, but rather, they invite listening in/through multiplicity, revealing the possible plurality of the heard. As one is listening to a glitched sound object, new interpretations can continuously emerge. Thus, rather than accidental ticks and faults in the system, I wish to challenge this common view of glitches, and suggest how they can be understood as an errant operation, which facilitates less concrete and more plural listening experiences. As Jo Scott explores in the next chapter of this book, the glitch displays multiple processes and reveals the uneasy intersections between them.

In her glitch studies manifesto, Rosa Menkman defines glitch as a 'wonderful interruption that shifts an object away from its ordinary form and discourse, towards the ruins of destroyed meaning' (2011: 340). While I agree with the conception of how these slippages modify the trajectory of listening, I am not entirely convinced by the extremity of 'ruins' which also downplays smaller trembles in the status quo. For Menkman, '[t]he glitch is often perceived as an unexpected and abnormal modus operandi, a break from (one of) the many flows (of expectations) within a technological system' (2011: 341). Expanding Menkman's definition, I approach glitch more broadly. From this perspective, *Lippy* is full of glitches, comprised of an excess of disruptions and delocations of voice, body and meaning. Dead Centre deliberately use accidents and disruptions to tear and defy synchronicity, straying away from the expected unity of voice and mouth, body and expression.

Beyond the aforementioned noises and agitations in *Lippy*, is song. Following the lip-reading experiment, the Sound Designer, Adam, initiates a round of 'When you were born you cried/And the world rejoiced./Live your life so that when you die./The world cries and you rejoice' (Dead Centre 2014: 27). He begins again, adding to the playback of the first round. And then again. And again. His voice is looped as he sings, clashing different lines and creating an open-ended echo. The glitched song seems to act as an incantation for the untold story of the Mulrooneys as the stage opens up and the dimly lit interior of their home appears. Filled with huge piles of shredded material, several forensics clad in full-white suits drift through the room – these are the Mulrooneys, ghosting their story, buffering the production and making every attempt to voice through the glitches and accidents the production affords (see Figure 6.3).

At one point, Bridg-Ruth is lying down while Josephine holds the microphone above her. Catherine swings the microphone like a pendulum: 'We hear the speech intermittently, only when the microphone is in range' (2014: 44). As the dialogue between the interviewer and lip-reader is suddenly muted, it continues in silence – 'lips moving, no sound' (27). Bridg-Ruth attempts to deliver a speech while the other women cover their ears and the sound of a signal failure interrupts her, swallowing most of her speech. When she tries again, she's interrupted by a coughing fit from Frances. Bridg-Ruth talks to Catherine, their lips move and sync with the words heard,

Figure 6.3 Dead Centre's *Lippy*. Photographer: Jeremy Abrahams

only their voices are extremely low-pitched male voices. Muffled speech is heard through a mask. A sudden lip-sync to 'Crying in the chapel', with the lip-reader as Don McLean's and the Mulrooneys as the backup vocals. Interrupting her monologue, Catherine covers Bridg-Ruth's mouth and a pre-recorded text continues. At some point, the lip-reader has stopped speaking while his voice carries on – 'It is, as if he is listening to something he has said in the past. Something that has never left him' (28). Text echoes between scenes. The lip-reader vocalizes inaudible mouth movements. Catherine appears to be speaking when suddenly her image is closed off and is replaced by a projection of a huge mouth covering the whole screen. A general hubbub fills the room: a recording of the audience from when they entered the auditorium. It is an interval that happens during the show and a chance for the audience to hear themselves.

This is how sound in *Lippy* glitches and loses sync; how voice and body are no longer (if they ever were) housed in the same (stable) figure. The visual and aural are pulled apart. Voices and bodies are stretched and reformed, extended and fragmented. Both the signal and the body disintegrate. Certainties and performances of fixed identity crumble. Whether it is a cacophony of voices, sharp noises or incoherent fragments, *Lippy* strains towards hearing *differently*. The performance troubles borders between bodies, and summons different, multiple meanings and manifestations of subjectivity through itinerant sonic expressions.

Two previous accounts approach *Lippy* through questions of representation
and the different modes of representation (or misrepresentation) the
performance employs (Sack 2015; Venn 2019), specifically within the
contexts of Ireland and gender, and with particular concern to issues of
authorship and the ethics of engaging with suicide. Daniel Sack, for instance,
notes how in the Don McLean lip-sync, the four women play 'the embodied
vessels for a men's quartet' and 'do not possess their own voices' (2015: 5). In
the same vein, as Catherine tries to say: 'It didn't happen like this ... I didn't
say this ... I didn't say any of this' (Dead Centre 2014: 36), a male voice utters
these words. Likewise, Jon Venn notes that Bush Moukarzel and Ben Kidd,
the creators of *Lippy* are not Irish, nor are they women, and as such they
might be telling a story which might not be theirs to tell (2019: 26).

– *Can I just say something? I think Sack and Venn both miss the point; the
  problem is the idea that Women's voices are disconnected from bodies.*[3]
– *I'm kind of fed up of the idea that women are vessels easily filled by the
  voices of others. Isn't Dead Centre's production about the searching for
  what the Mulrooneys said through the revelation of the conditions that
  silenced them? And what they perform is not their silence (far from it) but
  the emergence of their voices?*
– *Yes, it might not be the creators' story to tell, but they engage in the
  difficulty of telling it. Instead of speaking, they keep asking: what or who
  are you listening to?*[4]

Indeed, the perilous and unstable state/condition that the Mulrooneys find
themselves in is not alien to wider considerations of precarity. Especially
if precarity is understood as 'a condition that speaks to practices of
marginalization and invisibility' (Fragkou 2019: 4). However, to sidestep
the risk of a 'universalizing vocabulary of precarity', instead of continuously
rehearsing the Irish family's fragility and helplessness, I wish to focus on
'affective mapping of the possibilities for resistance' (Nyong'o 2013: 158).
So while the Mulrooneys can be seen as figures who did not always choose
to be placed in a vulnerable position, their actions and resistance can be
considered through LaBelle's formulation of the 'weak' put forward as 'a
position of strength, a feature whose qualities enable us to slow down and
attune to vulnerable figures' (2018: 20). In other words, their voice is not
necessarily being staged as that which is silenced or kidnapped by others.
Rather and paradoxically, by interfering with the clarity of voice, *Lippy*
draws more attention to these figures at risk, inviting the audience to listen
again and differently to these precarious subjectivities, or the traces they
have left behind. *Lippy* dislocates and delocates voice and body in ways that

deconstruct the expectation of 'accurately' representing or performing the Mulrooneys' story. For me, the inability to represent can be perceived as part of the failure to deacousmatize, to bring voice back to the body. As such, *Lippy* produces bodies and voices that are continuously displaced, politically delocated, trapped in a glitch. With their voices out of sync, the Mulrooneys become ghost-like figures, precarious entities of faulty avatars, echoing something (a voice, a story) that extends an unstable – if existing – origin. Much like Scott's notion of place-mixing which is 'avatoring' city wildness, in trying to refigure the flow that was glitched, *Lippy* tells us as much about *how* we listen, as opposed to how a story is told or represented.

Conclusion

Chekhov's First Play stages precarity throughout. Through the collapse of the text and theatrical labour Dead Centre play with the precariousness of audience, subjecting them to and subjectifying them with the work, by making audible the all-powerful yet unheard voice of the director or listening and performing as if they were Platonov. Played at such close proximity to the audience's ears, this production creates an avatar-audience. The delocated voice produces a precarious listener, a quasi-performer, who is interpolated into the work. *Lippy* presents its audience with almost the opposite; precarious subjectivities so far removed from their identities that they need significant sonic effort to arrive, glitching, interfering through faulty signals and the noise of disempowerment. In both cases, sound is no longer merely an effect, or there to support text and story. Instead, it becomes a tactic of transforming, reshaping and articulating contemporary subjectivities. Taking into account how within a postdigital culture, media technologies play a crucial role in performing and transmitting those subjectivities – and how it is exactly because of these technologies that acoustic ecologies are flooded with new and unexpected (yet unstable) voices – in this chapter, I've suggested how voicing identity is in the throes of theatre sound and sound-led theatre. It is through sound that bodies come into relation to voices, their politics expressed not by the cleaving, but by the reconfiguration of both through this act, whether by being attuned to sound's delocation and the unveiling of its power, or by setting listening loose via glitch to hear voices anew.

Earlier I asked, how does the *return* of the voice to the body *through performance* invite a resounding of identity, and whose? Perhaps the answer to this question is that subjectivities in *Chekhov's First Play* and *Lippy* are not necessarily found through identification. Rather, this work demonstrates a need to expose the precarity of subjectivity in and of itself, which they achieve through the aesthetics and difficulties of contemporary vocality. Furthermore, the sounds of Dead Centre's precarious subjectivities are a constant intervention in the visual sphere. Thus, the voice holds the capacity to disrupt what one sees, because, particularly in the case of *Lippy*, it is not possible to clearly see what they said.

Roy Sorenson asked the question, 'Are you *seeing* this sentence or are you *hearing* it?' (2009: 128, original emphasis). And in the introduction to this chapter I proposed that one can hear the voice of the writer, and that this might be instrumental in hearing me and not you. By me, I mean I and I (Lynne and Yaron), by you – the 'reader'. In terms of Dead Centre's theatre, this precarious 'author function' is intrinsic to the unsettling aurality of their work, from delocation to disturbance of voices, their work hinges on the collapse of certainty between the voice and identity, body and speaker.

- *Yet theatre has always been a place of vocal delocation.*
- *So what Dead Centre achieve is a sense of hope in their work. Their precarity is one that embraces this delocation as a way of bringing othered voices in, it generates hope or a call for action – that, in the case of Chekhov's First Play, we may see the power that the singular voice can attempt to exert; and that, in the case of Lippy, the Mulrooneys may be heard.*
- *And that I'll be a voice in your head, unless, like me, you already have one, in which case you'll have three.*

Acknowledgement

Lynne Kendrick and Yaron Shyldkrot would like to thank Dead Centre and especially Ben Kidd and Bush Moukarzel for their generosity and sharing footage of their work.

Notes

1   Though directorial practice has been notoriously difficult to capture other than through the 'artist of the theatre's' account (see Delgado and Heritage 1996; Giannachi and Luckhurst 1999; Schneider and Cody 2002; Shepherd 2012), accounts of Anton Chekhov and Konstantin Stanislavski's disagreements have provided useful evidence of the arrival of a 'director's theatre' (see Braun 1982). Of all Chekhov's contestations with Stanislavski's directorial autonomy, the presence of extraneous sound effects seems to

cause the worst offence; the notorious opening cacophony of church bells, drunkards, frogs and corncrakes for *The Seagull* (see Magarshack 1952) before a word of the text was uttered caused particular consternation as the director shifted to an authorial rather than a producerly function and, according to Chekhov, an inaccurate one at that.

2 For Chion de-acousmatization is an unveiling of the *acousmêtre*, and a loss of power at the revelation of its visual source. It also represents a coming to rest of the voice, a '*place* [where] the human and mortal body where the voice will henceforth be lodged (1982: 28). Subsequent scholars have developed the idea of a de-acousmatization as dismantling of the voice. Rather than a return to its source the journey of the voice may trouble the idea of a knowable 'speaker', rendering identity difficult (Verstraete 2011) or deacousmatization an impossible operation (Dolar 2006).

3 The fact that women's bodies first appear, then speak, is a common symptom of 'woman' as object, a normalized sexist bias of much literature, drama, cinema and theatre production, deeply rooted in a history of the disembodied – and dangerous – female voice: the Sirens. In twentieth-century production, much of the blame is levelled at the dominance of psychoanalysis, which key feminist critiques have sought to disrupt (Laura Mulvey, Helene Cixous, Julia Kristeva) celebrating the pre-semantic, vocalic nature of feminist discourse. More recently, Adriana Cavarero has offered alternative theories of voices as not singular but relational, as a way of disrupting the separation of voice from the (female) body that the vocalic still upholds. Her theory is not that women need to be reconnected with their voice, but that they already had it in the first place. For Cavarero (following Arendt) another political possibility of the female voice is at stake. She explains: '[I]n the western macrotext, the voice has always been a stereotypically feminine element. Instead of simply denouncing this stereotypical value (and the conceptual trail that carries it: woman/voice/body/animality/monstruosity/Sirens/lethality), my choice has been to valorize it, to give value to the voice as the expression of an embodied uniqueness constitutively relational and, as such, capable of disrupting logocentric structures' (Caverero in Thomaidis and Pinna 2018: 85).

4 Venn interestingly unpacks a complexity of lip-reading, which sits at the heart of *Lippy*, and is introduced initially as a 'mechanism of surveillance', when the lip-reader mentions he was hired to look at CCTV footage to decipher what the Mulrooneys said. Lip-reading then, as Venn posits, is 'an attempt to forge a voice out of the visual. The Lip Reader takes the silent moving lips and grafts a meaning out of their motions. [it is] an active and forceful implantation of meaning' (2019: 27). Of course, 'taking silence and manufacturing voice' holds the possibility of 'misunderstanding, of incorrectly putting words to lips' (2019: 28) – something which *Lippy* makes evident quite early on, as the lip-reader fails to interpret the interviewer's words correctly. For Venn, the power of interpretation

risks taking advantage or even reclaiming a silent voice. The lip-reader is speaking out a dialogue, as the Mulrooneys mouth words that become his (2019: 27). However, the problem here is the implication that there is only one fixed interpretation and one either gets it right or wrong.

References

Berry, D. M. and M. Dieter, eds (2015), *Postdigital Aesthetics: Art, Computation and Design*, Basingstoke: Palgrave Macmillan.

Braun, E. (1982), *The Director and the Stage: From Naturalism to Grotowski*, London: Methuen.

Cavarero, A. (2005), *For More Than One Voice: Towards a Philosophy of Vocal Expression*, Stanford: Stanford University Press.

Chekhov, A. and K. Stanislavski ([1904] 1952), *The Seagull Produced by Stanislavski/The Seagull by Anton Chekhov Production Score for the Moscow Art Theatre*, trans. D. Magarshack, London: Dobson.

Chion, M. (1982), *The Voice in Cinema*, trans. C. Gorbman, New York: Columbia University Press.

Dead Centre (2014), *Lippy*, London: Oberon Books.

Dead Centre (2016), *Chekhov's First Play*, London: Oberon Books.

Delgado, M. and P. Heritage (1996), *In Contact with the Gods? Directors Talk Theatre*, Manchester: Manchester University Press.

Dolar, M. (2006), *A Voice and Nothing More*, Cambridge, MA and London: MIT Press.

Fiumara, G. C. (1990), *The Other Side of Language: A Philosophy of Listening*, trans. Charles Lambert, London: Routledge.

Fragkou, M. (2019), *Ecologies of Precarity in Twenty-First Century Theatre: Politics, Affect, Responsibility*, London: Bloomsbury Publishing.

Giannachi, G. and M. Luckhurst (1999), *On Directing: Interviews with Directors*, Basingstoke: Palgrave Macmillan.

Ihde, D. (1986), *The Consequences of Phenomenology*, Albany: SUNY.

Ihde, D. (2007), *Listening and Voice: Phenomenologies of Sound*, Albany: SUNY.

Kendrick, L. (2017), *Theatre Aurality*, London: Palgrave Macmillan.

Klich, R. (2017), 'Amplifying Sensory Spaces: The In- and Out-Puts of Headphone Theatre', *Contemporary Theatre Review*, 27 (3): 366–78.

LaBelle, B. (2017), 'Restless Acoustics, Emergent Publics', in M. Cobussen, V. Meelberg, and B. Truax (eds), *The Routledge Companion to Sounding Art*, 275–86, Oxon and New York: Routledge.

LaBelle, B. (2018), *Sonic Agency: Sound and Emergent Forms of Resistance*, London: Goldsmiths Press.

Menkman, R. (2011), 'Glitch Studies Manifesto', *Video Vortex Reader II: Moving Images beyond YouTube*, 336–47.

Nancy, J. L. (2007), *Listening*, trans. Charlotte Mandell, New York: Fordham University Press.

Nyong'o, Tavia (2013), 'Situating Precarity between the Body and the Commons', *Women & Performance: A Journal of Feminist Theory*, 23 (2): 157–61.

Ridout, N. and R. Schneider (2012), 'Precarity and Performance: Introduction', *TDR*, 56 (4): 5–9.

Sack, D. (2015), 'Not Not I: Undoing Representation with Dead Centre's *Lippy*', *European Stages*, 4 (1): 1–9.

Schneider, R. and G. H. Cody (2002), *Re:Direction: A Practical and Theoretical Guide*, London and New York: Routledge.

Shepherd, S. (2012), *Direction: Readings in Theatre Practice*, Basingstoke: Palgrave Macmillan.

Sorensen, R. (2009), 'Hearing Silence: The Perception and Introspection of Absences', in M. Nudds and C. O'Callaghan (eds), *Sounds and Perception: New Philosophical Essays*, 126–45, New York: Oxford University Press.

Thomaidis, K. and I. Pinna (2018), 'Towards a Hopeful Plurality of Democracy: An Interview on Vocal Ontology with Adriana Cavarero', *Journal of Interdisciplinary Voice Studies*, 3 (1): 81–93.

Truax, B. (2017), 'Acoustic Space, Community, and Virtual Soundscapes', in M. Cobussen, V. Meelberg, and B. Truax (eds), *The Routledge Companion to Sounding Art*, 253–64, Oxon and New York: Routledge.

Venn, J. (2019), 'It Didn't Happen Like This: Suicide, Voice and Witnessing in Dead Centre's Lippy', *Journal of Interdisciplinary Voice Studies*, 4 (1): 21–36.

Verstraete, P. (2011), 'Radical Vocality, Auditory Distress and Disembodied Voice: The Resolution of the Voice-Body in The Wooster Group's *La Didone*', in L. Kendrick and D. Roesner (eds), *Theatre Noise: The Sound of Performance*, 82–96, Newcastle: CSP.

7

Postdigital Place-Mixing in the Wild City

Jo Scott

Preamble: The wild city

This city is wild

Not in the ways you might immediately imagine, though those are there too ... wild, code breaking, 'free-will' asserting, spontaneous human acts.

There are also the wild processes that ferociously destroy and reshape the lived environment. The vertiginous lift towers, looming moodily into the sky to indicate another space of development. The cranes and cranes and cranes, loping above us. The churning lorries and HGVs carving up the streets. Of course, these are human processes, made up by us, dreamed and designed by us and built by us, but somehow, it all feels a little beyond what we have control of – more like what Jack Turner calls the 'ceaseless process of the ever new, the generative power of autonomous processes and self-organisation' (2013: 49).

Perhaps it is understandable to feel this sense of edgy unsettled fervour in the face of mass redevelopment – that which is out of control, that which is beyond. Michael Taussig describes wildness as 'the spirit of the unknown and the disorderly, loose in the forest encircling the city and sown land' (1987: 289). No longer encircling the city – its wild and ferocious energy emanates from within, arises from the pavements, coalesces and releases in the swirling air around the lift shaft, the low ominous groan of the machinery, the slap of mud and grit.

And yet ... here and now, that wildness – the ferocious hunt for capital and the scraping of pockets of land to find it – is somehow distant. Here, on the litter-strewn streets, with the overflow of human life, everything remains the same. The tendrils of that pioneer spirit, breaking ground again and again, recede into boarded up buildings and overflowing bins. A different wildness here then.

Different again, those wild, green spaces, sunk by the river, lost in self-contemplation, echoing with ghosts of human activity, while sloughing off the past to revel in the rich processes of the present – growth, renewal, decay and ceaseless activity. Not the countryside, not the park, not the escape from the city or the ordering of nature, but wild spaces, where nature has us in its grip, reclaiming just a slice of what the ground-scraping automatons have left behind.

And between these spaces sits an entanglement of wild energies and forces, not battling, but intermingling and sparking and restlessly unsettling. Taussig claims that wildness 'challenges the unity of the symbol', that it 'pries open this unity and in its place creates slippage and a grinding articulation between signifier and signified'. He claims wildness as 'the death space of signification' (1987: 219).

Here, in the wild city – the city of wild and unfettered development, the city of overflowing waste and burning buildings and smashed windows, the city of sharp green Spring growth and the majestic overrunning of ivy and balsam and buddleia and all those inimitable plants that just *grow*. Here, there is no 'unity' of the symbol. It has been pried and forced and nail-splittingly heaved open – the city grinds against itself, failing articulation, failing in representation and exploding in its own ongoing, ceaselessness. It doesn't mean anything, it doesn't say anything – it is the 'death space' of signification.

Introduction

The preamble above evokes feelings and shapes of wildness that I connect with the experience of living in a city now. The preamble text 'walks before' this chapter in order to offer a flavour of the 'wild city' and the different ways it manifests, grows and reshapes itself, through a range of human and non-human processes. It also insinuates itself into the arguments and practices offered below – an insistent growth in and through the forming of my thoughts about the work I am making in this area. These are ideas I am writing with and there is an instability inherent in that act – particularly the wish for the wild ideas to flow through and interrupt the neatly serried ranks of letters on the page. This connects to Kendrick and Shyldkrot's opening question in the adjacent chapter as to how voices manifest through writing in their chapter. Their roaming voices at large feel like wild forces such as those characterized above, escaping confinement and singular form, making insistent incursions into our thoughts, our ears, our imaginations, 'always already there' and ready to 'burst through'.

This chapter offers an account of practices that I have come to think of as 'place-mixing' in wild urban landscapes. These practices have a relationship with wildness – the wildness of the city, nature and the digital processes that underpin and inform how they are made. They also have an oppositional tinge or flavour, if not a particular force or intent. They are made in a questioning way – a way that queries how the digital device and its computational processes meet the processes of the city and those of nature in urban spaces. As such, they sit within an emergent postdigital lineage of practice that attempts to unpick some of the relationships between the material and the digital, the computational and the world it represents and reshapes. In this writing, I want to open up the processes that constitute postdigital place-mixing and particularly its relationship with the wildness of contemporary urban landscapes.

As part of this opening up of very current making processes, I propose a positioning of this practice that is distinct from place-*making*, particularly when that making is understood as a process 'by which we can shape our public realm in order to maximize shared value' (Project for Public Spaces 2018), with a focus on 'beautifying, cleaning, and regenerating public spaces for promoting development and attracting investment' (Bedoya in Toolis 2017: 186). As Alesia Montgomery points out in her study of 'market-driven place-making' in Detroit, such practices are aligned with a commercial agenda, through 'increasing commerce and rents in an area by crafting vibrant streetscapes' (2016: 776–7). As outlined below, the various activities of place-making in cities often exceed and counteract such agendas, but their intent is still often about making places better, and not always for current residents. Place-mixing has a different intention and focus. It constitutes a series of encounters with city-places as a 'set of processes, meeting and weaving together at a particular locus' (Massey 1994: 154). The curious, but broadly sceptical approaches to digitally mixing wild elements of that urban landscape are a way of feeling and thinking through those elements in active and interrogative ways – it is a way of finding out. As a practice, place-mixing is longitudinal, speculative, searching – it takes place over time through a series of encounters and crucially, it does not seek to make or remake the places in question; rather it seeks to discover and to question the forces and processes at play in the wild city.

The chapter also works to engage and combine a number of discourses, mirroring the ways in which the practices in question enact an exploratory mixing of elements to 'rupture, unsettle, animate, and reverberate' (Vannini 2015: 5). The lines of enquiry range through theories of wildness, ideas of place-making and postdigital theory, practice and philosophy, led by a non-representational perspective and interest in relations between these ideas and practices – 'associations, mutual formations, ecologies, constellations, and co-fabrications' (Vannini 2015: 8). Both the writing and the practices seek 'affective resonances' or 'novel reverberations' between materials and movements, feelings and perspectives (12). In this way, the chapter echoes the 'affective resonances' that happen in my repeated encounters with the city as an entanglement of wild energies and forces, meeting and mingling in the vast computational energy and 'reverberations' of a digital device.

Intermedial practices and place-mixing

We begin with the practice – its actions, directions and perspectives. I have been making what I broadly term intermedial practice for the past eight years. Arising from a dissatisfaction with what my body provided in its capacities to perform and create, this dissatisfaction was aligned with a wish to disrupt, outsource, redirect and re-form creative responses to the world through technological interfaces. I became particularly drawn to using such interfaces to mix a range of materials in real time – video and sound, voice and song, text and object – and the fleeting feelings that this mixing practice generated between the materials, my actions and the technological processes in play. From experimentation with how to mix materials in live events and in conjunction with those present, I then started to explore how these mixes might be employed to respond to particular ideas, contexts and frameworks.

My move to the city of Salford (see Scott 2017) was the catalyst for using these acts of mixing to address place, specifically this new, urban place I had made my home. The practices started to reach out into the city through digital mixing workshops for local residents, fixed media installations, performances and online artworks.[1] Here, sound, song, video and text were combined to offer an unsettled perspective of the contrasts, grafts and uncomfortable counterpoints I experienced in the city between rapid redevelopment and urban decay, between riotous green spaces and the slew of human waste, between the wild imaginings of the future and the echoes of the past – regeneration, tradition, heritage, abandonment.

The practice is inherently restless. Arising primarily from improvised live events, the mixes I make are still formulated through live processes of recording and capturing sound, text, song and image, and are rarely refined or shaped in any meaningful way beyond their mixing in live events or the initial combinations I create on my laptop. This rough, always-forming, never-quite-finished approach to making is led by chasing affects that manifest initially in the encounter between me, a digital device and a place/subject and then shift, rupture and re-form in the live mix with other materials and actions. This resonates with understanding affects as forces, arising from and passing through various human and non-human forms as 'properties, competencies, modalities, energies, attunements, arrangements and intensities of differing texture, temporality, velocity and spatiality' (Lorimer in Vannini 2015: 5). In relation to this practice, it means understanding feeling, not as something that is experienced by and contained within a singular human form, but as moving forces happening between the various elements in an encounter, mix or 'arrangement'. An example, evoked in the preamble, is walking through a city environment and encountering a void, ready for redevelopment. The space seethes with a strange energy created through both its emptiness and ferocious activity, through its textural carving out of the landscape, the velocity of its happening and the catch of breath in my throat, as I encounter the scale of the lift shaft that has shot up through the lens of a camera phone. As Massumi (2002) characterizes, these 'autonomous' forces escape confinement in individual bodies and emanate within and through particular shifting engagements and arrangements in the world. Crucial to this practice is engaging with affects as forming through active encounters and relations (Spinoza in Thrift 2008) between bodies and things. In the practice of 'place-mixing', these active encounters happen between digital devices, places and bodies, both in the initial meeting of these elements and then 'in the mix' of their reformulation through software and code.

My encounter with contemporary Salford (as referenced above) formed this interest in 'place-mixing' – how the digital-material mixes I was making might speak of and to the city, might find routes through its contradictions, might form a productive encounter with its feelings and materials. In particular, this most recent phase of place-mixing has focused on wild, green city spaces, also known as 'urban wildscapes'. This term describes

> urban spaces where natural as opposed to human agency appears to be shaping the land, especially where there is spontaneous growth of vegetation through natural succession. Such wildscapes can exist at different scales, from cracks in the pavement, to much more extensive urban landscapes, including woodland, unused allotments, river corridors and derelict or brownfield sites.
>
> (Jorgensen in Jorgensen and Keenan 2012: 1)

These spaces – exhibiting simultaneously human neglect and non-human abundancy – are dense with meanings and feelings. They are often celebrated and relished, alongside contemporary urban ruins, in writing that revels in their playful, wild and oppositional qualities (Edensor 2005; Farley and Symmons Roberts 2012; Jorgensen and Keenan 2012), particularly the alternative they represent to ordered and homogenized urban places. However, urban wildscapes are also often situated in deprived neighbourhoods, where they can be signs of ruination, poverty and neglect, existing in abandoned, devalued and unloved places. The complexity of these places and what they mean in the broader context of the city are of interest to me as a practitioner and researcher, along with the diverse affects that emerge in and through their material growth and symbolic decay.

This interest is represented in some early place-mixing that focused on a nearby 'urban wildscape' called Kersal Dale (see Scott 2020) and resulted in mixes such as *Sycamore* (2018).[2] The Dale is a lush, green, wild urban woodland, established as a local nature reserve in the wake of landslides in the 1920s that ruined the houses of rich industrialists who had settled there and effectively ended its time as a space of human habitation. My fascination with this place happens at the intersection of the ghosts of its past – in the ruins of grand houses, now covered in moss, avenues of trees and ornamental ponds gone wild – and its present as a space of riotous green growth. It also happens in the duality of the dale as a peaceful haven in the city and the threat that is associated with wild, urban woodlands of this nature. As Jorgensen and Tylecote (2007) indicate, after a survey of residents' attitudes towards surrounding woodland in Birchwood, Warrington New Town, 'a quarter of those who identified local green and woodland spaces as their favourite places in the locality also said that they would feel unsafe if they were alone in them' (444).

As I articulated in a previous article, the practice 'occupies this "ambivalent interstice", in its imaginings of the dale's captive past – enacted mainly through text and song – in combination with digital manipulation of the feral present of the woodland, through video mixing' (Scott 2020). The initial mixes emerged from solitary walks in the dale, where I 'sampled' the environment through capturing video, images and sounds and then remixed these with refrains and scraps of layered vocals that were recorded quickly following each walk. The video mix was created in real time, using the software Modul8[3] to manipulate the footage, resulting in intersections between live animation and the footage, as well as 'tiled' images of natural growth in the wildscape that I reflect on below in more detail.

Though many of my place-mixing encounters emerge from urban wildscapes in my immediate vicinity, they also find echoes in the wider contexts of the cityscape (evoked in the preamble) – re-forming, resisting, ceaseless and careless – particularly the ways in which the cities of Manchester and Salford are currently in the throes of mass, corporate redevelopment. This political, social and material process of extensive change sits beyond the abandoned wildscapes of my practices and yet still rears and appears and interrupts the forming and thinking and feeling of the work – an affective echo or strain that passes through its processes and occasionally, as Taussig describes, 'encircles' its making in a more concerted way. This wild feeling and its 'grinding articulation' are particularly evident in my work in places like the Meadow in East Salford – a teardrop wild green space, existing in a loop of the River Irwell and increasingly overhung and encircled by mass blocks of new development. In this mix,[4] the forces of capital and the processes of nature, the hazy pastel visualizations of the future buildings and the tangled present energies of natural growth and construction work meet uneasily (see below for further analysis of the mix).

At first, I was not engaged critically with the digital processes involved in the making and rather these were experiments in how my pre-existing live mixing practice might meet, explore and interrogate the complexity of an urban wildscape. However, all the work arises from experimentation with digital devices, technologies and interfaces – the mixes are made with phones, cameras, digital sound recorders, loop pedals, samplers and synthesizers. They are mixed with software and they are primarily formed of code. A growing recognition of my lack of awareness and understanding of the functioning of these devices has led to a new thread in the research. I am now engaged in thinking through and in response to the opaque computational processes of such devices in relation to the unknowable, wild, beyond and innumerable processes of city life and natural growth. This understanding of digital networked spaces as wild prompts consideration of how we intersect with the scale and speed of the 'ceaseless process of the ever new' (Turner 2013: 49) that is present in the endless, but minute by minute accretion of content made available to us, through mobile, digital devices.

For me, the 'spirit of the unknown and disorderly' (Taussig 1987: 289) also speaks to the autonomous and hidden processes that happen within my digital devices. As a proponent of the broad tenets that a postdigital perspective offers to an artist working with digital tools (see below), part of my practice is now in the process of turning in on itself, questioning the capacities of its technologies to represent and account for the wildness of the city and also enquiring as to what is happening between the digital, organic and material processes present in a place-mixing encounter. As evoked by Taussig again, 'wildness is the death space of signification' (1987: 219) and as Jack Halberstam comments in relation to Taussig's characterizations, 'it cannot mean because it has been cast as that which exceeds meaning' (2014: 140). In this sense, exploring a common wild energy that is present within a digital device and a place is not a search for meaning, but a play with what arises at the points and moments when the computational meets the material, where the digital meets the actual. It also has some resonance with the 'itinerant voice at large' referenced by Kendrick and Shyldkrot in their chapter. This relocated, *moving* voice, which emerges from the actor's body in one space, but is simultaneously experienced in close proximity to the audience member in another, through headphones for instance, seems to me to have a wild and roving quality to it that exceeds the conditions of its transferral and exists in motion, at large, challenging 'the unity of the symbol' (Taussig 1987: 219) and occupying spaces between the voice as emanation, as digital process, as breath, as sound wave.

Finally, and as referenced above, I have something to say about where this work sits in relation to what might broadly be termed 'place-making practices', a range of activities that often involve an effort to re-form or remake a place or experience of that place, through material intervention or more ephemeral activity. In finding a positioning for the practice outlined here, I attempt some formulations of what place-making constitutes, how it is currently used and adopted and the ways in which the form and function of place-*mixing* represents a departure from these practices. Examples of the practice in process complete the chapter, accompanied by the thoughts and ideas that constitute a formulation of what postdigital place-mixing is and might be and some conclusions related to productive intersections of digital devices, creative practices and the wild processes of urban places.

Discourses of the digital and postdigital in theory and practice

Postdigital place-mixing, as its name suggests, is a practice that is critically and practically engaged in what it means to be making creatively with digital devices after the advent of the digital, in a context where digital and computational processes are embedded in our lives. As such, the practice aligns with a set of contemporary ideas which attempt to wrestle with this context for making and engage actively in thinking through what it means.

David Berry has written extensively about the functioning of code and software, and the philosophical and practical implications of how we currently use and engage with computation. In his 2011 monograph, *The Philosophy of Software*, he lays out some key ideas about code and software processes that are not just relevant to, but active in my consideration of digital wildness in postdigital place-mixing. Berry describes the affordances of code and software which make them distinct from previous ways of organizing and processing the world. He points to the increased 'speed' and 'volume' of computational processes, linking this to the convenient delegation of 'mental processes' to code, which in turn 'instils a greater degree of agency into the technical devices' than would have been previously possible. In addition, he argues that 'networked software' in particular 'encourages a communicative environment of rapidly changing feedback mechanisms that tie humans and non-humans together into new aggregates'. These new aggregates happen when our clicking and browsing combine with an algorithm to collectively decide what we might watch or listen to next, or when our sense of time is aggregated with the digital processes of a device, which might suggest when we set our alarm, how long it should take to walk to our chosen destination, or automatically remind us of memories that have drifted out of view. Finally, Berry points out that there is a now a greater use of 'embedded and quasi-visible technologies' (Berry 2011: 2) due to the fact that computational devices have 'an internal state which is generally withheld from view and is often referred to as a "black box", indicating that it is opaque to the outside viewer' (15).

Each of these distinctions is of interest to me, as a postdigital place-mixer and non-expert, who is not versed in the language of coding and who therefore interacts with technologies (as most of us do) through their 'visible' properties – interfaces, apps and the surfaces of devices. The lack of expertise is important, as it offers a flavour to the critical, exploratory and speculative practices, which is imbued with what Berry and Dieter call 'agnosis', a postdigital condition whereby 'computation facilitates a systemic production and maintenance of ignorance' and, in turn, directs us towards 'passive trust in widely delegated, yet obfuscated actions' (2015: 5). These practices work *from* that ignorance as a productive starting point for intersecting with computation, allowing the ignorance to be a leading, pushing, probing factor of the work that disrupts, if not reveals those 'obfuscated actions'. This strand of my practice acknowledges that there is something to critically engage with – to encounter in a questioning way – in relation to the invisible functioning of code and software. With regard to the 'agencies' of the devices with which I work, the aggregates that are formed between us and the embedded and only barely visible nature of the computational processes being employed have become part of my place-mixing process (see below), particularly through my efforts to try to understand, if not with more clarity, then certainly with more thought, how those processes meet the places I am mixing and shape my embodied encounters with those places.

This is particularly interesting in relation to Berry's articulation of software as 'a tangle, a knot, which ties together the physical and the ephemeral, the material and the ethereal, into a multi-linear ensemble that can be controlled and directed' (2011: 3). The querying and indeed the practising of different modes of direction and control in the practice is a core part of place-mixing, particularly when the practice offers a space for considering those controls and directions within the creative output itself. For example, in my recent wanderings in Kersal Dale, I deliberately experimented with disrupting the flow of a smoothly panned digital image. The panning function on a phone camera allows for an unusually wide image of a landscape to be captured, through moving the phone smoothly and horizontally across the area you want to record. The simple control mechanism that the phone enacts is to direct you to keep the image even with a kind of digital spirit level on screen that you can follow as you pan and an instruction to 'slow down' when the phone cannot capture the panned imaged at the speed you are moving the camera. Through counteracting these instructions and erratically moving the phone around at various speeds and in a number of directions during the pan, a number of sometimes quite beautiful digital glitches appear (see Figure 7.1).

Such simple practices are a playful intersection with the affordances and control mechanisms of the computational device. They do not undo or 'hack' those processes, but there is an inherent question about the digital residue, so often hidden in our crisp and clear high-definition images, that comes to the fore in the act of creation and its result. Equally, it brings the wild, organic processes of the wildscape into discourse with the computational processes of the device, as I expand on below.

If we accept that 'devices are in a constant stream of data flow and decision-making which may only occasionally feedback to the human user' (Berry 2011: 14), then these practices draw attention to that decision-making and the '*hidden* affordances' (15) of the device in its processing of experience. As referenced above, this is not quite the 'postdigital hacker attitude of taking systems apart and using them in ways which subvert the original intention of

Figure 7.1 Glitched digital images of a wildscape, formed through 'incorrect' panning on an iPhone

the design' (Cramer 2015: 20). Rather, I find methods and ways of working with the computational device (from a position of ignorance) that interrogate the visible workings on the surface, putting these into a playful mix with the visible, material surfaces of the places in question. Perhaps this is akin to 'challeng[ing] the unity' (Taussig 1987: 219) and smooth impenetrability of digital images, prying them open a little, so underlying processes are brought to the fore. It also links to Kendrick and Shyldkrot's discussion of 'voice-as-glitch' and particularly the precarity this induces, troubling 'the apparent fixity of theatre's acoustic ecology'. Kendrick and Shyldkrot explore glitches as 'intentional interventions in the aural sphere' that can 'resist, unsettle or problematize different structures of power'. In a similar way, I induce glitching in my image-making to make more porous the relationships between the processes I encounter and the digital processes of 'capturing' the natural world.

This deliberate 'unsettling' is also enacted in a mode of digitally 'tiling' natural environments that has emerged in my mixing of wild green spaces (see Figure 7.2).

Again, this has involved engaging actively with a digitally enabled process of mixing an image or video, which is offered by my VJ-ing software, where images can be duplicated, 'tiled' and repositioned on the screen, so that they appear kaleidoscopic. In the video versions of these kaleidoscopes (see *Sycamore* (2018)), the images retain the breath of the natural energy of the landscape – wind moving the branch of a tree, sun darkening the shadow of the undergrowth – but that process is mathematically and

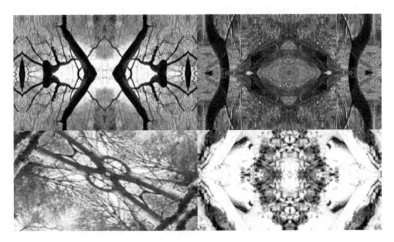

Figure 7.2 'Tiled' images of wild, green spaces (captured from video footage)

precisely reformulated in the tiled version, so that something of the growth, movement and materiality of the natural landscape is trapped in its digital form, existing uncomfortably and sometimes strikingly in conjunction with its computational re-processing. My fascination with these digitally patterned images of natural growth – which has its own distinct patterns and formulations – sits precisely at the intersection of the diverse processes in play and some of the uncomfortable grafts between them. These uneasy intersections are always present in the numerical code underpinning digital images, but often hidden, and are deliberately brought to the fore in this mixing process and in the glitched images discussed above.

Through such methods, a postdigital mixing practice emerges. Like computation itself – often conceived as ephemeral, outside or in opposition to materiality – the practice is actually 'experiential, spatial and materialized in its implementation, embedded within the environment and embodied, part of the texture of life itself but also upon and even within the body' (Berry and Dieter 2015: 3). Such practices aim to playfully mix and graft together the digital and the material, the organic and computational. However, underlying the creative play, sits a questioning of and unease with a world formed through digital-material intersections and modes of representation, particularly the hidden and coded forms of direction and control these involve.

This links place-mixing to an emergent lineage of postdigital art, including the work of Ingrid Burrington, who engages in practices that reveal the materiality of the internet, in projects such as *Networks of New York* (2014–16), described as 'a field guide to finding the internet on the streets of Manhattan', through documenting 'different signs of buried network infrastructure and easily overlooked network objects' (lifewinning n.d.). On the other hand, exposure and visibility, as practised through surveillance in various different digital forms, is a concern for Trevor Paglen. He 'make[s] visible the workings of the modern-day surveillance system', through diving into the oceans to photograph 'choke points', where 'clusters of fibre-optic cables connect the continents to each other' and which are therefore the 'places that the NSA [National Security Agency][5] taps for access to international communications data'. Here, as Paglen outlines, 'you are able to surveil a tremendous amount of the internet because you put a tap on the bottlenecks and everything's got to go through it'. Through photographing these 'choke points', Paglen points to the material places where the more abstract processes of 'dataveillance'[6] happen. He describes this photographic practice, in an echo of Burrington's concerns, as part of an effort to reveal that 'infrastructures of power always inhabit the surface of the earth somehow, or the sky above the earth. They're material things' (Paglen in Jobey 2015). In another manifestation of what could be considered postdigital practice, the Critical Engineering manifesto claims 'Engineering to be the most transformative language of our time, shaping the way we move, communicate and think', outlining that '[i]t is the work of the Critical Engineer to study and exploit this language, exposing its influence' and the 'inner workings' of technologies, as well as looking beyond the 'awe of implementation' to determine methods of influence and their specific effects (Oliver, Savicic and Vasiliev 2011).

All these practices are in a dynamic relationship with what is visible and over-exposed in our world through the functioning of contemporary digital technologies, as well as the 'self-surveillance' many of us practise through the sharing and imprinting of our lives in digital-networked spaces. On the flip side, there is also a consistently critical relationship with what is hidden, what escapes us, what sits beneath our attention and indeed what is so deliberately complex as to escape comprehension in our interactions with digital code and technologies and where those technologies materially exist in the world. Samuel Arbesman argues that 'when faced with such massive complexity, we tend to respond at one of two extremes: either with fear in the face of the unknown, or with a reverential and unquestioning approach to technology' (2016: 5), with the latter enabled by '*abstraction*' or 'the process of hiding unnecessary details of some part of a system while still retaining the ability to interact with it in a productive way' (23). This consistent hiding or abstracting of the actual and material processes of code and software that are happening at our behest, but also on our behalf and despite us – escaping control and comprehension – constitutes a core element of the 'wildness' of the digital. The burgeoning, ever-renewing space of process is also autonomous and self-willed – a place where signification consistently fails, breaks and falters in the wake of complexity; 'the death space of signification' (Taussig 1987: 219).

In these ways, I connect place-mixing to broadly postdigital approaches, and also perhaps to a postdigital gaze, which is adopted in relation to what is seen within a particular digital encounter with place, as well as what is not seen, but sensed and present within that encounter. Such a gaze is not predicated on seeing through the layers of obfuscation and abstraction referenced above, but on acknowledging this layered and stratified experience in the practice, along with the practices of control laced through my intersection with the visible surface of my digital device. This in turn links back to what is particular to the critical creative practice outlined in this chapter which is the link I form between ideas arising from the digital doings happening in the world and theories of wildness – this particular theoretical graft informs both the making and thinking associated with this work.

Digital wildness

Wildness, Robert Macfarlane states, can be seen as 'an energy both exemplary and exquisite'; a 'quality of aliveness' or 'self-ablazeness' or 'continuous coming-into-being' to which Chinese *Shan-shui* artists gave the name *zi-ran* (2007: 31). Giving attention to the consistent newness of the natural world – its 'constant and fecund present' (177) – means also seeing wildness 'as process, something continually at work in the world, something tumultuous, green, joyous' (234).

Conversely, a range of other ideas circulate around the term that have an altogether different and darker flavour. Taussig's evocation, referenced above, is of wildness as an encircling and predatory force, as 'the spirit of the unknown and disorderly', creating spaces of 'slippage' and a 'grinding articulation between signifier and signified' and finally, and most evocatively as creating 'spaces of darkness and light in which objects stare out in their mottled nakedness while signifiers float by' (1987: 219). This conception of wildness arises from Taussig's research into the violence inflicted on indigenous people by colonists in Colombia. Taken up by Jack Halberstam, as part of a reflection on the untimely death of Jose Esteban Muñoz, Halberstam reads Muñoz's writings through Taussig's ideas that 'Colonialism … projects a wildness, a violence, and a savagery onto the other and then seeks to counter the senseless brutality that it imagines inheres to this other order of being with a senseless brutality of its own' (Halberstam 2014: 139). In response, Halberstam transposes the vivid imagery of Taussig's accounts and recasts wildness as 'a kind of queer-eco-critical endeavor' (2014: 138), specifically connecting these ideas to 'the modes of knowing and unknowing that emerge in the encounter between capital and chaos, privilege and struggle, myth and countermyth … those places of slippage between language and experience and life and death' (147).

It is in the rich confluence of Macfarlane's reflections on wildness as a tumultuous, green and joyous process and Taussig's references to 'grinding articulation' and objects 'staring out in their mottled nakedness' – as well as broader etymological associations with 'self–will', meaning that '*wild* indicates autonomy and agency, a will to be, a unique expression of life' (Van Horn 2017: 2) – that real resonance arises with core elements of this research. The wild tumultuous beyondness of the computational sphere meets the ferocious growth of a pioneer plant in an urban wildscape, pushing aside tarmac and concrete just to *be*. This in turn hits the ravenous force of urban redevelopment, swooping and sweeping, razing and raising, emanating with a quality of something more than human, in its ferocious formulations and reshapings of the city.

I see the thread of wildness through the elements of this place-mixing practice, in the edgelands and urban wildscapes referenced above. These are places where human agency is not in charge – the disordered and naturally abundant places that do not exist in pristine separation, but which edge into and intersect with our managed, urban spaces, speaking of something beyond this imposed order – leaning us towards the slippage of the unknown. Also pressed up against us and sinuously entwined in our human doings is the 'network' described by James Bridle as an 'agential soup' (2018: 5) of knowing and unknowing created between us and our technologies. These quick moving, self-willed and expansive technological agencies with which we share our lives are also wild – beyond, unknowable, disorderly and unmanageable. Just look at the two evocations below of sleeping in a meadow and what computation is enacting as we sleep:

> I could hear the ongoing business of the meadow – the shifting of grass stalks, the shy movements of animals and insects – and again I felt a sense of wildness as process.
>
> (Macfarlane 2007: 234)

> Networks of machines silently and repetitively exchange data. They monitor, control and assess the world using electronic sensors, updating lists and databases, calculating and recalculating their models to produce reports, predictions and warnings.
>
> (Berry 2011: 1)

The endless business of the meadow and the machines, of natural growth and computation, surrounds us, but often sits beneath our notice, unlike the more brashly evident sweep of the shifting built environment of the wild city, and yet all these processes meet through the notion of something that exists beyond our human capacities, that exceeds and swamps us in distinct ways. Equally, the notion that this quality of wildness exists, not as an opposition to order necessarily, but 'in the encounter between capital and chaos, privilege and struggle, myth and countermyth' (Halberstam 2014: 147) seems to speak strongly of some of the forces in play both in the contemporary city and more broadly in the network forming and developing between human actions and computational processes.

Place-making and place-mixing

As referenced above, this confluence of forces, energies and activities is also reflected in viewing places themselves as 'processes' (Massey 1994: 155). In encountering and remixing the processes happening between places, bodies and digital devices, this practice has connections with place-making activities. Place-making itself is something of a slippery concept. Rethink Urban (2019) – a Canadian company 'dedicated to improving safety, wellbeing and quality of life in communities' – describes it as 'the process through which we work together to shape our public spaces', pointing to 'community-based participation' as being core to this. However, as the brief discussion in the opening of the chapter reveals, such practices can be co-opted for commercial means, as part of 'market-driven place-making' which aims to improve the look and feel of areas, so that they become more economically valuable and investable, leading to increased rents for residents. This concern is echoed by Elaine Speight (2013) in a critical account of the role of place-making in the regeneration of UK towns and cities. She outlines:

> Although rarely defined, the term has become shorthand for the practice of 'creating somewhere with a distinct identity' (Cowan 2005: 292) through an on-the-ground approach to urban design and planning. In particular, place-making advocates the involvement of communities and the application of local knowledge as ways to engender local distinctiveness and a strong sense of place within urban regeneration schemes.
>
> (26)

Her critique comes in how place-making – particularly its intersection with art-making – has been used in this context: 'Place-making became seen as an effective way to improve the external perceptions of blighted areas and to transform them into attractive places. The commissioning of art was regarded as an integral part of this process' (26). There is therefore an argument that a type of 'art-washing' is employed as part of place-making practices, alongside a nominal amount of community involvement in largely predetermined and commercially minded development schemes – just enough of both to give the appearance of positive engagement in regeneration led by private companies, whose primary aim is to make a profit. This argument is taken up by Heather McLean (2014) in her consideration of 'arts-led regeneration' (2156) and the potential complicity of artists 'in naturalizing colonial gentrification processes at multiple scales' (2156) in such contexts.

Place-making activities have proliferated in recent years, perhaps specifically to counter the homogenization of spaces impacted by globalized capital and culture. The wild underbelly of these practices though is the overflowing and ongoing reaches of corporate development – the scooping up and scooping out of places to accommodate an increase in returns for investors. The arguably much more pallid, but entirely marketable response to any critique as to the ways in which our cities are 'up for grabs' is the promotion of practices where communities have at least some role in re-forming, remaking and revaluing their own places.

It is important to say at this point that not all place-making activity is co-opted in this way and that there is a wealth of creative practice engaging with place which does not fit this commercial model. For example, Sally Mackey's research in this area uses temporary, ephemeral acts of performance in places, to offer participants 'new ways of considering, and dwelling in, the present' (2016: 121) of such places (see Performing Places n.d.). Equally, there are organizations, such as zURBS who address urban place through a 'socially-engaged artistic approach', focusing on 'an open participatory process that enables participants to articulate their experiences of their city on their own terms, and this way raise people's consciousness about the structural conditions that shape their lives' (zURBS 2020). In both these examples, playful, creative activities located in places prompt 'an additional layer of unexpected experience in the *same* environment' (Mackey 2016: 119), rather than looking to materially change it. According to zURBS, there is a role for imagining in these activities, where 'imagination can be seen as the first step towards collectively producing our cities, by playing a critical role in expressing desires for urban worlds that are radically better or different, and insisting that other worlds can be imagined and constructed' (zURBS 2020).

These practices are not necessarily engaged in any active re-making of a physical environment and rather look to creative activities in places as a way of reviewing or re-forming a relationship with a present place or indeed imagining its future. Place-mixing also has different intentions from activities that seek to re-form and remake, as well as those that engage participants with places to 'reveal, expose, heal, enhance and alter people's response to their inhabitation and dwelling' (Mackey 2016: 107). This practice functions as a speculative, exploratory mode of feeling through those present relationships, opening up a mix of forces and drawing attention back to the affective and material processes in play within the encounter. The act of place-mixing is also one of resistance to any easy connections of place-making to positive affirmations of 'place attachment'. Place attachment is defined by Altman and Low (1992) as 'the bonding of people to places' (5) and they claim that 'we form a stronger bond to a place if it meets our needs, both physical and psychological, and matches our goals and lifestyle' (9). As Mackey points out, 'place-making and place attachment are phrases that have become popular as incitements to change in policy reports' (2016: 112). However, the idea of matching places to goals, lifestyles and identities, in the context of market-driven place-making, is problematic. As Montgomery argues, 'to secure public order and place capital, placemaking must do more than redesign streets – it must guide eyes and feet. To do so, it insinuates itself into private space, it monitors the poor and discontented, and it harnesses the memories and dreams of suburbanites' (2016: 788). As such, questions arise as to whose goals and lifestyles are being matched with newly 'remade' places and whose are discounted 'on the basis of dollar returns and enhanced city image' (787).

Equally, market-driven place-making activities do not or cannot encompass or acknowledge the complex and contradictory forces in play and often seek to smooth over such troubled, elusive and immaterial forces through activity to make somewhere look and feel better. As Erin Toolis comments in her account of 'critical placemaking' in the United States, 'the focus on commonality rather than difference can obscure the plural and often contested nature of communities', while 'Placemaking's "revitalization" efforts frequently focus on beautifying, cleansing, and regenerating public spaces for prompting development and attracting investment, while neglecting considerations of economic and racial inequality' (2017: 186).

In contrast, an interrogative act of place-mixing is specifically aligned with the 'unfixed, contested and multiple' (Massey 1994: 5) nature of places. Place-mixing revels in the contrasting, incongruous, uneasy elements of a place, encountering what is present in a speculative way – whether that is the surface of a mobile device, the visualization of a future development or an abandoned plot of land. Equally, the open, searching, 'live' nature of this roughly-hewn mixing practice aims to disrupt and reveal some of the forces of control and containment in the city and the device. The provocation of this practice, in response to the narratives of place aligned with particular, exclusive visions of their future, is to allow and invite a set of forces to be present and shifting in an encounter, opening up messy and uneasy relationships between these forces, with no movement to resolve them. In addition, the place-mixer in the wild city has a perennial interest in that which exceeds the senses, which is riotous, beyond signification and tumultuous in nature, culture, material and digital processes. This attention to the wild, urban world, as manifest in the built cityscape, nature and a digital device leads the explorations of place in an open and querying way, which is echoed in the subsequent mixing of materials through the types of lo-fi, intuitive and unfinished ways outlined above. The result exists in a perennially suspended, shifting space, where the materials and encounters in question rub up against each other and are not resolved.

By no means am I claiming that this work can completely escape any of the contexts I outline above in relation to the co-opting of place-making practices or that it has a particularly sharp critical voice in opposition to the wildness of regeneration agendas in our cities. What I am interested in is how the gaze, approach and actions of postdigital place-mixing constitute a resistant, speculative and interrogative act; how a feeling encounter with wild processes might prompt a reconsideration of such processes and how they meet, overlap and exchange. Equally, as Mackey points out, digital technology's 'connection with place-making is as yet under-explored' (2016: 122). This speculative, enquiring practice is one way to start to unpick the relations between the materialities, meetings, disconnections and exclusions of a place and the insistent threads and practices of digitality as we engage them in processing what is happening around us. In order to articulate and ground these thoughts, I turn now to some of my experiments in this area in order to illuminate how these emergent practices happen, before completing the chapter with principles, approaches and ideas that have emerged so far from my postdigital place-mixing in the wild city.

Place-mixing in practice

As referenced above, an early place-mix focused on a space in East Salford called the Meadow – a teardrop wild green space caught in a loop of the River Irwell and increasingly overhung by a range of new developments that fringe the outer edge of the river.[7] The Meadow sits right next to Chapel Street, an area where Salford meets central Manchester, and which is consequently at the very sharp edge of an aggressive redevelopment agenda on the part of the city council and attendant commercial developers.

In this case, the initial encounter with the meadow was a walk where snatches of video footage and text were gathered, particularly reflecting my engagement with the unfettered natural growth of the space in relation to the wild, energetic throwing up of buildings and eerie, disjointed sounds of construction echoing around. I also pulled in the strangely lonely, digital visualizations of the future buildings to intersect uncomfortably with my raw, shaky footage, while singing and speaking the text I had created on the walk and that from the marketing material for the new Adelphi Wharf developments that sit on one side of the river.

The echoing of wild and self-willed processes in the natural elements of the Meadow and the human-made actions surrounding it generated an unsettling and excited feeling, also holding an edge of despair – the sense of things running through fingers, always-escaping and exceeding what is possible to capture. Part of the mixing of these materials was an engagement with those feelings and ideas through a rough editing process and also through some very deliberate digital processing choices, which highlight the mixing and reformulation of the materials. These include the tiling of imagery referenced above, the shifting of colour and the very deliberate moving and overlaying of the materials. The initial video mix was done live with little conscious thought and never really developed beyond that first edit in any meaningful way, manifesting in an eternal rough cut, never to be refined. This type of rough-hewn graft of digital materials is characteristic of my postdigital place-mixing, deliberately showing the edges of things and denying the ability of the digital edit to smooth them out. These types of mixes are also, as referenced above, deliberately engaged with showing the processing of the image, if not through revealing the code that underpins it, then certainly through accentuating the digital glitches and traces that emerge, both sonically and visually.

In a development of this work, a recent project aimed to share practices arising from a natural wildness that I experienced in Kersal Dale – the urban wildscape near my home referenced earlier in the chapter – as mirrored in the digital processing of my smartphone, when I attempted to use the latter to capture the former.[8] This particular mix is more engaged with disruptive strategies that can shift the initial encounter between digital and natural processes, as opposed to adding that layer in an edit. As such, and as referenced above, I played with forming glitched panned images of the trees and undergrowth, as well as employing the device in unusual ways in the space – leaving it to record without looking at what it captured, observing its visible processes, trying to listen for its invisible workings, singing to it … These represent attempts – without actually re-forming any of the underpinning code – to counteract and playfully intersect with some of the familiar ways I use the phone's digital processes in relation to the environment, particularly more obvious affordances of capturing, sampling and digitally slicing the space into video and image.

These first attempts at mixing digital and natural wildness also include a set of musings, thoughts and musical responses, as well as proposed prompts for activity, thinking through both the device and place as sets of related processes, patterns, happenings and landscapes for 'corporeal practice' (Wylie 2007: 214). Two examples of these prompts for place-mixing activity are outlined below:

> *Put the phone into the environment – somewhere where it doesn't fit and make it do something – record or play sound, image, video. Place its automated happenings in relation to all the other processes happening here. Don't look through the device – look at it in this space. What does it look like? Why is it here? What is it hiding? Record your responses to these questions, if you want.*
>
> *Leave the phone somewhere in the space to film/record sound/take pictures, then run towards it fast, pick it up and turn it out into the space.*

The image will move with your breath, which is good – that will change how the environment is. Feel the breath of the body in the image, the impossibility of stillness, the moment formed between body, device and place.

(Scott 2019)

As both these prompts indicate, this emerging mixing practice focuses on the body, device and environment in a present encounter and the relationships that form in that encounter that might help us to rethink the positioning of each in relation to the other. It attempts to surface the shared wild processes happening within and between the body, device and natural space. It also creatively engages with what Berry calls the 'new aggregates' (2011: 2) that are formed between humans and non-humans in the software-soaked contemporary world. It attempts to bend and reshape some of the practised relationships between these elements, where, for instance, we consistently view or engage with an environment through the phone's framing and hidden processing.

These initial experiments – arising from my intermedial practices, in combination with an interest in a postdigital perspective and a sense of wildness as present in nature, urban places and digital processes – represent the starting points for developing a postdigital place-mixing practice. Alongside these early experiments, I offer below, by way of conclusion, some emerging thoughts about the practices and ideas that circulate here, particularly the principles and approaches that underpin them.

Postdigital place-mixing practices: Some principles and approaches

A live mixing practice is not able to offer a unified or singular perspective of a place and does not seek to; mixes hold the multiple in a suspension that is only temporary, before those parts fly apart and re-form into something else. Above, I describe place-mixing as a restless practice and indeed, even in its fixed forms, it is fleeing and chasing. Mixing is also about a first encounter and then a re-encounter. The mixer first meets the place through a digital engagement, often using a device to capture something of that. Such processes of 'capture', as discussed above, are deliberately unseated and shifted through a wild symbiotic methodology, that seeks feral threads in all that it encounters and feels the bottomlessness of the ecologies of computation and natural growth; that revels in, but is threatened by what is beyond our capacity to see and understand and what is consistently happening on our behalf. In this first encounter, the place-mixer makes futile efforts to attune themselves to those processes, to what is actually happening when the fake red button is pressed, when the camera casts its digital eye towards the veneered brickwork of this new development or that intense green carpet of ivy or moss.

This is not an untroubled encounter. The place-mixer holds their device in their hands and feels a little queasy as to what it contains, how it exceeds, how it threads out into the world and what it can never account for. The place-mixer regards what is around them with a similar queasiness, with ignorance certainly, but also with a feeling, from which a querying and speculative encounter might arise. They then allow that encounter to result in a few lines of computational code to be made manifest in sound or image.

In the re-encounter with these digital materials through a mixing practice, the glassy exterior and dead-eyed look-back of the digital image and footage belies the ferocious energy beneath that is played out through the code and software, re-forming, reordering and recalculating material into new shapes and processes. Though the non-expert place-mixer does not have the capacity to plumb the depths of the layers of code, they are consistently paying attention to how the computational processing might become active and visible in the ways the mix reformulates the encounter between the processes of the body, digital device and place. The mix itself is never that well-formed, it's never that beautifully shaped – it could be better – but what arises (either in performance or in a fixed media output) is a feeling encounter, opened up and pried to the surface by a particular wild imagining and querying, coming into being through a process of choice-making that acknowledges what is beyond control. Like the 'postdigital gaze' I gesture to above, it engages with what is not seen, but sensed and present in the layers of the experience and the act of digital mixing, a precarious and unsettled engagement that resonates with Kendrick and Shyldkrot's account of *acousmatic* sounds that we experience 'without the visual presence of their cause or source'.

I have written before (Scott 2016) about being led by materials and environments in my mixing, being pulled by forces in the mixes as they are made manifest. I have reflected somewhat on the affordances of the technologies I use and what they offer to me. Up until this point, I have eschewed the layers and stratification and giddy drops and depths of code and computation that are made and formed and re-formed in this work. As a place-mixer, I now want these signs in the mix – the digital hiss of the microphone in the wind, the residue of an echo that disrupts the sound of bird song, the glitch that emerges when that is looped, the breath of wind in the tiled image and the sense that nothing is complete and fixed, but in a frustrating, moving amalgam, only a part of which I will ever touch or will ever touch me. In this way, nothing is ever completed. Materials are just pushed and pulled, stretched and poked, licked and tasted and then discarded or included. The mixes are inherently unsatisfying and always reach for something more – a better, truer representation of what is there. They fail, and in failing, they activate the stumbling and not-quite-formed encounters we have with the world, with the city, with nature, the digital and ourselves. They reach for and grasp at the wild processes of the city evoked in the preamble, in a sustained condition of 'uncertainty or relationality' which links the practices to the precarious subjectivities in play in Kendrick and Shyldkrot's account of contemporary vocality.

As this chapter reveals, these are emergent thoughts and practices. There is more work to do here, more encounters to form, more questions to ask, more approaches to test. However, what is arising distinctly through the thinking and making of this work is a collection of resonant concepts and practices around the wild city. I am feeling towards a sense of what that means as a condition of both city dwelling and postdigital existence, where certain senses of vitality, powerlessness, excitement, fear and bewilderment arise in relation to the boundless processes happening in these spaces. If this wild synergy of disparate elements holds anything, it holds something of how it feels to be alive today and resident in a city, full of both stasis and rampant change, where computational threads meet the forces of capital which in turn lean over abandoned spaces of natural growth. Through postdigital place-mixing, some creative and critical engagement with this synergy is enabled, a speculative acknowledgement and recognition of that which is wildly beyond us.

Notes

1   Documentation of these practices is available at www.joanneemmascott.
    com – see Projects/'Mixing the Irwell' and 'The Broughton Oratory' in
    particular.
2   The mix, *Sycamore* (2018) is available to watch through this link: https://
    www.youtube.com/watch?time_continue=305&v=yjIUpmdHnng&feature=
    emb_lo
3   Modul8 is a piece of VJ-ing software, 'designed for live performance
    and real-time video mixing' (garageCube 2017). It allows videos to be
    manipulated and layered, as well as offering a range of effects that can be
    added to the footage.
4   See https://www.youtube.com/watch?v=GzIQHk6b8YI to view the
    resulting mix, titled *Adelphi*.

5   The mass surveillance activities of the US National Security Agency
    (NSA) were brought to wide public attention through Edward Snowden's
    revelations in 2013.
6   Dataveillance is the practice of monitoring and collecting digital data. Goos
    et al. (2015) note that the term was coined by Roger Clark in the 1980s 'to
    capture the spread of computers and the possibilities to process data that
    came along with that'. They explain that new modes of surveillance were
    added to a revised definition in 2003 which included 'Internet tracing,
    digital rights management, chip-based identification, biometrics, person
    locating and tracking' (72).
7   See https://www.youtube.com/watch?v=GzIQHk6b8YI to view the
    resulting mix, titled *Adelphi*.
8   See materials published as part of the Theatre, Dance and Performance
    Training special issue on digital training in the Blog section: http://
    theatredanceperformancetraining.org/2019/07/new-processes-for-digital-
    encounters-with-wild-gren-spaces-by-jo-scott/

References

Altman, I. and S. Low, eds (1992), *Place Attachment*, New York: Plenum Press.
Arbesman, S. (2016), *Overcomplicated: Technology at the Limits of
    Comprehension*, New York: Penguin.
Berry, D. (2011), *The Philosophy of Software: Code and Mediation in the Digital
    Age*, Basingstoke and New York: Palgrave Macmillan.
Berry, D. and M. Dieter, eds (2015), *Postdigital Aesthetics: Art, Computation and
    Design*, Basingstoke and New York: Palgrave Macmillan.
Bridle, J. (2018), *New Dark Age: Technology, Knowledge and the End of the
    Future*, London and New York: Verso.
Cowan, R. (2005), *The Dictionary of Urbanism*, Tisbury: Streetwise Press.
Cramer, F. (2015), 'What Is Post-Digital?' in D. Berry and M. Dieter (eds),
    Postdigital Aesthetics: Art, Computation and Design, 12–27, Basingstoke and
    New York: Palgrave Macmillan.
Edensor, T. (2005), *Industrial Ruins: Space, Aesthetics and Materiality*, New
    York: Berg Publishing.
Farley, P. and M. Symmons-Roberts (2012), *Edgelands: Journeys into England's
    True Wilderness*, London: Vintage Books.
garageCube (2017), 'Modul8'. Available online: https://www.garagecube.com/
    modul8/
Goos, K., M. Friedewald, C. Webster, and C. Leleux (2015), 'The Co-evolution
    of Surveillance Technologies and Surveillance Practices', in D. Wright and R.
    Kreissel (eds), *Surveillance in Europe*, 51–100, New York and Oxon: Routledge.
Halberstam, J. (2014), 'Wildness, Loss, Death', *Social Text 121*, 32 (4): 137–48.

Jorgensen, A. and M. Tylecote (2007), 'Ambivalent Landscapes – Wilderness in the Urban Interstices', *Landscape Research*, 32 (4): 443–62.

Jorgensen, A. and R. Keenan, eds (2012), *Urban Wildscapes*, London and New York: Routledge.

Jobey, L. (2015), 'Trevor Paglen: What Lies Beneath', *The Financial Times*, 31 December. Available online: https://www.ft.com/content/beaf9936-a8ff-11e5-9700-2b669a5aeb83

lifewinning (n.d.), 'lifewinning'. Available online: http://lifewinning.com/

Oliver, J., G. Savicic, and D. Vasiliev (2011), 'The Critical Engineering Manifesto', *WIRED*, October. Available online: https://www.wired.com/2011/10/the-critical-engineering-manifesto/

Macfarlane, R. (2007), *The Wild Places*, London: Granta Books.

Mackey, S. (2016), 'Performing Location: Place and Applied Theatre', in J. Hughes and H. Nicholson (eds), *Critical Perspectives on Applied Theatre*, Cambridge: Cambridge University Press.

McLean, H. (2014), 'Cracks in the Creative City: The Contradictions of Community Arts Practice', *International Journal of Urban and Regional Research*, 38 (6): 2156–73.

Massey, D. (1994), *Space, Place and Gender*, Cambridge: Polity Press.

Massumi, B. (2002), *Parables for the Virtual: Movement, Affect, Sensation*, Durham and London: Duke University Press.

Montgomery, A. (2016), 'Reappearance of the Public: Placemaking, Minoritization and Resistance in Detroit', *International Journal Of Urban And Regional Research*, 40 (4): 776–99.

Performing Places (n.d.), *Performing Places Website*. Available online: http://www.performingplaces.org/

Project for Public Spaces (2018), 'What Is Placemaking'. Available online: https://www.pps.org/category/placemaking

Rethink Urban (2019), 'Placemaking'. Available online: http://rethinkurban.com/placemaking/

Scott, J. (2016), *Intermedial Praxis and Practice as Research: 'Doing-thinking' in Practice*, Houndsmills and New York: Palgrave Macmillan.

Scott, J. (2017), 'Salford Samples', *Journal of Artistic Research (JAR)* (14). Available online: https://doi.org/10.22501/jar.301815

Scott, J. (2019), 'New Processes for Digital Devices in Wild Green Spaces', *Theatre, Dance and Performance Training*, 10 (1): 205–7. Available online: http://theatredanceperformancetraining.org/2019/07/new-processes-for-digital-encounters-with-wild-green-spaces-by-jo-scott/

Scott, J. (2020), '"It's Cowboy Country Up There": Ruination and *Ruinenlust* in the Wilds of Broughton', *Research Catalogue*. Available online: https://www.researchcatalogue.net/view/565417/565418/0/0.

Speight, E. (2013), '"How Dare You Rubbish My Town!": Place Listening as an Approach to Socially Engaged Art within UK Urban Regeneration Contexts', *Open Arts Journal*, 1: 25–35.

Taussig, M. (1987), *Shamanism, Colonialism and the Wild Man: A Study in Terror and Healing*, Chicago and London: University of Chicago Press.

Thrift, N. (2008), *Non-Representational Theory: Space I Politics I Affect*, London and New York: Routledge.

Toolis, E. (2017), 'Theorizing Critical Placemaking as a Tool for Reclaiming Public Space', *American Journal of Community Psychology*, 59 (1/2): 184–99.

Turner, J. (2013), 'The Wild and the Self', in P. Hasbach and P. Kahn (eds), *The Rediscovery of the Wild*, Cambridge, MA: MIT Press.

Van Horn, G. (2017). 'Introduction', in G. Van Horn and J. Hausdoerffer (eds), *Wildness: Relations of People and Place*, Chicago and London: University of Chicago Press.

Vannini, P., ed. (2015), *Non-representational Methodologies: Re-envisioning Research*, New York: Taylor and Francis.

Wylie, J. (2007), *Landscape*, Oxon and New York: Routledge.

zURBS (2020), 'The Theory'. Available online: http://zurbs.org/wp/biographyintro/theoretically/

Index

acousmatized voices 142–3, 148
acousmêtre 142–3, 157
acoustic ecology 147–51, 171
Adams, Matt (Blast Theory) 51
Aeon, 116, 117–20, 123, 131, 132.
    See also Dunn, Lz
aesthetics of wrongness 10–11, 76–7,
    92–3, 94, 96, 99, 101, 102, 106,
    108
agnosis 169
Alexenberg, Mel 118
algorithmic relationships 50
algorithms 25, 47–51, 57, 82, 84,
    94–6, 100, 107, 169
All The Queen's Men 116, 128–32.
    See also Coming Back Out Ball
Altman, Irwin and Setha M. Low 177
Arbesman, Samuel 173
artificial intelligence (AI) 89, 98, 100,
    108
arts-led regeneration 176
art-washing 176
Auslander, Philip 3, 24–6, 35, 124
Avatar (film) 21, 29–32
avatars
    aural avatars 138
    avatar (as written word) 138–9
    avatar-audiences (in headphone
        theatre) 8, 155
    avatar identities/bodies (in *Avatar*
        (film)) 30–1, 33
    avatars of deceased actors/
        relatives 92, 98–100, 106
    Avatar performers (in
        Ontroerend Goed's *A Game of
        You*) 103–6
    embodied avatar (in Blast Theory's
        Karen app) 42–3, 47, 50–1

    motion tracking/virtual puppet
        avatar 20
    performance capture 6

Balázs, Béla and Siegfried Kracauer
    25
Bandersnatch (television
    programme) 47. *See also Black
    Mirror*
Bassermann, Albert (actor) 17–18,
    27, 35
Bay-Cheng, Sarah 3, 6
Benjamin, Walter 18–19, 27–8
Bennett, Jane 146
Berry, David M. 4, 6–7, 139, 168–9,
    175, 181
big data 4, 46, 49, 53, 60, 100
Birringer, Johannes 35
Black Mirror (television programme)
    47
Blas, Zach 28
Blast Theory 39–61
Bolter, David 4, 121
bots 7, 8, 72, 84, 98
Brecht, Bertolt 27–8
Brexit 46
Bridle, James 175
Burrington, Ingrid 172
Butler, Judith 59

Cage, Nicolas (deepfakes) 89–93,
    95–6, 101, 106. *See also*
    Franken-Cages
Calpurnia Descending 116, 120–8,
    131–2. *See also* Sisters Grimm
Cambridge Analytica 46, 98
Cameron, James 21, 31, 34
Carnicke, Sharon Marie 22–3

Cascone, Kim 5, 91, 118–19
Causey, Matthew 1, 3–6, 43, 91–2
Chapple, Freda 2
Chatzichristodoulou, Maria 52
cheapfakes 90. *See also* shallowfakes
Chekhov, Anton 141, 156–7
Chekhov's First Play 137, 140–5, 149,
    155–6. *See also* Dead Centre
Cheney-Lippold, John 45
Chion, Michel 143–5
chronophotography 20
Cixous, Hélène 157
Coming Back Out Ball 116, 128–32.
    See also All The Queen's Men
Complicité 138
Couldry, Nick and Andreas Hepp 39,
    43, 56–7
COVID-19 1–2, 129
Cramer, Florian 5–6, 170–1
Cushing, Peter 33, 98–9

Darkfield 138
data role-play 42, 45, 56–7, 60
databodies 8, 42, 46–9, 62
datafication 4, 12, 21, 39–40,
    42–3, 45–6, 49, 51–2, 54–6, 57,
    59–60, 62
dataveillance 4, 12, 21, 29, 40, 42, 44,
    46, 49, 52, 60, 172, 184
deacousmatization 145, 148, 157. *See
    also* Chion, Michel
Dead Centre 8, 137–56. *See also*
    Chekhov's First Play; Lippy
deepfake-ification 92, 94–6, 103–4,
    106–8
deepfakes 8–9, 77, 81, 89–102, 103–4,
    106–8. *See also* cheapfakes;
    shallowfakes
deepfakes algorithm 94–5
Deeptrace 102
Der Andere (film) 18, 27
disinformation 5, 90, 92, 94, 108
diva dromology 126
Dixon, Brandon (*Hamilton*) 80–1

Dixon, Steve 121
drag remediation 121
Dunn, Lz 116, 117, 120. *See also Aeon*

Edelman, Lee 131
ELIZA (computer programme) 98.
    See also Weizenbaum, Joseph
Elleström, Lars 4
Esteban Muñoz, Jose 174
eterni.me 92, 99

face-swap 90, 96–7, 101–2
face-swap porn/revenge porn 94,
    101–2, 106, 108
fake news 90
FakeApp 89
Fischer-Lichte, Erika 12
flocking 116–17, 142
Flusser, Vilém 93, 97, 100, 105, 107
Flyway 117. *See also* Dunn, Lz
Foucault, Michel 2
Fragkou, Marissia 138, 140, 147–8, 154
Franken-Cages 89–93, 96, 105
Franklin, Benjamin 115

A Game of You (Ontroerend Goed)
    93, 103–6
generative adversarial networks
    (GANs) 93, 95, 97, 103–5, 108
gerontology 116
glitch/glitching 5, 12, 100, 115–16,
    118–20, 126, 132, 138, 140,
    148–53, 155, 170–1, 172, 180,
    182
Glitch (television programme) 115, 132
glitch art 9, 91
glitch-camp aesthetic 127–8
Grusin, Richard 121

Halberstam, Jack/Judith 131, 167,
    174
Hamilton 8, 80–1, 98
Hansen, Mark 43, 56
Harding, James 27, 29, 34, 40

Hayles, N. Katherine 9–10, 43–4, 56, 58, 107
Helper, Roslyn 93, 100–1, 107
Hepp, Andreas 39, 43, 56–7
hypermedium 2, 6. *See also* Kattenbelt, Chiel

Ihde, Don 137–8, 142
Ilter, Seda 39, 49, 51–2, 59
Imaginarium Productions 22
Industrial Light and Magic 98–9
intermedial turn 1
intermediality 1–5, 7, 9, 12

Jackson, Peter 21, 23

Kafka, Franz 17–19, 27, 35
Kanemaki, Yoshitoshi 9
Kant, Immanuel 115
Karen (app) 8, 39, 41–2, 45–61. *See also* Blast Theory
Kattenbelt, Chiel 2
knot not 7, 10, 12
knot topology (mathematics) 10–11
Koopman, Colin 7
Kracauer, Siegfried 25

Labelle, Brandon 146–8, 151, 154
Leeker, Martina 8–10, 44
LGBTI elders 9, 116, 129–32
Lifestyle of the Richard and Family 93, 100–1, 107. *See also* Helper, Roslyn
Lilley, Chris 93, 101–2, 106. *See also* Lunatics
Lippy 139, 149–57. *See also* Dead Centre
Loukola, Mijou 59
Lunatics (television programme) 93, 101–2. *See also* Lilley, Chris

Macfarlane, Robert 174–5
Mackey, Sally 177, 179
Macpherson, Crawford Brough 107

Magritte, René 96–7
Marey, Étienne-Jules 20
Massumi, Brian 165
Matzner, Tobias 43–5
McLean, Heather 176
Mee, Erin 50–1
Menkman, Rosa 152
micro-subjectivities 8, 43–4
misinformation 94
Montgomery, Alesia 163, 177
Mori, Masahiro 21
Morrison, Elise 28–9, 32
motion capture 19–20, 22, 26, 29, 36, 98–9
motion tracking 20
Muybridge, Eadweard 20

Na'vi 21, 30–2

Obama (deepfake)/synthetic Obama 8, 89–91, 98–9, 105–6
Ontroerend Goed 93, 103–7. *See also* *A Game of You*

Paglen, Trevor 172–73
Peirce, Charles Sanders 24–5
performance capture 6, 8, 12, 17–36, 43–4, 56
performative turn 9
Perry, Katy 126–7
Phelan, Peggy 2–3
place attachment 177. *See also* Altman, Irwin and Setha M. Low
place-making 163, 168, 175–9
place-mixing 147, 155, 161–9, 172–4, 175–181, 183
postdigital aesthetics 5, 89, 94
postdigital aesthetics of wrongness 89, 94
postdigital gaze 173, 182
postdigital queer time 131–2
postdigital subjectivities 12, 39, 41–2
postdigital turn 5, 100
Post-History 97. *See also* Flusser, Vilém

post-human 19, 29, 31, 33, 35, 40–2, 45–6, 53, 55–61
precariat 138, 142
precarity 4–5, 10, 137–45, 147–9, 151, 154–6, 171

quantified self 49, 60
queer ecology 119–20
queer postdigital flocks 9
queer theory 116, 131

Rainbow, Randy 8, 9, 65–86, 103, 106
remediation 4, 121. *See also* drag remediation
Rethink Urban 176
Ridout, Nicholas 142
Rise of the Planet of the Apes (film) 8, 24, 32
Rogue One (*Star Wars*) 33, 92, 98–9
Rolnik, Suely 146

Schneider, Rebecca 142
Selvaggio, Leo 28–9
Serkis, Andy 8, 21, 22–6, 27. *See also* performance capture
shallowfakes 77, 89–90. *See also* cheapfakes; deepfakes
Short Organum (1948) 28. *See also* Bertolt, Brecht
Sisters Grimm 116, 121–2, 126. *See also Calpurnia Descending*
Snowden, Edward 3
social media 1, 5–6, 8, 21, 54, 65–6, 68–9, 71–4, 76–8, 80–5, 98, 102, 127, 132, 139
Sontag, Susan 121
Sorenson, Roy 156
Speight, Elaine 176

Stanislavski, Konstantin 141
States, Bert O. 25, 27
synthetic identity theft 94

Tandavanitj, Nick (Blast Theory) 46–7, 50, 52–5
Taussig, Michael 161–2, 166–8, 171, 173
technological turn 9
techno-performativity 42, 49, 56, 58, 60–1
thispersondoesnotexist.com 96–7
Toné, Yasunao 118
Toolis, Erin 178
transmedia 1
Truax, Barry 147, 150
Trump, Donald 8, 46, 65, 67–77, 79–81, 83–5, 90, 98
Turner, Jack 161, 167

uncanny valley 21, 92, 108. *See also* Mori, Masahiro
urban wildscapes 165–6, 174
URME project 28–9

verfremdung 27. *See also* Bertolt, Brecht
Virilio, Paul 126
virtual actor 34

Weizenbaum, Joseph 98. *See also* ELIZA
WETA digital 21–2, 26, 32
wildness 161–3, 167–8, 174–5, 178, 180–1

zi-ran 174
Zimmerman, Eric 57
zURBS 177

Lightning Source UK Ltd.
Milton Keynes UK
UKHW020154161221
395626UK00003B/237